Love and Latrines

IN THE LAND OF SPIDERWEB LACE:

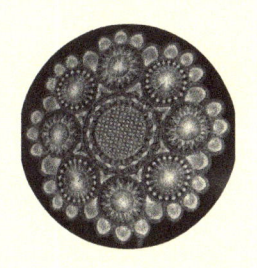

A Peace Corps Memoir

Mary Lou Shefsky

The cover photograph shows the author's special design of a spiderweb lace symbolizing the Peace Corps.

The inner circle contains a dove that represents the Peace Corps as well as the red, white, and blue of the U.S. and Paraguayan flags.

Starting at one o'clock and continuing clockwise:

Hookworms and blood • Health

Growing cornstalks • Agriculture

Books • Education

Hands • Cooperatives

Bombillas & *guampas,* used to drink *yerba mate*
• sharing and friendship

Anthuriums • hospitality

Sunflowers • good luck, truth, honesty, loyalty

Gladioli • remembrance

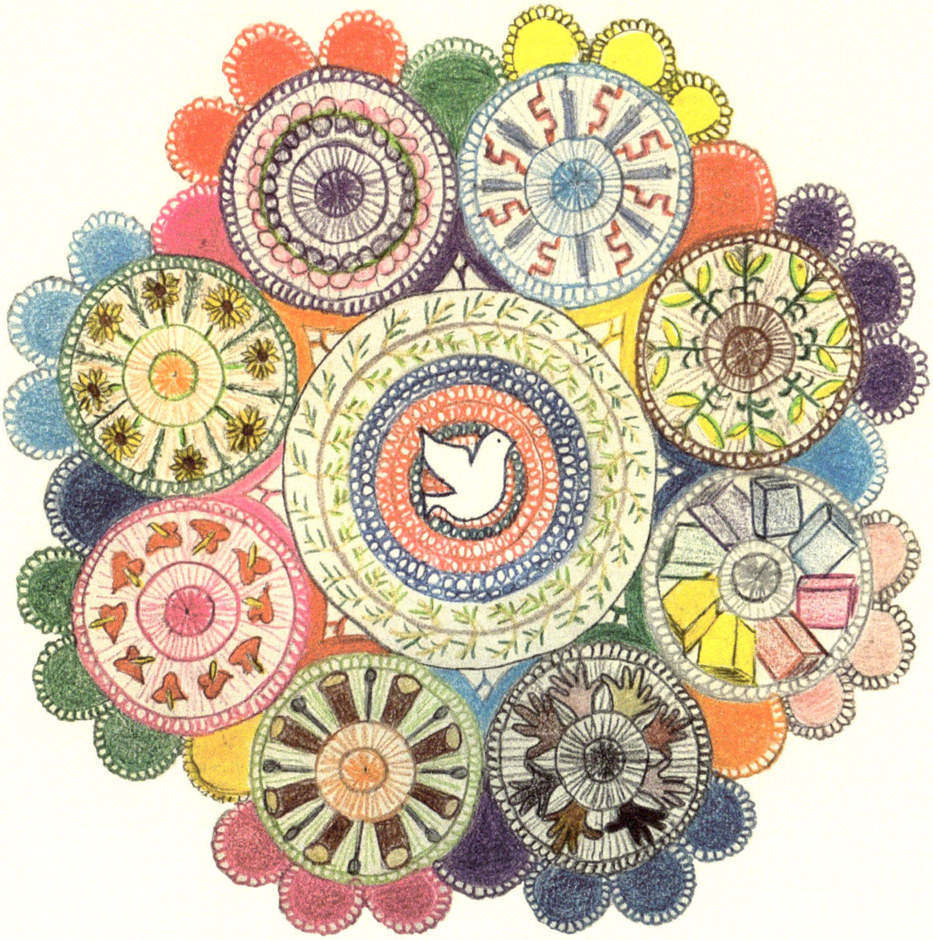

Copyright © 2021 Mary Lou Shefsky, MPH. All rights reserved. No part of this book, including front and back cover images, may be reproduced or utilized in any form or by any means, electronic or mechanical, including photocopying, recording, or by information storage and retrieval system, without written permission from the author. Photographs are owned by the individual or organization to whom they are credited. Photographs without a specific credit are the property of the author. Photographs may not be reproduced or utilized in any form or by any means without written permission from the owner/photographer.

Design by BookCreate
Redmond, Washington USA

Printed in USA

ISBN 978-1-7373635-2-1

Dedication

To Stephen,
with my love and deep gratitude,
and in memory of Ña Niní.

Preface

Before relocating from Florida to the Pacific Northwest in 1989, Mother gave me a box containing the letters and tapes I sent to my parents from Paraguay, where I served as a Peace Corps Volunteer from 1974 to 1976. Mom had saved them for me because she valued handwritten letters. During World War II, she saved over 700 letters that my father wrote her from his training sites and then from his radar operating stations, ultimately atop Mt. Suribachi on Iwo Jima. I wasn't as prolific a writer as my father, but I recognized the personal importance of the contents in my box.

My husband, our two young boys, and I moved into a house in Toppenish, Washington, where my box was stored in the basement, untouched for nine years. In 1998, we moved it to the basement of our newly built home in Granger, Washington. When the boys grew into young men and left for college, I began cleaning out our storage area. I rediscovered the box but was too busy to do more than glance through it. Finally, in 2014, I found more time on my hands. I opened the box, removed the letters from their envelopes, and placed them one by one into clear plastic holders that fit into a large loose-leaf binder. It was finally time to decide what to do with them.

Over the years, I often told anecdotes about my time in Paraguay to family and friends. Co-worker Lynn Harlington, after hearing a story or joke about my service, would often comment, "Mary Lou, you ought to write a book." She said it sincerely and frequently enough for me to take her advice. One day in 2015, I sat at the computer and typed an outline of my Paraguay experiences. With my letters and other mementos at hand, I began writing *Love and Latrines in the Land of Spiderweb Lace*.

My intent is to leave something of my Peace Corps experience, along with insights into Paraguayan history and culture, for family and friends to enjoy and remember me by, particularly sons Matthew and Daniel, grandson Oliver, and any other grandchildren that might come along. I also want to add my story to the impressive literature on Peace Corps service that has been published over the past 60 years. However, unlike most Peace Corps memoirs, this story also reveals how my service has had a lasting impact on my life.

Weekly meetings of the Writing Club at the Harman Center in Yakima, Washington, motived me to draft my book. Vicki, Anna, John, Elizabeth, Gean, Roger, Brice, and Pat made suggestions, asked for clarifications, and always positively encouraged me. Others who contributed comments and suggestions were Returned Peace Corps Volunteer Karen Brozovich, my cousin Nancy Wishart, my dear friend Dr. Susan Ellis, and my swimming pal Pat Bieze. Pat did the good deed of referring me to her brother, writer Kirk Landers, who in turn recommended substantive editor Chris Nelson. Kirk supplied me with numerous good ideas and tips, and Chris provided me with detailed input and ideas for smoothing out my story flow. Kirk also recommended Ruth Beach as a copy editor, and Ruth's work helped refine the manuscript. William Hoard designed this book for me, providing his superb professional advice during the last stages of producing it. I am indebted to all who are mentioned here.

I acknowledge and embrace the people, both named and unnamed, who played parts in this memoir—the Volunteers who served with me, Peace Corps staff, and the array of Paraguayans who taught me about their culture and lives and welcomed me into their homes. In some cases, I have changed names when I felt that was the best thing to do. I feel love and deep gratitude for Ña Niní and the Feltes family as well as Tomasa and her family for their love and support across the miles and through the years.

Words in Guaraní, the indigenous language of Paraguay spoken by most of the population, are difficult to read but fun to pronounce. I have included some rough pronunciation guides in parentheses after many of the words and phrases in this book. I have not done so for words in Spanish, but remember that the five vowels each have only one pure sound—a, e, i, o, u are pronounced *AH, EH, EE, OH, OO* (or *U*)—and you should be close to correct.

Although the writing is mine, it is also Stephen's story. He read all of it, correcting details, elaborating in places, and occasionally suggesting deletions. I cannot imagine writing this book or living my life without him.

Table of Contents

Part One
Peace Corps Paraguay ▪ 1

Chapter 1
Stone Piece of the Rosary ▪ 2

Chapter 2
The Special Project in My Last-Choice Town ▪ 28

Chapter 3
An Interlude ▪ 62

Chapter 4
Fighting Intestinal Parasites in Capiatá ▪ 78

Chapter 5
The Move to San Lorenzo and a New Assignment ▪ 100

Chapter 6
The Trip Home through Latin America ▪ 120

Part Two
Life After Peace Corps Paraguay • 127

Chapter 7
Returned Peace Corps Volunteers (RPCVs) • 128

Chapter 8
Did We Make a Positive Difference? • 135

Chapter 9
Growing Families • 151

Chapter 10
Adventurous Vacations • 159

Chapter 11
Celebrating the Peace Corps and Reflecting • 181

Chapter 12
Where We are Now • 199

Love and Latrines in the Land of Spiderweb Lace

Route from training in Puerto Rico to Asunción, Paraguay, 1974

PART ONE

❧

PEACE CORPS PARAGUAY

From a 1973 Peace Corps recruitment poster

CHAPTER 1

Stone Piece of the Rosary

As long as poverty, injustice and gross inequality exist in our world, none of us can truly rest.
—Nelson Mandela

I suspected nothing serious when the health center's midwife took me aside a month after I arrived in Itacurubí del Rosario. The small northern Paraguayan town, eight hours by bus from the capital of Asunción, was an isolated place for a Peace Corps Volunteer. Five hours of the bus ride were on a dirt road. The town was one of ten sites offered to the dozen Volunteers in my training group, and Itacurubí (EE-tah-ku-ru-BEE) del Rosario had been my top choice. Perhaps the midwife would offer me a tip about a new living arrangement.

I was temporarily living with Kate, the agricultural extension Peace Corps Volunteer, during my initial adjustment as a health education Volunteer. While I enjoyed living with her, I was ready for my own space. It really didn't have anything to do with Kate accidentally dropping our last roll of toilet paper down the latrine hole, or with her dropping a flashlight into the hole. It really didn't bother me that the flashlight had new batteries, was still on, and was pointed up, because after a few trips to the latrine, the flashlight was buried. (Those things did happen.) I worried that perhaps my efforts at learning the guitar sometimes got on Kate's nerves, since I sometimes irritated myself with my slow progress learning to play the instrument. However, the bottom line was that I really didn't want to wear out my welcome in Kate's home.

Kate rented a small whitewashed house with a thatched roof and a sanitary latrine in the back yard. For water, she used a neighbor's well. A spunky young woman with short blonde hair who wore earrings to give herself a feminine look, Kate made people laugh with her delightfully dry sense of humor. On our first evening together, she had me chuckling at her description of a dance she had attended a distance away from town, requiring a ride standing up in the back of an open truck with other attendees. She had taken care to bathe and dress up for the dance only to arrive covered by red road dust kicked up by the truck, as were all of the other riders. Her facial expressions and manner of describing the event were typical of how Kate interacted and communicated with others. Her wry sense of humor made people laugh and smile at situations and themselves. While Kate, who had been in Paraguay almost a year, was the first Volunteer in town, I was the first to work in health education.

I followed the midwife, Ña Marta, a petite woman dressed in a white medical lab coat, to an unoccupied room in the modest white one-story rural health center. (Ña, short for *Doña*, was a title of respect for married women.) I had already learned a great deal from Ña Marta and Dr. Yinde, a slight, clean-shaven man in his thirties with a kind, calm manner and steady hands when treating patients.

"Dr. Yinde is leaving us, Marilú," Ña Marta told me in a soft, sad voice. She explained that the local pharmacy owner had complained that Dr. Yinde was sending health center patients to his wife's new pharmacy. Ugly threats had been made toward the doctor and his family. Dr. Yinde was granted his request for a Ministry of Health assignment elsewhere. As Ña Marta was speaking to me, the doctor was preparing for his departure, and he soon would be gone. She conveyed his deep regrets to me. While everyone hoped another physician would soon be assigned to our town, things tended to work slowly in Paraguay. We would have to wait and see.

Ña Marta went to inform the other health center employees, leaving me alone in the room. I was stunned, numb, and empty. In my short time in the town, I had grown to love the atmosphere of the isolated place and its people, particularly when I was in the health care setting. Now, I feared my time in Itacurubí del Rosario would end. Because the local doctors supervised the health education volunteers in Paraguay, the Peace Corps would likely reassign me unless a replacement for Dr. Yinde came quickly.

I stayed alone for a bit, and I recalled that the name Itacurubí del Rosario means "stone piece of the rosary." Had I been a Catholic with a rosary in my pocket, at that moment, I likely would have used it to pray that I would be allowed to stay in the town.

As I walked to Kate's house, I mulled over this turn of events and reflected on how I had reached this current situation. My mind worked in a slow-motion replay, the opposite of my life flashing before my eyes in a moment of crisis. During the rest of the day and into evening hours, my thoughts continued to wander through recent months, interrupted only by a conversation with Kate about Dr. Yinde's departure and a bit of guitar strumming.

The town only had electricity for about three hours each evening when the generator ran. On my before-going-to-bed trip to the latrine after the town's generator was shut down for the night, I turned off the flashlight to gaze in awe at the incomprehensible galaxies of twinkling stars filling the sky. During a new moon in a place without electrical lighting, the spectacle was a breathtaking glimpse into infinity. The two constellations I could readily recognize were the Southern Cross, not seen from the northern hemisphere, and Orion the Hunter, who appeared upside-down from this southern hemisphere view. The Big Dipper, the Little Dipper, and the North Star are not seen in the skies south of the equator. I felt miniscule but alive and in awe of this land-locked country in the heart of South America.

∞∞∞

Upon arriving in Itacurubí del Rosario on the last day of May in 1974, three months after beginning my Peace Corps journey, I jumped into my job as a health educator and began presenting short, formal talks to patients waiting to be seen by the doctor or midwife. Two months of Peace Corps training in Ponce, Puerto Rico, and an additional month in Paraguay had prepared me for this quick start.

I had been one of twelve Ponce trainees who became Peace Corps Volunteers in Paraguay after extensive language training, cross-cultural orientation, and technical training. Among the trainees were Marty, Pauline, Wyn, Burl, Larry, and Steve. Marty from California would become my roommate during training in Paraguay. Whereas most of the trainees started with Spanish instruction, Marty, Pauline, and I immediately began Guaraní (gwah-rah-NEE) classes because we were fluent in Spanish. The Paraguayan government recognizes both Spanish and Guaraní as official languages. Spanish is the dominant language in public life (commerce, education, and politics), but Guaraní is the preferred language in homes and social settings. While about 90% of Paraguayans speak Guaraní, there are many people in rural areas with very limited Spanish-speaking skills.

During our lunch break, we trainees gathered in the training center's small cafeteria and socialized. Wyn turned out to be the sister of Gwyneth, a Spanish major a year ahead of me at Albion College in Michigan. Burl was a vegetarian from my hometown of Detroit. He asked us to call him *Reynaldo* because "Burl" was too close to *burro*, which means donkey or ass in Spanish. Larry, who had spent some of his childhood in Aruba, dreamed of becoming a chef and someday owning a restaurant. Steve from Connecticut was a tall, quiet, curly-haired guy who had majored in psychology.

Our Guaraní classes started with the basic grammar of the language and common phrases, such as ¿Mba-éi-xa-pá? (Mba-EHee-shah-PAH, how are you?) and the response, *iporâ* (ee-poh-RÂ, fine). The "a" in *iporâ* has a nasal tone, as indicated by the little upside-down vee mark above it. The vowels in Guaraní, including "y," can be either regular sounds or nasal versions of them. Whether the word has a nasal sound or not can change the meaning. An example is the one-letter word "y." The regular sound of it is what you might make if you are socked in the stomach (similar to UH), and it means "water." The expansive, impressive falls between Argentina and Brazil close to their borders with Paraguay, majestically shown in the 1986 film *The Mission* starring Robert Di Nero and Jeremy Irons, are called *Y-guazú*, meaning "water-big." (The official spelling is "Iguazú.") Yes, they are big waterfalls. When the sound is nasal, the meaning changes to "without." We had to effectively learn to make these nasal sounds *without* pinching our noses. Knowing how the change of one vowel in a word completely changes the meaning, I worried that flipping a nasal sound to a regular one might create an embarrassing word.

The women in our group would become health educators and the men would work in environmental sanitation. To prepare us for our assignments as Volunteers, our trainers in Guaraní helped us to write and practice some simple talks on common health topics in the Indian language—sanitary latrines, hookworm and other common intestinal parasites, tuberculosis, diarrhea, dental hygiene, hand washing, prenatal care, vaccinations, and even tetanus (lock-jaw), a vaccine-preventable disease.

"It is heart-breaking to see a newborn die from tetanus," our instructor lamented. "It is a painful way to die for a person any age. The disease is caused by a toxin made by a bacterium commonly found in dirt and manure." During my childhood, I learned about the need to get a tetanus vaccine periodically throughout life to prevent the disease. A special booster is needed if someone steps on a dirty or rusty nail that penetrates the foot. The instructor continued, "If the umbilical cord is cut at birth with an unclean knife, the baby can die of tetanus. People in the countryside call it *el mal de siete días* (the evil of seven days) because it takes about that length of time to result in a baby's death. I hope you never see a baby suffer from the painful muscle spasms, a high fever, and trouble swallowing caused by this disease." Simple sterilization of the cord-cutting instrument and vaccinating women late in pregnancy can prevent *el mal de siete días*. I could picture myself conducting classes, with the guidance of Paraguayan professionals, to educate lay midwives and reduce infant mortality due to tetanus.

While my language skills in Guaraní were only somewhat beyond basic by the end of Peace Corps training, I was ready to present talks on diarrhea, tuberculosis, tetanus, and hand washing with the help of pieces of poster board. On the front of each piece was a hand-drawn picture, and on the reverse was the script in Guaraní. I had only to read the text while holding it in front of my face. It was an effective way of building a health vocabulary and conversation skills. Appropriately responding to questions in Guaraní was beyond my language level at that point, but I was prepared with a brief statement to that effect. I would rely on the health center staff to bail me out as needed. At 23 years of age, I knew the basics of health education from Peace Corps training and was eager to continue learning.

Starting with my first day in Itacurubí del Rosario, I gave my prepared health talks and pitched in to assist the health center staff whenever asked. One of the tasks I helped with when the nurses were busy was taking blood pressure measurements. That was something I had done a few times in training situations. On my first morning, my initial real patient was a stooped, elderly woman with wrinkles that told of decades of living in the Paraguayan countryside. Her eyes twinkled in spite of the milky glaze of cataracts. As we exchanged basic pleasantries in Guaraní, she reacted with a sweet smile at my foreign-sounding accent. She continued to smile as I put the blood pressure cuff on her arm. After correctly placing the stethoscope, I pumped up the cuff and watched the dial until it reached 200. I then slowly let out the cuff's air, listening intently for the first hint of the systolic sound. As it dropped below 120, it hit me that the wizened old woman certainly didn't have high blood pressure, with normal being 120/80. I continued listening intently, slowing down the release of air so as not to miss the first sound. It dropped below 80, then 70, then 60, and still I heard nothing. With her eyes fixed on me, I tried to maintain a professional demeanor. I finally heard the pulsating sound at 48, which was the systolic pressure. I stopped hearing it at 32, which was the diastolic pressure. I wondered if her blood pressure really could be only 48/32. If that were the case, it would be a wonder that she had the energy to walk around.

Trying to maintain a calm demeanor, I asked her to wait a moment while I hurried to tell Dr. Yinde what I thought the woman's blood pressure was. He smiled at me with sadness in his eyes. Assuring me that I had heard correctly, Dr. Yinde said that she walked to the clinic every day it was open to have her blood pressure checked. There wasn't anything the doctor could do for her—she was suffering from "old age." He returned with me, greeting her with the respect due an elder. He told her that her blood pressure was stable and that she could come to the clinic any time to have it checked. She was never charged for these brief visits. The doctor shook hands with her, and I gave her a brief hug with the customary kiss on each check before she slowly walked out of the health center. I could not venture a guess at her age, but I knew that she had walked in the Paraguayan sun for many years.

A short time later, Dr. Yinde called me into a small exam room to show me the results of a serious post-injection infection in an elderly woman. Although the infection had fortunately resolved, a deep hole in the buttock remained. The doctor explained to me that anyone in Paraguay can give an injection. No prescriptions were required for any medications or medical equipment. The doctor urged the patient to seek medical care in the future only from qualified people. Later that morning, Dr. Yinde said the same to the mother of a year-old baby who had disturbing amounts of pus slowly oozing from a post-injection site in the buttock. He prescribed an antibiotic for the child.

Patients were generally seen in the mornings. During those consults, Dr. Yinde treated me as part of his medical personnel, including me in his own brief teachings to the staff and sometimes explaining medical conditions one-on-one. Weather permitting, in the afternoons the staff often piled into the health center's new VW van to vaccinate children in outlying areas. With the doctor driving and our materials and ice-and-vaccine-packed Styrofoam cooler stowed in the back, we ventured into these communities when we were expected. As instructed, I moved supplies and swabbed arms with alcohol-soaked cotton balls before other staff gave the shots. Dr. Yinde and Ña Marta determined which vaccines to give. I asked about keeping records of the 150 shots that we gave one afternoon. The doctor said that they relied on the parents to tell them what vaccines children already had. It seemed a little relaxed to me, but that was how things were handled at that time.

"*¡Marilú, ejú, rápido!*" (Come quickly!) Above the patter of the rain one cold morning, I heard the voice outside the room shout with an urgent edge. I had been casually reviewing my health talks in Guaraní, pondering new ones to develop. Due to the rain, it was slow at the health center, but medical emergencies occurred regardless of the weather.

Following the direction of the voice, I turned to the right, dashed down the corridor, and entered the humble operating room. A 26-year-old pregnant woman was lying on the table while being prepped by a nurse. The patient looked well into her 30s to me, but I knew that the heavy work, childbearing, and sweltering summer sun that Paraguayan women in the countryside endure can prematurely age them. I learned that she had two children at home.

The rain sounds accelerated into a roar, invading the room through the large open windows along with the chilly air. A low-to-the-floor charcoal hibachi was emanating some modest heat. The windows were open because burning charcoal in a closed room can cause asphyxiation. June, the beginning of winter in Paraguay, could have temperatures close to freezing at night. I had layered on clothing that morning, with my unlaundered-for-two-days white lab coat on top like the other health center personnel. Nobody seemed concerned about maintaining a sterile operating environment.

The 12' x 12' high-ceilinged room with pastel-painted plaster walls and a reddish-brown brick floor was clean and sparsely furnished with only the surgical table and an adjacent instrument cart. The windows let in some daylight, but there wasn't enough illumination for a surgery on the stormy dark morning. The town's generator wouldn't provide electricity for several hours. Not only was I about to see my first delivery and first surgical operation, but I would also participate on the team of seven. Dr. Yinde would perform the procedure, assisted by the midwife. Two nurses would hold retractors, and one nurse would tend to the baby once it was born. Oscar was present to help as needed. My job would be to hold the flashlight.

Dr. Yinde had scrubbed up in another area of the health center using water hauled from the well, as the town had no running water. Now he adroitly pulled on surgical gloves while waiting for the nurse to finish her prepping.

The doctor murmured some words in Guaraní to everyone and then told me in Spanish that a Cesarean section had to be done because of a placenta previa. The placenta, a round and flattened organ attached to the inside of the uterus during pregnancy to nourish the fetus through the umbilical cord, was blocking the cervix where the fetus had to exit. Placenta previa can cause severe bleeding in both the mother and the fetus during pregnancy or at the time of delivery. At our health center, we had no capability of transfusing a patient needing blood. We lacked even basic supplies, such as a microscope and a centrifuge for blood or urine analysis. Transporting this woman to Asunción was out of the question due to the distance and the bad weather. An attempt would be fatal to both mother and baby. This health center did not have general anesthesia available either. A local anesthetic would have to suffice. What could be done would be done right in front of me with what we had available.

After someone handed me a flashlight, I was directed to stand near the woman's head. I extended my arm up above her chest, firmly clutched the flashlight in my fist, and aimed the beam of light at her pregnant abdomen as Dr. Yinde injected several doses of numbing Novocain at two-inch intervals from her belly button to her pubic bone. He followed the brownish stain of the iodine solution the nurse had used to clean the skin. After waiting a few moments to allow the area to numb, the doctor began his long abdominal incision. As her insides were exposed to the room's cold air, vapor arose from the woman's body, like steam escaping from a boiling kettle when the lid is slowly lifted. Our patient only occasionally moaned. Otherwise, she maintained a stoic manner of handling her pain, typical of Paraguayan adults who have lived through many difficult physical trials in their lives. The two nurses holding retractors blotted away blood from the completed abdominal incision as Dr. Yinde lifted the scalpel to begin a second cut to open the bulging uterus.

At this point, the beam from the flashlight began to fade—the batteries were becoming depleted! "Shake the flashlight, Marilú!" I was directed. The beam became a bit stronger with my shaking and trembling, only to fade a few seconds later. Dr. Yinde barked an order to have the health center's errand boy run to the nearest store for new batteries. Next, he told me to remove the batteries and switch them around in the hope of stimulating sufficient light to continue the C-section. I did as told, but the beam was only slightly better for some fleeting moments. As my flashlight faded away completely, my mind's eye saw the dying Tinker Bell's light fading in "Peter Pan." In semi-darkness, the nurses blotted up the blood while Dr. Yinde spoke soothingly to our patient.

Shortly, the boy returned and helped me load the new batteries into the flashlight cylinder. The operation continued, the uterus was opened, and the baby was lifted out. Everyone stopped breathing until the baby gasped and cried out with its first breath, which was quickly followed by seven staff members and the mother all sighing with relief. Dr. Yinde announced that it was a boy, passed him to the nurse at his side waiting with a clean blanket in her outstretched hands, and clamped and cut the umbilical cord. The infant weighed in at about 6½ pounds. A cap was placed on the infant's head to retain as much body heat as possible in the cold room. Next, the doctor removed the placenta from low in the uterus where it had been blocking the cervix, checked it to make sure it was complete and intact, and proceeded to stitch up first the uterus and then the outer abdominal incision under the bright beam of my flashlight. We all displayed huge smiles when the last stitch was made. It was at that moment I became aware of the distinct earthy smell of giving birth—a combination of amniotic fluid, blood, and human sweat—mingling with the odor of burning charcoal.

Two days later, I visited the mother and observed the nurse changing the dressing. I was amazed to see a rather healthy-looking scar forming from navel to pubic bone, except for one minor inflammation with a small amount of pus draining near the navel. The nurse applied an antibiotic ointment to the reddish area. On the fourth day, the mother and her newborn went home. What I had witnessed changed me forever. I was in awe that this mother had withstood the pain of major surgery with only local anesthetic and had survived with only a minor infection in spite of the lack of sterile conditions. When I asked Dr. Yinde how the woman had avoided a major infection, he replied that lifetime exposures to a variety of bacteria force adults to develop strong immune systems.

The rain stopped the day after the C-section. The sun, known in Guaraní as the *mboriajhú poncho* (mbor-yah-HU, poor man's poncho), rose in the sky to dry out the rural roads and warm our hearts. That day, Dr. Yinde asked if I wanted to meet a patient with an interesting problem before he sent her to Asunción. As he explained the problem and situation directly to the patient, I listened and watched intently. Dr. Yinde told her that she had an impaction in the large intestine, a blockage that he was not able to treat in town. I clearly saw that her large intestine was distended and outlined on the abdomen as distinctly as a drawing in an anatomy book. She had been constipated for a couple of weeks. The doctor wrote a transfer note for her to take to the public hospital in the capital, and she left to wait for the next bus that would take her on the eight-hour trip on the now dry, dusty road.

∞∞∞∞

Dr. Yinde left and I was in limbo. Nobody knew if or when another doctor would replace him. Over the next few days, only a few women came to the health center to see the midwife, and our collective activity and morale plummeted. In an effort to do something positive, Ña Marta decided we could still vaccinate in outlying communities, but the good midwife lamented that the doctor had been the only person at the health center who knew how to drive. To complicate matters, the van had a standard transmission. "I can drive it, and I have a Paraguayan driver's license," I offered enthusiastically to the staff. "And I'll teach Oscar and Ña Marta how to drive!" My father had taught me to drive an automatic transmission in 1966. Six years later, I learned to drive a standard transmission while a VISTA (Volunteers in Service to America, a domestic poverty program) member at the Utah Migrant Council. My friend and supervisor John had the patience and courage to teach me in his brand new car.

I laughed to myself remembering when I obtained a Paraguayan driver's license during our training. Although I had had no desire to get behind the wheel of a vehicle and join the chaotic traffic on the narrow urban streets of the capital, I thought that perhaps I might drive in a rural area. So I went along with what the Peace Corps told us to do. To get a license, we simply filled out a form and answered some oral questions. I was still trying to tune into the Paraguayan accent in Spanish at that time and often asked people to repeat things. But when asked, *"¿Tiene Ud. problemas en escuchar?"* (Do you have any problems with your hearing?), I felt chagrined by my too-quick response: *"¿Qué dijo?"* (What did you say?).

With renewed energy, I drove the enthusiastic Oscar and the reticent Ña Marta to a straight and level stretch of road just outside of town for their first lesson. After stopping the van, I slowly went over the steps of restarting the vehicle. "This is the gear shift," I said. "I can shift gears when I have the clutch pedal pressed to the floor with my left foot." I showed them the four gear speed positions, along with neutral and reverse. "We are going to use neutral and first gear today. First, make sure the emergency brake is on." I continued talking them through it while restarting the van.

After repeating the demonstration, I let Oscar take the wheel. He did well for his first attempt, giving us only very mild whiplash. I repeated the steps of starting the van and driving in first gear. Oscar made a second go of it and did better.

When Ña Marta's turn came, she was visibly trembling. I urged her to take it slowly, step by step, but the mind and hands of the practiced midwife struggled to learn a new skill that she perceived was predominantly male in nature. Gear grinding noises, abrupt jerks, and her deep sighs of despair caused me to conclude the first lesson with a promise we would keep trying.

During subsequent sessions, we covered how to shift to second and third gears. Oscar continued to improve while Ña Marta made painfully slow progress in first gear. I wrote home, "If I teach her to drive, I will have accomplished a great deal in this town. The midwife knows a lot about delivering babies, but she wasn't really sure what a steering wheel is for."

On our next vaccination trip, Oscar drove until we neared the populated area. He did well, maintaining control in the road's sandy areas where the van slid and swayed while the tires attempted to retain some traction. After subsequent lessons and vaccination trips, I had confidence that Oscar would become a good driver. Someday, Ña Marta might make a viable backup driver. I reminded her how helpful driving would be when the need arose to reach a laboring pregnant woman whose life and fetus were in danger.

The health center staff worried that Peace Corps would not let me stay without a doctor in town. I shared their concern and privately had the sinking feeling I would be assigned to Ybycuí (uh-buh-ku-EE), my dead last choice on the list of possible sites. Trying to picture in my mind what Ybycuí might be like, I reflected on two other rural sites I had visited.

Toward the end of training in Asunción and before receiving a placement, we trainees had left the capital to see some of rural Paraguay. Our group had two weekend trips scheduled during which each trainee individually traveled to a site to stay with an experienced Volunteer to get a taste for rural work and life.

My first site visit was with Ellen in Itaguá (ee-tah-GWA). It took only a 45-minute bus trip from Asunción on the paved road heading due east toward Puerto Presidente Stroessner on the Paraná River, bordering Brazil. At the time, it was one of only two paved roads in the country outside the capital. The other one went southeast from Asunción to the city of Encarnación further down the Paraná River at the border with Argentina. Both paved roads had only one lane going in each direction. During the quick trip to Itaguá, I gasped a few times as my bus passed vehicles on the narrow road with little spare space to avoid hitting the oncoming traffic.

As I stepped off the bus in Itaguá for this first visit, I admired the large ñandutí (nyahn-du-TEE, spiderweb lace) tablecloths displayed along the roadside, enticing travelers to stop and buy. The Guaraní word for spider is "ñandú," and the ñandutí lace is reminiscent of delicate spiderweb patterns. Much of Paraguay's ñandutí is made in and around the town of Itaguá.

Evolved from European lace in the sixteenth century and passed down through generations of women, Paraguay's ñandutí can be made with thread ranging from coarse cotton to fine silken strands. First, fabric is attached by string onto a wooden frame and stretched taut. Next, circular patterns are sewn onto the fabric as an outline for the piece. Once the outline is done, the rest of the ñandutí threads are attached onto that outline in an array of patterns from nature. One of the most delicate and difficult patterns is often used in the center of the lace. Composed of tiny circles and knots, it looks like the center of the guayaba (or guava) fruit when cut in half. Other patterns have aptly descriptive names such as cornflower, snail, jasmine flower, cattle tick, parrot's beak, cow's footprint, passionflower, anthill in a cornfield, ox footprint, and frog's anus. A finished piece of ñandutí can be left on the frame and displayed on a wall, or the fabric backing up the lace can be cut off to leave a lovely doily. I was in awe of the artistic beauty and vivid colors of this lace.

The intricate spiderweb lace of Paraguay is artfully described in a book by Annick Sanjurjo entitled *Ñandutí, encaje paraguayo* (*Spiderweb Lace, Paraguayan Lace*), and I highlight some of its background here. The lace might be linked back to the Middle Ages when priests' habits and altar cloths were made with trimmings of silk, silver, or gold thread. It definitely has connections to European lace, particularly the Spanish styles. Paraguay's *ñandutí* has been directly traced to the Spanish Canary Islands. In 1724, families from the Canaries helped found Montevideo in what today is Uruguay. Based on similarities of the patterns, it is possible some of those families influenced lace making in Paraguay.

Interestingly, in 1731, a group of people from the Canaries arrived at what we now call San Antonio, Texas. The Franciscans working in the area founded communities for the local indigenous people, including the Mission of San Antonio de Valero, later called the Alamo. By the end of the 18th century, Spain sent a couple thousand people from the Canaries to what is now Texas to protect its border with the French in the area now called Louisiana. The lace from this region along the U.S.-Mexican border is very similar to Paraguayan spiderweb lace. In the 1990s, a Peace Corps Volunteer from Texas who had served in Paraguay observed that his mother was buying *ñandutí* in the border cities with Mexico.

In 18th century Paraguay, girls were taught to make thread, sew, weave, make lace, and embroider, tasks that were the responsibility of women. The lace designs began to mimic aspects of the landscape and objects of daily rural life. Once the lace was cut away from the stretched fabric upon which it was made, it looked like a lovely spiderweb. Many people say it's similar to the yellowish webs of a black spider, *Epeira socialis,* found in the jungle undergrowth in Paraguay.

Napoleon Bonaparte's invasion of Spain in 1808 led to Spain's decline and the subsequent loss of its colonies in the Americas over the following decade. Paraguay declared its independence from Spanish colonial rule in 1811. Three years later, the Congress of the new country made José Gaspar Rodríguez de Francia its supreme dictator. Francia, who ruled until his death in 1840, consolidated his power and developed a distinct national identity by isolating Paraguay and encouraging the preservation of the Guaraní language. He closed the borders, banning outsiders from entering and residents from leaving, and he stopped international trade. During the years of isolation of the Francia dictatorship, women had to make everything—threads, ponchos, capes, tunics, blouses, shirts, skirts, vests, netting, etc. The two dictators following Francia, Carlos Antonio López and his son Francisco Solano López, continued Francia's practices to some degree. Being isolated perhaps allowed the Paraguayan style of *ñandutí* to develop in communities like Itaguá, Guarambaré, and Carapeguá.

The *ñandutí* label might have been used first by the British brothers Robertson who lived in Paraguay off and on from 1807 to 1815. The word appeared in an 1838 book they published in London about Paraguayan hospitality in which they mentioned *"los ejemplares selectos de ñandutí"* (the selected examples of *ñandutí*), but they failed to describe them. There are pieces of *ñandutí* from the middle of the 19th century that survive today, and they possess the general characteristics of the spiderweb lace in modern Paraguay.

After admiring the samples of this local craft displayed on the roadside, I stopped in one of the ñandutí stores to ask for directions to the house of Ellen (*Elena* to the locals). An older woman flashed a quick smile and provided me with easy directions. Approaching the tidy house a short distance away, I clapped my hands, which was the Paraguayan way to "knock on a door." Ellen was expecting me.

Petite, curly-haired Ellen quickly became a helpful friend and role model due to her efficiency, practicality, and hard work. Ellen oriented me to bucket baths, daily health talks at the health center, and socializing with people in town. Everyone I met in Itaguá seemed to like and respect Elena. She did the big favor of teaching me elementary lessons of daily hygiene and personal maintenance in rural Paraguay.

The trick to enjoying a good bucket bath was the right amount of water at the right temperature. Ellen advised that two buckets of well water would suffice. She demonstrated by first pulling one bucket from her deep well, protected by a circular rust-colored brick wall about a yard tall. A sturdy frame above the well held a pully with a strong rope threaded through it. The rope attached to the handle of an aluminum bucket, which dangled directly below the pully. Ellen grabbed a piece of the rope that was neatly coiled on the well's ledge and let it slip through her hands, allowing the bucket to disappear out of sight into the darkness of the well. Watching her, I recalled one of the first Paraguayan adages I had learned describing hard times: "*I-po-í la piola,*" meaning "The rope is thin." After we heard a kerplunk of a splash from deep within the well, Ellen paused to allow the bucket to fill with water. She then began the hand-over-hand pulling on the rope to raise the filled bucket. Each time her right hand released the rope, it guided the formation of the coil I had seen when we approached the well. When the bucket appeared, Ellen reached with her free hand to grab it, haul it toward her, and pour the contents into the waiting aluminum pot so that it could be heated to boiling on her small stove top. She then hauled up a second bucket of water, poured it into a basin, and carried the basin into the bathing stall in the back yard. Once the pot of hot water was ready, Ellen instructed me to carry it to the stall, mix it with the cold water, and enjoy my first bucket bath. "Use the enamel cup in the stall to get yourself wet," she advised. "Then shampoo and soap up completely. Most of the water is needed to get well-rinsed, in a cup-by-cup fashion."

For hand washing, Ellen poured water into an enamel-coated aluminum basin, wetted her hands, soaped up, and then rinsed off in the basin. For dishwashing, she heated enough water for a soapy cleaning and for a rinsing basin. I observed her efficiency and imitated it from that point on.

One of Ellen's strengths was that she could laugh at herself. She shared with me that during one talk in *Guaraní* at her health center, she had meant to say, "Wearing shoes on your feet prevents hookworm." But instead of the word for feet, she said a word that meant penis. The response was delighted laughter by the women in the group, one of whom said, "No, no, Elena, that prevents babies!" She laughed along with them.

A personal bonus to my site visit was purchasing some quality pieces of *ñandutí* with Ellen's expert advice. I left Itaguá with the confidence that I would survive and maybe even thrive as a Volunteer.

During the last weekend of training, I spent my second site visit with a female Volunteer about three hours outside of Asunción in a town on a dirt road. Again, I traveled by bus. This trip was an adventure well into the countryside, like going back in time to a life devoid of modern amenities. The town was without electricity. Automobile traffic in rural areas was sparse in 1974. Every once in a while, a bus going in the opposite direction would kick up a cloud of dust on the dirt road. More commonly seen were people on foot balancing parcels or belongings on their heads or people traveling in ox carts. A reliable but slow form of transportation, the ox cart typically had two enormous wooden wheels and was pulled by a pair of large oxen yoked together. Along the roadside I saw land dotted with palm trees and rough-looking ground cover interrupted by occasional conical mounds several feet high that I learned were termite hills. This remote area of the world had a primordial feel to the scenery, evoking the fancy that a dinosaur or two might suddenly appear.

My second experienced Volunteer was pleasant and welcoming, and I appreciated her willingness to host me. As I accompanied her at work and around town, I saw that she was a hard worker who meant well but seemed less connected with her community than Ellen. After she had completed her service and returned to the States, I heard through the Peace Corps grapevine that people in her town gossiped that this Volunteer did not wear any underwear. Although she sent most of her clothing out to local women for washing, she had made a point of washing her own underwear because of the rough treatment clothes undergo when washed by hand. There is quite a bit of scrubbing with a stiff brush and beating with a wooden paddle. But in small towns, where gossiping is a common pastime, guessing and speculation become a form of entertainment and are often the source of untrue "facts." When I heard this, I felt trepidation about becoming a target of gossip.

After completing our site visits, we trainees were given a list of the available site assignments and had to fill out a form about what kind of a living and working situation we preferred. Although we could make a request, Peace Corps would make the final decisions. All of us anxiously reviewed the possibilities, knowing that we would spend two years of our lives at our assigned locations. The two sites requesting a male and a female Volunteer were Mallorquín and Puerto Presidente Stroessner. Both were on the paved road close to the border with Brazil. Villa Hayes asked for a sanitation Volunteer. Located in the Chaco across the river from Asunción, it was named for U.S. President Rutherford B. Hayes and was pronounced EYE-jehs. Sites wanting female health educators included Yaguarón (jah-gwa-ROHN) and Ypacaraí (uh-pah-kah-rah-EE), towns near the capital; Villa de San Pedro in the north; Caraguata-y (kah-rah-gwah-tah-UH), a couple of hours by bus from the capital and a short distance off the paved road to Brazil; and Itacurubí del Rosario, about eight hours from the capital. Then there was Ybycuí.

Chuck, the Peace Corps physician and health program director, had devised "The Program to Eradicate Intestinal Parasites." His goal was to eliminate parasites, particularly hookworms, from the population of a rural Paraguayan town. After talking with a number of health and sanitation Volunteers, Chuck selected Ybycuí, a town of about 3,000 people only three hours by bus from the capital, for the project. He proposed a multi-agency collaboration. Foremost would be the involvement of the Peace Corps and the Health Ministry, which included the *Servicio Nacional de Saneamiento Ambiental* (National Environmental Sanitation Service) that was referred to as SENASA (say-NAH-sah), Health Education, and Ybycuí's health center. Other collaborators were the Treasury Ministry and the U.S. Agency for International Development (USAID). A local committee in Ybycuí would be organized, and the director of the project would be Dr. Orihuela, the physician at Ybycuí's health center. Peace Corps would assign five Volunteers to do the work.

The plan called for a complete sanitation census of the town, a comprehensive educational campaign, a random stool sample study to estimate the rate of parasite infestation in the population, the building of sanitary latrines where needed, a distribution of anti-parasite medication to the population, and a second random stool sample study to confirm that parasites had been eradicated. All of this was to be done by November 1975, only 18 months after our service started. Chuck's grant proposal to USAID for financial support to buy laboratory supplies and medications was already approved. Implementation of the plan began a few months before my group arrived in Paraguay.

After listening carefully to Chuck's dream project, I began to understand why Ybycuí had been selected. First, it was the site where Martina, an active and conscientious Volunteer, had worked successfully in the health education program. Although she would soon complete her service, she was enthusiastic about a comprehensive project and was helping to launch it before leaving. Second, Dr. Orihuela at the health center was amenable to working with Chuck on this project. Lastly, there were no Paraguayan sanitation workers in Ybycuí. Volunteers in other towns had struggled working with their sanitation counterparts and had complained that some SENASA inspectors were difficult to work with. They told Chuck that many were merely political appointees who collected the salary but did no work. Chuck had intentionally selected a town without this perceived obstacle for the special project, but he had still included SENASA as a collaborating agency. Undoubtedly, the Peace Corps physician had other reasons for his choice, but these three stuck in my mind.

I definitely did not want to be in a town saturated with other Volunteers. The tendency would be to hang out together, making it more difficult to develop Paraguayan friendships and become involved with life in the town. I thought that the timeline of the Ybycuí project was overly ambitious, and I was puzzled as to how time had been budgeted for building sanitary latrines without knowing how many were needed. I also wondered about the lack of SENASA inspectors as counterparts for the Volunteers and how this would be accepted by administrators at the national sanitation agency. Hearing comments made by the other trainees in my group, I realized their perceptions were similar to mine.

When the assignments came out, I breathed a sigh of relief. I was granted my first choice and was headed to Itacurubí del Rosario. Pauline and Larry were assigned to Mallorquín, and Burl/Reynaldo was going to Villa Hayes. Marty was assigned to Villa de San Pedro. Wyn would work in Caraguata-y. The remaining Volunteers in our group would be sent to other towns on the list that they had requested. Steve was the only Volunteer in our group destined to work on the special project in Ybycuí. During our site discussions when others had spoken up to claim towns that interested him, Steve had remained calm and silent until only Ybycuí was left.

After our swearing-in ceremony with the U.S. Ambassador at the American Embassy in Asunción on May 23, 1974, we officially became Peace Corps Volunteers with a two-year commitment to serve to the best of our abilities. After the ceremony, the Ambassador graciously invited us Volunteers to use the swimming pool at the American Embassy when we were in the capital. By the pool was a small eatery where American-style hamburgers were sold. We were also happily informed that the Embassy's plumbing was adequate for flushing toilet paper down the toilet.

In Ponce, an experienced Volunteer had warned about the disposal of toilet paper in Paraguay. Pat, a tall woman with a mane of thick, light brown hair and a twinkle in her eye, was flown up from Paraguay to help with our training. This self-confident woman in her mid-twenties bluntly advised us, "Don't throw toilet paper into a flush toilet or into the latrine hole. It will plug up the toilet or too rapidly fill up the hole. Put the used paper into the basket or box provided for this purpose and periodically burn the used material." Pat continued explaining other aspects of bathroom and latrine hygiene. The basket should have a lid on it to prevent flies from spreading disease. When no basket is available, used toilet paper should be thrown onto the latrine or bathroom floor. Toilet paper was available, although the common type had the look and feel of stretchy, rough crepe paper and was less absorbent than the more expensive variety. Other options were stripped corncobs, leaves, newsprint, or other types of paper. Peace Corps regulations, it was commonly joked, were especially good because they came hole-punched for a loose-leaf binder, making it convenient to hang the paper on a nail driven into the latrine wall.

As we left the American Embassy as Volunteers instead of trainees, Pat's overall best advice from the Ponce training played back in my brain. "Maintain a sense of humor," she told us. "Reduce stress and break down personal barriers by laughing." Pat assured us that rural Paraguayan adults appreciated earthy humor with sexual innuendos. She told us a good example of this. Pat had purchased a horse with her Peace Corps transportation allowance and had thoughtfully named him *"mi novio"* (my boyfriend). People in her town snickered and giggled when they asked her, "Where are you going?" They already knew her response, "I'm going to ride/mount *mi novio*." With those mental reminders, I was ready to transition to rural Paraguay and my first-choice town.

∞∞∞∞

Two months later, I fought off the doom-and-gloom prospect of a transfer to Ybycuí. I had spent some time with Steve from Connecticut during a recent trip to Asunción to check for mail (Kate's and mine) and shop for some personal items. On that first trip away from my new town, I boarded the bus at dawn. It was already quite crowded with people and bundles, but I found a seat in the very back and settled in for the ride. The first five hours on the dirt road turned out to be exceptionally unpleasant. A seat closer to the front would have had less dust coming through the windows and would also have been less painful. By the time we arrived at the asphalted highway, my body ached from the battering and pounding, likely caused by a faulty bus suspension system without shock absorbers on the bumpy dirt road. The last three hours, with diminished dust and smooth sailing on pavement, went quickly. In Asunción, I transferred to a city bus that took me to the Peace Corps office. Once there, I checked the mailboxes for both Kate and myself—yes, we had letters from home. I tucked those in my tote bag.

My next stop was the Peace Corps library, and that's where I saw Steve perusing books. I chatted with him while picking out reading material to borrow and mentioned I was thinking about buying a guitar. I was itching to try some of the printed guitar lessons I had brought from the States. Steve's face lit up as he shared that he played a bit of guitar and was thinking about buying one, too. We approached Felicita, the receptionist at the Peace Corps, to ask where we might buy guitars. Helpful as always, she gave us directions and the bus numbers to take to the town of Luque near the airport, where there were several small shops selling Paraguayan guitars, harps, and cases for them. Steve and I agreed to meet at the Peace Corps office the next morning for a trip to Luque.

The ride on the asphalted road to Luque was smooth and quick. We boarded the half-empty bus and gave the driver's assistant two red 10-guaraní bills each. The fare was only 15 guaraníes (gwah-rah-NEE-ehs), about $0.12. The assistant, called a *guarda,* folded the paper bills lengthwise and filed them according to their denominations between the fingers on his left hand. He curled the middle of each stack around his fingers so that the back of his hand looked like the accordion-folded tail feathers of a paper turkey. Because his palm was unencumbered, his hand could still be used for other things. Then with his right hand, the *guarda* plucked two blue 5-guaraní bills, imprinted with the sketch of a young Paraguayan woman in traditional dress, and handed them to us for change. In the early months of service, watching the *guardas* flip through their bills was a novelty akin to observing someone skillfully do math calculations on an abacus.

The Peace Corps paid Volunteers in guaraníes, correctly spelled with a small "g." The symbol for the currency was similar to our dollar sign, but a "G" rather than an "S" was used with a vertical line through it. Because Peace Corps directly deposited our living allowances in the *Banco Nacional de Fomento* (National Development Bank), each Volunteer had to open a bank account in order to get paid. In 1943, the guaraní had replaced the Paraguayan peso, with one guaraní worth 100 pesos. At that time, guaraníes came in paper bills, but there were also aluminum-bronze coins in céntimos. Well before 1974, the céntimos fell out of use due to inflation making them essentially worthless. The formal exchange rate in 1974, used by Peace Corps and the Paraguayan government, was 126 guaraníes to the dollar. Monthly allowances, also called stipends, in rural sites in 1974 were 18,900 guaraníes, or $150. According to usinflationcalculator.com, this amount is the equivalent of $796 in 2021 dollars. When I converted my small savings of U.S. dollars and traveler's checks I brought with me, I could get 136 guaraníes to the dollar in an exchange house in Asunción. The pastel colors of the currency easily caught the eye. The 5,000 guaraní note, worth about $40, was bright red, while the 1,000 guaraní bill, at almost $8, was a muted purple. More commonly in my pocket were the orange 100 guaraní bills ($0.80) and smaller denominations.

With our bus fare paid, Steve and I found two seats together and watched out the window until we saw the small guitar shops along the side of the road, one after the other, with their wares displayed to entice shoppers. Leaving the bus, we approached the nearest store and stared at the shellacked guitars of various yellow-orange-beige earthy wood tones. Price determined which ones we would purchase, but it was pleasurably entertaining to listen to a vendor's description of each instrument's virtues.

At the third store, we lingered to admire the fine craftsmanship, obvious even to my untrained eye. It was a shop owned by Agustín Sanabria, who had learned the skill of guitar-making from his father. (There is now a fourth generation Sanabria named Gustavo who carries on this family tradition—see gustavosanabria.com.py.) We each purchased a Sanabria guitar for about $30, along with inexpensive cases to protect them. The guitar heads, where the tuning pegs are located, had lovely designs carved into the wood.

Catching a return bus with new guitars in hand, Steve and I discussed how things were going in our respective sites. I was curious how the special Ybycuí project was working out. Although Steve was the only new Volunteer in the town, Martina and Dave were veteran Volunteers wrapping up their Peace Corps service by starting up the project.

The three of them were currently preparing the hookworm and latrine educational materials for the elementary schools. Martina had sketched out a story translated as *Barefoot Pepe and the Hookworm* that could be printed on both sides of a paper and tri-folded into a booklet. The story simply related that a little boy named Pepe went barefoot and became tired and weak. When he went to the health center, the doctor gave him medicine and told him he should wear shoes and always use a sanitary latrine. The boy was ill because hookworms passed through the skin on his feet when he went barefoot. The little worms ended up in his intestine and sucked blood, making him ill. The worms also laid lots of tiny eggs that left his body when he pooped. If he didn't poop in a sanitary latrine, the eggs could develop into larvae that might get into other people who go barefoot. The larvae develop into tiny adult worms once inside a human body, and the cycle repeats itself. Pepe follows the doctor's advice and becomes healthy again.

Martina typed the initial mimeograph stencils for the story, drew the pictures into them by hand, and produced copies at the Peace Corps office. (Photocopy machines would not be available in Paraguay for at least another six years.) They also developed a one-page handout on "What Is a Sanitary Latrine?" and mimeographed copies of it. These two handouts would be given to the children when the Volunteers taught about hookworms and latrines in the elementary schools.

Their sanitation census was underway and involved systematic home visits of the roughly 700 houses in Ybycuí. Initially, Dave and Martina were each accompanied by a nurse from the health center. Once word spread around town about the census, the Volunteers began working on their own. When Steve arrived, Martina pulled out of the process. Dave and Steve worked together until Steve felt comfortable on his own. Approaching a house, they would practice proper Paraguayan etiquette by clapping their hands outside the front gate until someone appeared. After introducing themselves and exchanging pleasantries, they explained that the health center was conducting a sanitation census of every house in town. Interestingly, they encountered very little resistance to their saying, "Hi, we're North Americans. We would like to look at your latrine."

They recorded their findings on forms, one for each house, according to the official SENASA ratings. There were no homes rated as having a #1 facility, because there were no modern bathrooms on city running water. Ybycuí was several years away from having running water. Steve said there were some nice homes with modern plumbing operating with water from a private, elevated tank. Electric pumps filled the tanks with water, and gravity allowed the water to flush the toilet. These were rated #2. A sanitary latrine was deemed a #3. This meant that the latrine had walls and an easily cleaned cement floor. Paraguayan outhouses were typically squat latrines with a cement slab with a hole in the middle. On each side of the hole were raised foot pads, but there wasn't a throne to sit upon. A #3 sanitary latrine also needed a roof, a door that closed to keep out animals, and a cover over the hole to keep out flies. It was located a safe distance from the well to avoid water contamination. And of course, fecal material was not overflowing onto the floor. An unsanitary latrine lacked one or more of the needed items of a #3 and was ranked a #4. "No latrine" was rated #5. Steve commented that on a few occasions people told them that their latrine was too ugly for the North Americans to see, and he or Dave made an educated guess that it was a #4.

I asked how Dave happened to be assigned to the Ybycuí project. Steve explained that Dave had spent three-quarters of his service as a sanitation Volunteer in Puerto Rosario, several hours north of Asunción on the Paraguay River, and was fluent in Spanish and Guaraní. When he found himself in a politically difficult situation in town after speaking out a little too bluntly and negatively regarding the health center's doctor, Dave asked for a transfer elsewhere to complete his service. He confided to Steve that he was convinced the doctor, an immigrant to Paraguay from Germany after World War II, was an ex-Nazi. During training we had heard rumors about Nazis hiding out in Paraguay, including Dr. Josef Mengele, the notorious "Angel of Death" responsible for cruel and deadly medical experiments on children in the Auschwitz concentration camp during the war. It was a disturbing thought. (In fact, historians have confirmed that Mengele entered Argentina in 1949, fled to Paraguay in 1959, and entered Brazil in 1969. He lived in Brazil until his death in 1979, successfully resisting extradition requests by West Germany and evading Nazi hunter and Holocaust survivor Simon Wiesenthal.)

Steve wasn't sure what would happen when Martina and Dave completed their service in October. He hoped that the census would be done by then. The three of them were working as fast and efficiently as they could, but they were already behind in their timeline. In addition to the census, the education program in the schools had premiered with the showing of an entertaining cartoon movie in Spanish that taught about hookworm and the importance of sanitary latrines. Steve and Dave borrowed the movie and a projector from Peace Corps for this activity. Each audience of children saw the movie twice—the first time with the Spanish soundtrack and the second with Dave's narration in Guaraní.

Steve chuckled as he related a blooper Dave had made at the presentation for the Catholic primary schoolchildren when narrating the film in Guaraní. In one segment of the movie, there is a cross-section drawing of a latrine showing a cartoon figure with hookworms in his intestine. He was "doing his business" in the latrine. The eggs laid by the hookworms, along with the feces, fall into the latrine and die. Dave meant to say that when someone with hookworm uses the latrine, *"La jhupi-á jho-a-pá-ta jha omanó-ta"* ("The eggs will fall out and die"). However, instead of j*hupi-á* for "eggs," he changed the "u" to an "a" and said j*hapi-á,* which means penis. Although Steve was busy running the movie projector, he retrospectively thought that the nuns looked a little funny and some of the children giggled. One little boy, taking Dave at his word, went home and told his mother that he wasn't ever going to use the latrine again! After discovering the reason, the mother told the doctor's wife, who told Martina, who told Dave about the error, involving the difference of one letter.

Steve and I recalled another language blooper that occurred during our time in Ponce. Pat, the experienced Paraguay Volunteer previously mentioned, ordered a salad at the training center's small food counter staffed by an elderly Puerto Rican man. As Pat sat down to eat it, she noticed a bug in the salad. Returning to the man behind the counter, Pat pointed to the salad and calmly said, "*Señor, hay un bicho en la ensalada*" (Sir, there's a bug in the salad). I saw the man's face pale when he staggered back a few steps, and it looked like he was having a heart attack. (He wasn't.) While in Paraguay the word *bicho* means a bug or bothersome thing, in Puerto Rico it is a crude slang word for penis. A Peace Corps staffer intervened to explain and diffuse the situation, which served as a humorous lesson on vocabulary variation among Spanish-speaking countries. Steve and I could only wonder how this slang word had come about.

I confessed to him an embarrassing slip of the tongue while a college student in Bogotá, Colombia. I had not enjoyed the food there until my classmate Paulette and I vacationed on the northern coast. While guests of a family there, we were treated to a delicious rice and coconut dish laced with sautéed seafood morsels. They called it *arroz con coco* (rice with coconut). The bland, boring white rice I had eaten as a main part of my diet was transformed into a culinary delight. Back in Bogotá talking with a group of Colombian students, someone asked me what my favorite Colombian dish was. After a brief moment when nothing came to mind, I remembered that meal on the coast and blurted out, "*Arroz con caca*." Yes, I really said, "Rice with poop." Just the difference between "o" and "a." I commented to Steve that it was almost as bad as using the word "*coger*" in Colombia. While in other places the word means "to grab or catch," in Colombia and a few other countries it is a crude word for sexual intercourse. A story circulated among the North American college students in Bogotá that when one innocent English speaker had asked a local person in rudimentary Spanish where he could "catch the bus," he was told, "at the exhaust pipe."

We agreed it had been odd to spend two months hearing Puerto Rican Spanish and experiencing a culture different from that of our Peace Corps host country. Throughout our two months in Ponce, we trainees wrestled with the Puerto Rican version of the Spanish language. I told Steve about hearing a man yelling in downtown Ponce, "Hamón, Hamón," with an initial hard guttural "h" sound, which in Spanish would be a "j." I thought he was shouting, "Jamón, Jamón," which meant, "ham, ham." When a second man a short distance away responded to the shouting, the light bulb came on in my head—he was calling out the name *Ramón* (Raymond in English). It became apparent to me that the trilled "r" in Spanish turned into a harsh guttural "h" sound in Puerto Rico. A single "r" was often pronounced as an "l," giving the island the name of "Puelto Hico." The dropped "s" at the end of words and quick slurring of sounds were common as the tongue took shortcuts. Paraguayan Spanish was a lot easier to understand, we agreed.

During my time in Asunción with Steve, we enjoyed reflecting on our Peace Corps training and service thus far. He and I hadn't talked much, except for passing comments, since our journey down to Paraguay. At the end of our training in Puerto Rico, Peace Corps booked our training group on Braniff Airlines, at the time the only U.S. carrier flying into Paraguay. We were routed via Barranquilla and Bogotá, Colombia; Lima, Perú; and La Paz, Bolivia, where we were to change planes for a non-stop flight to Asunción. Although trips with fewer stops were available on foreign carriers, the U.S. government required Peace Corps personnel to travel on U.S. airlines.

During the stop in Lima, Perú, a flight attendant's voice announced the names of everyone in our training group, asking that we gather our belongings and leave the plane. The next leg of the flight was overbooked, and we lacked confirmed reservations. We would have to wait for the next Braniff plane with space available, which could be several days. Stranded with limited cash, we made our way to the local Peace Corps office, where the staff notified Peace Corps Paraguay regarding the delay and provided us with local currency and hotel advice.

With the unexpected time in Lima, I recalled that the Ponce trainers had mentioned that if we were ever in Perú, the Larco Museum in Lima had an archeological exhibit worth visiting. The museum features artifacts from the Moche civilization, which dominated the northern coastal and valley areas of Perú from the first century to 800 A.D. It produced some of the finest burial tombs, pottery, and jewelry of gold and silver in the Americas. The trainers recommended that we view the Larco's "special exhibit," but they declined to give us any details about it. Feeling more comfortable touring with just one other person, I asked Steve if he might be interested in going with me to the museum. He was willing.

Steve and I went the following day, paid our admission, and looked around for the exhibit. Because no signs were posted, I approached one of the military guards armed with a rifle. Before I even finished my question, with a bored look he pointed to an unlabeled room. As we entered the room and focused on the nearest display, a cabinet of several shelves packed with artifacts, my jaw dropped. The exhibit was an eye-opening collection of pre-Colombian erotic art that had escaped destruction by the Spanish conquerors and their Catholic priests. I was too shocked to be embarrassed. The scores of human and animal clay figurines, some colorful and others a cinnamon-brown, demonstrated a variety of sexual acts, celebrated maternity from pregnancy to delivery to breastfeeding, and depicted erotic interactions between humans and various animals. (For more information, see atlasobscura.com/places/larco-museums-erotic-art.) After Steve and I gawked at these artifacts, we enjoyed a Peruvian lunch together.

A few days later, at the end of April, our training group resumed the journey on Braniff Airlines, flying from Lima to La Paz. Next, rather than flying directly to Asunción, we proceeded to Santiago, Chile, where we had the option to deplane. I felt safer staying onboard. Steve and a few others from our group got off the plane, only to be kept under stern scrutiny in a room guarded by rifle-wielding soldiers. In September 1973, only seven months earlier, Chile's General Pinochet had seized power from the democratically elected government of Dr. Salvador Allende in a bloody coup covertly supported by the U.S. government. The coup would be followed by 17 years of Pinochet's vicious, brutal repression. Even in an airport holding room for transient international passengers, the military presence was intimidating.

From Chile, we continued our convoluted trip around the southern part of the continent by proceeding to Buenos Aires, Argentina, and changing planes there to enter Paraguay, finally, from the south. Our logged mileage from Lima to Asunción was roughly 4,100, almost double the direct distance as the crow flies. Our flight path looked to me like an upside-down question mark, bringing to mind curious thoughts about what our futures held. After being in the presence of rifle-toting soldiers during our brief time in Peru and Chile, we were about to enter Paraguay under the military dictatorship of General Alfredo Stroessner.

A month into our actual Peace Corps service, it was emotionally helpful to reflect with someone from my training group about what we had experienced and learned in recent weeks. When Steve asked how I was doing, I told him about holding the flashlight for the C-section, vaccinating children in outlying areas, and giving health talks. Looking forward to returning to Itacurubí del Rosario the next day to resume my work, I was silently glad I hadn't been sent to Ybycuí. Perhaps Peace Corps would soon figure out some way to provide Steve with the support needed to continue the project, but I was glad not to be involved in it. I was quite content in my town in the north.

∞∞∞∞

Back in Itacurubí del Rosario, I began practicing on the guitar by spending evenings learning some basic chords and simple songs from the U.S. Starting with "Tom Dooley" because it had only two chords, I haltingly played while singing, pausing to rearrange my fingers and then proceeding smoothly on beat until the next chord change. My frequent hesitations while changing chords probably bothered Kate more than my singing, as I noticed that she was softly attempting to sing along only to be thrown off by the intermittent pauses. I gradually improved, and over the next two years, I would expand my North American folk music repertoire to include a number of Paraguayan songs.

But now I faced the real possibility of being transferred to Ybycuí. I pondered what I might possibly do about it, hoping that a new doctor would soon come to Itacurubí del Rosario. A psychiatrist from a town an hour away began coming on Mondays and Fridays to see patients. People lined up by the scores for a consultation with the doctor.

To keep busy, I followed a suggestion of another Volunteer to prepare a filmstrip. First, I cut two strips of clear plastic. Next, with permanent markers, I drew on one strip the instructive hand-washing pictures of the health talk entitled "Panchita Po Ky-á" ("Francis Dirty-Hands") acquired in the Peace Corps Office. Then, I used an iron (made of cast iron and containing hot charcoal) to fuse the second strip on top of the first. Lastly, I prepared the script in Guaraní. I presented it on a Friday morning to an audience of waiting patients. I pulled the fused plastic strips through a battery-operated filmstrip projector provided by Peace Corps. As the images projected frame by frame onto the wall of the darkened room, I read the story in Guaraní. The crowd applauded me.

One Friday, the visiting doctor took a local patient he labeled as "crazy" back to his health center in order to cure him. The patient's mother had insisted that he was throwing up live frogs, bees, and wasps. At the same time, I heard about a freak show coming to town. A man supposedly would lie down on two chairs, one chair under his head and the other under his feet. While in this position he would have five men sit on his chest. Due to rain, the super-chest show was cancelled. All of us in town were disappointed.

With my future in question, I told myself that somewhere, somehow, I would complete my two-year commitment. I had first considered Peace Corps service when in college. During my last semester at Albion College, I applied to both the Peace Corps and VISTA, and the latter organization responded first with an opportunity to serve in a program helping migrant and seasonal farm workers in the picturesque Rocky Mountain region. I accepted. A short time into my work in the Adult Basic Education Program of the Utah Migrant Council, Peace Corps offered me a physical education teaching position in Venezuela. I opted to complete my year in Utah, subsequently adding a six-month extension to cover another agricultural summer cycle, when sugar beets, potatoes, fruit trees, and vegetables required hand labor. Migrant families came from the Rio Grande Valley of Texas to work the crops. My VISTA housemate Peggy extended as well.

I had often translated for my other VISTA housemate, Punkin, a registered nurse whose job was to set up some basic health screenings and perform medical outreach services to migrant farm workers and their children. One day, she brought home a centrifuge and equipment to perform hematocrits, a simple screening test for anemia. She informed me, "I'll show you how to do it, and we can do screenings together. First, I'll stick your finger." After a quick wipe with an alcohol swab, she poked my finger with a lancet, drew the blood up into a thin plastic capillary tube, gave me a band-aid for my finger, and placed the tube into the centrifuge. "Now, you stick my finger," she said. Following her process but not wanting to hurt her, I made a first, feeble attempt. "Come on, Mary Lou, you have to put a little force behind it," she instructed. I took a deep breath and stabbed her finger with considerable force. Punkin yowled; I felt horrible. After composing herself, she forgave me and watched me fill a capillary tube with the blood oozing out of her finger. Then we spun my first ever lab test. Neither of us had anemia, but I was anxious to learn more. I didn't want to actually do the hands-on nursing things, but I wanted to become a health educator.

In addition to our regular duties in the education program in Utah, Peggy and I became involved in organizing extra activities for migrant children, including ice skating in an indoor rink, attending a circus with donated tickets, and short hiking trips in the Wasatch Mountains. On Halloween of 1973, Peggy and I completed our extended obligation.

After my VISTA service, I returned to my parents' home in Detroit and received a Peace Corps Nicaragua offer to work as a health educator. Although the job description enticed me, my Uncle Bob, a public administration professor at Penn State University with extensive international development knowledge, advised me to decline. "The Somoza regime is brutal," he said, "and I don't see a happy ending to it. There is growing violent opposition to the dictatorship." (Anastasio Somoza Debayle, the third in his family to lead Nicaragua, ruled the country from 1967 to 1979. In the early 1970s, the Sandinista movement opposing him grew in strength and eventually toppled him from power. Uncle Bob was right.)

My mother hoped Uncle Bob would say the same about the invitation to Paraguay that came a couple of months later. Instead, he encouraged me to accept it. "Yes, it's a dictatorship, but it appears to be a stable one. Give it a go." In early 1974, I responded favorably to the offer to serve as a health educator in Paraguay. (Years later, I learned that Peace Corps extended only three invitations per applicant at that time—three strikes and you're out.)

I bided my time in Itacurubí del Rosario for a couple of weeks, but then a fateful phone conversation took place. Effective communication was a complicated process in Paraguay in those years. Pat, the Volunteer trainer in Ponce, had given us suggestions about communicating with other Volunteers in the country. In rural areas, a telephone conversation was somewhat rare, quite costly, and time-consuming, particularly if a call was to someone without a phone. A call could be made to the government phone building in a town, and an errand boy would have to search for the person receiving the call. If found, the person would go to the phone building and attempt to connect back with the caller.

Telegrams were cheaper but didn't always work as anticipated. Pat told of a telegram she received from a Volunteer in her group working in a nearby town which said, *"Hay animales aquí"* (There are animals here). She thought, "Okay, there are animals everywhere in Paraguay, so what's the big deal?" When she next saw her friend, Pat asked for an explanation. Her friend explained that there were a couple of German tourists passing through her town. Knowing that Pat spoke some German, the friend thought Pat would hop a bus for a visit. The telegram should have said, *"Hay <u>alemanes</u> aquí"* (there are Germans here). Pat never found out if it was her friend or the Paraguayan at the telegraph office who committed the error.

In early July of 1974, the fateful phone call was a pre-arranged conversation between Kate and her supervisor Bob, the man in charge of Peace Corps' agricultural extension program. While Peace Corps director Jerry was on leave, Bob was acting director. At the time, Chuck was also away in the U.S. for some needed surgery, leaving Bob in charge of everything. While at the town's small telephone building and on the phone with her boss in Asunción, Kate mentioned my predicament of slow work due to Dr. Yinde's departure. Martina from Ybycuí happened to be in the Peace Corps office that day and heard about the situation. She telegrammed me, asking that I visit her in Ybycuí.

Rainy weather and the subsequent closure of the dirt road happily delayed my planned travel to Asunción to review my situation with Peace Corps staff. Watching the raindrops make fleeting pockmarks in the puddles in Kate's yard, I recalled my first experience with rain in Paraguay.

During our first full day after arriving in Paraguay, our group of trainees walked 25 minutes from the hotel where were staying to the Peace Corps office for our first training session. Fortunately, that day it didn't rain, and we were able to take in the sites. Old Spanish colonial-style buildings with tall adobe walls lined the narrow streets. The city was coming alive. Businesses were opening, multi-colored diesel buses were picking up and discharging passengers, horns honked, a red trolley car clanged its bell, and people were moving toward destinations unknown to me. Passing through the busy Plaza Uruguaya, a shady square adjacent to the old train station, I heard street vendors hawking food and goods. Leaving the plaza, I noticed the first and only supermarket in the country at the time. Called *El Mercado del País* (Market of the Country), it was less than a quarter the size of a modest urban U.S. grocery store. Later that week, a veteran Volunteer told me it was the only place in Paraguay selling peanut butter.

During that first walk with other trainees, I saw some of the ongoing efforts to modernize Asunción. Thankfully, because the city already had a clean, reliable running water system, we didn't have to worry about getting sick from the water in the capital. Other amenities were on the way. Stop lights, installed at the busiest intersections only a month or so before, were gradually beginning to control traffic, although running red lights was still a common danger. Along one side of the Plaza Uruguaya were enormous storm sewers awaiting installation. When it rained in Paraguay, people generally stayed home, both in urban and rural areas. In urban areas without storm sewers, a downpour could turn streets into fast-flowing rivers. Rural roads were packed dirt that turned into muddy messes when it rained. Although there were occasional cobble-stoned streets in rural towns that held up better in the rain, the wet dirt roads were closed to trucks, buses, and cars because heavy vehicles can quickly destroy them. Only motorcycles were permitted. Ox carts were allowed to travel alongside the roads. In order to prevent people from driving vehicles on wet dirt roads, there were barriers that could be swung out to block the road until the rain stopped and the roads dried. These were similar to what we use at railroad crossings, but they were manipulated manually.

A few days after our arrival in Asunción, we experienced our first big rain and learned what happens in areas of the city without storm sewers. We had rain gear—rain ponchos for everyone and umbrellas for the females. Males in Paraguay at that time did not use umbrellas, which were considered effeminate.

Because we thought that our training would occur as scheduled, we donned our rain gear and ventured out. We noticed very few people and minimal traffic at a time when the streets were usually crowded. It was still pouring buckets when we crossed the Plaza Uruguaya to find that the street in front of the *Mercado del País* had turned into a fast-flowing river a foot deep. No wonder curbs and sidewalks were so high! Although the city terrain wasn't particularly hilly, water treacherously flowed toward the nearby Paraguay River.

As an option to wading in the flood waters to cross that street, we could pay five guaraníes, or about 3¢, to walk on the boards supported by cement blocks that some entrepreneurial pre-teenage boys had assembled. The boys would remove their planks when the rare large vehicle came along. Then, when potential customers approached, they quickly set up boards again.

A few of us paid our five guaraníes and balanced our way, one by one, across the street and above the rapid current. Others in our group decided to wade. It did seem a little odd to pay young boys up to their knees in water so that we wouldn't have to wade through it. When we reached the Peace Corps office, all of us drenched in spite of our rain gear, we discovered that our training for the day had been cancelled. Upon reading the national newspaper *ABC Color* the next day, we learned that a woman attempting to drive a Volkswagen beetle down that street we had crossed had been swept into the Paraguay River and drowned. Thereafter, we decided to follow the common Paraguayan wisdom to stay inside when it rains.

Waiting for the rain to stop and the roads out of Itacurubí del Rosario to dry out, I passed the time talking with Kate or the health center staff while we shared the ritual of drinking *yerba mate* (YAIR-bah MAH-teh), the ubiquitous cultural tea-drinking habit. Cold *tereré* (teh-reh-REH) keeps people hydrated in the scorching summer, and hot *mate* warms them in the winter. It was July, winter in the southern hemisphere, and we drank the hot version.

I had come a long way since my first *yerba mate* experience in Ponce with Volunteer Pat only a few months previously. After my training group arranged our chairs in a circle, Pat sat down with the accoutrements for cold *tereré*—a *guampa* (GWAM-pah), a tea receptacle made from a cow's horn; the loose tea; a pitcher of ice-cold water; and a *bombilla*, a metal straw with a perforated bulb on the end that serves as a tea filter. (In other countries where Spanish is spoken, *bombilla* means "lightbulb.") After shaking tea leaves from a paper container into the *guampa* until it was about half-full, Pat nestled the *bombilla* into the *guampa*, poured in water, let it brew briefly, and then slowly slurped the tea until a sucking noise indicated the water was gone. With a grimace, she commented that the first serving is sometimes so potent that the server will spit it out onto the ground. With one person serving the others, Paraguayans drink the tea in a counterclockwise order that goes round and round until all participants are sated. When a participant says *"gracias"* (thank you) upon handing back the *guampa*, it indicates that he or she doesn't want any more.

Refilling the *guampa*, Pat asked who would like to try it first. I volunteered, accepted the *guampa*, sniffed a little to get an idea of what the flavor might be like, and gingerly sucked on the *bombilla*. As the pungent tea invaded my mouth, I gulped hard to swallow it without gagging. With a forced smile on my face, I attempted to return the *guampa* to her. Pat promptly refused, reiterating that I had to slurp all of the tea in the *guampa* before handing it back. It was a strong and bitter half-of-a-cup volume. I stoically managed to draw on the *bombilla* until everyone heard the loud slurping sound. As I passed the *guampa* to Pat, I promptly told her *"gracias."*

Everyone tried it, but nobody cared for it. Pat bluntly stated that drinking *yerba mate* was an important daily social opportunity to discuss the weather, the latest happenings in town (*chisme*, or gossip), work, and life in general. To keep our session going, she explained that for hot tea, the container is a gourd, called a *mate* like the tea itself. The same circle process is used. She cautioned that there's a risk of burning one's lips on the metal *bombilla* as it heats up when hot tea passes through it. She advised us of another risk—inadvertently clogging up the *bombilla* with tea, just as a trainee, vigorously sucking to no avail, began to stir with the *bombilla* in a futile attempt to unclog it. Pat motioned with her hand for the return of the *guampa*, and she gently rotated the *bombilla* to loosen the tea from the bulb perforations.

At the end of our first *yerba mate* session, someone accidently (or on purpose?) dropped the *guampa*, spilling the deep green *yerba mate* leaves on the white tiled floor, leaving a streaked stain. We shared *tereré* several more times during training, occasionally eyeing that permanent green floor stain. After a few months of frequent imbibing since then, I had a fondness for the social bonding ritual as well as for the taste of the tea itself.

∞∞∞

I finally left for the capital early on July 23rd to meet with Bob about my situation in Itacurubí del Rosario. Once at the Peace Corps office in the late afternoon, I tore into my mail from home and read *Time* magazine with heightened interest, enjoying the distraction from my personal dilemma. The U.S. Supreme Court had directed Richard Nixon, embroiled in the Watergate investigation, to turn over the clandestine White House tape recordings he had been guarding under executive privilege. I had been following the news as closely as possible since the U.S. House of Representatives opened impeachment hearings the previous May. It all seemed unreal.

After meeting with Bob, it was clear the Peace Corps wanted to transfer me. The following day, I traveled three hours by bus from Asunción to Ybycuí to meet with Martina. Only the last hour was on a dirt road. Returning to the capital the next day, I wrote to my parents the simple statement, "It looks like a good place to work. I'm going back to Itacurubí del Rosario tomorrow to pack my things." I had lived there just a few days less than two months. My heart was heavy.

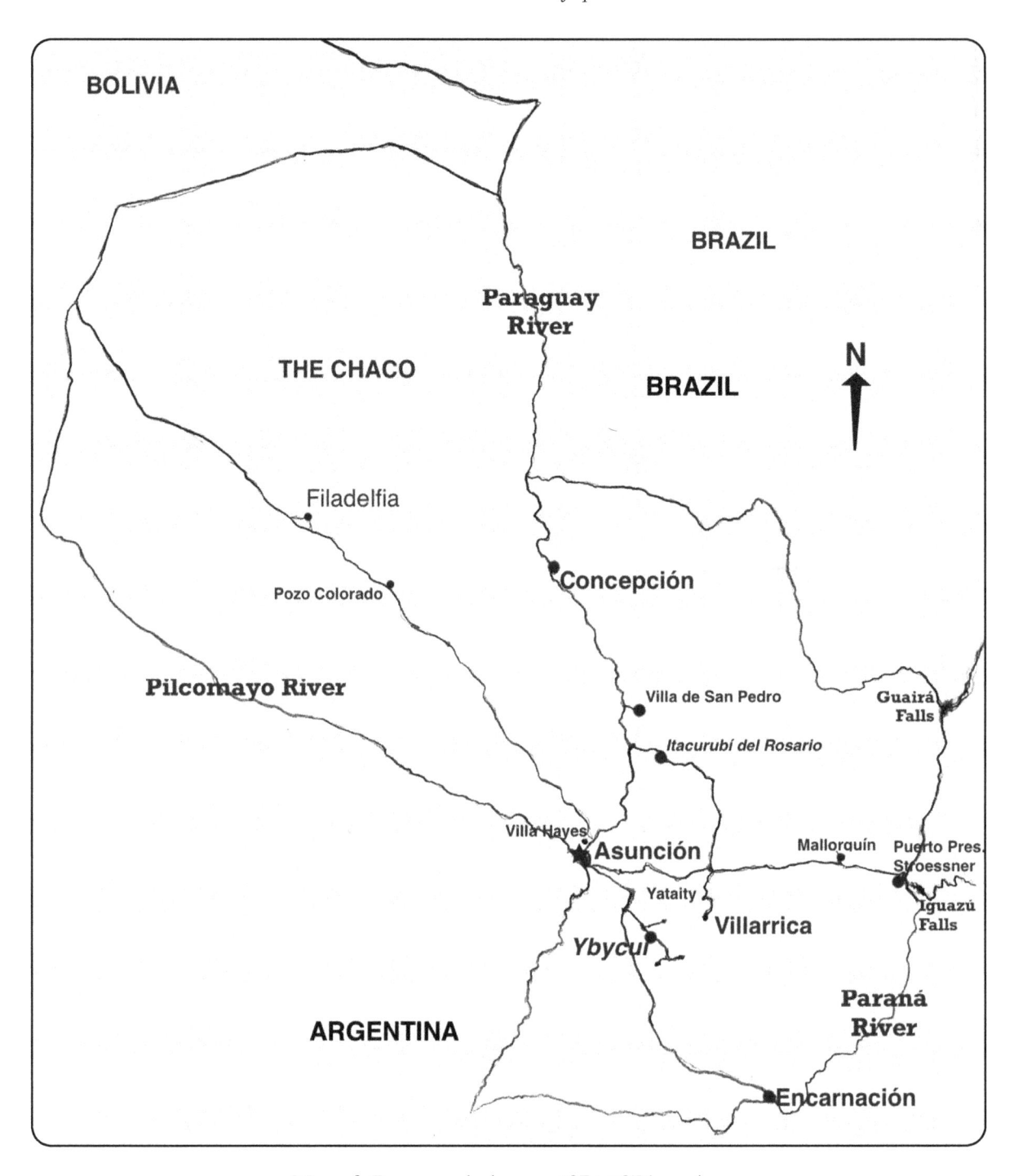

Map of Paraguay, during my 1974-1976 service

Our swearing-in ceremony at the American Embassy in Asunción, left to right: Steve, Cathy, Cindy, Wyn, Mary Lou, Pauline, Marty, Burl, Karen, Loni; not present: Larry and John. (Courtesy of Peace Corps Paraguay)

Kate's rented house in Itacurubí del Rosario

Ready to vaccinate near Itacurubí del Rosario;
the midwife is on the left, and Oscar is second from the right.

Spiderweb lace displayed on the highway through Itaguá, my first rural site visit

Standing by a termite hill, much larger than my 5'2" frame

CHAPTER 2

The Special Project in My Last-Choice Town

Start where you are. Use what you have. Do what you can.
—Arthur Ashe

Abel deftly guided the Peace Corps pickup truck on the smoothest parts of the dirt road, avoiding the ruts and potholes. I was relieved I didn't have to haul my belongings from Itacurubí del Rosario to Ybycuí by bus. It would have taken me two days and two different buses. In addition to what I had brought to Paraguay, I owned a simple wooden-framed bed with leather strips crisscrossed to support a rather thin mattress stuffed with lumpy cotton. For my clothing and other personal things, I had purchased a wooden armoire, a free-standing closet. Paraguayan houses did not have built-in closets because they would trap humidity and result in a mold problem.

Laying on top of my pile of belongings was the lightweight but bulky mosquito net for my bed, an essential item to prevent bites by that annoying nocturnal insect. Early on, I had developed the nighttime ritual of tucking the bottom end of the mosquito net under the mattress edges and searching the interior of the netting with a flashlight for mosquitos trapped inside with me. Although heavy, targeted DDT spraying throughout Paraguay during the previous decade had eliminated the *Aedes aegypti* mosquito that transmitted yellow fever and the *Anopheles* mosquito that carries malaria, there were swarms of other mosquitoes alive and thirsty for blood in Paraguay. Even the upper-class families in Asunción used mosquito nets rather than installing screens on their windows, as people felt that screens cut down on air circulation desired in the summer. I had also purchased a kerosene lamp, useful for reading after the generator in Itacurubí del Rosario had been turned off. My Paraguayan guitar rounded out my acquired belongings.

As the Volunteer coordinator for the men in the agricultural extension program for the Peace Corps, Abel was well-versed in Paraguay and things Paraguayan. He had been a Volunteer in Ybycuí for three years before taking on his program's coordinator position. Each program area in Paraguay had experienced Volunteers willing to extend their length of service to assist Peace Corps staff in administering the programs. Now he drove extensively throughout the country, visiting agricultural extension Volunteers to provide technical assistance and general support, screening locations for possible Volunteer placement, and moving Volunteers when necessary.

We zigzagged our way on dirt roads in a general north-to-south direction for about 175 rural miles. Abel slowed down as we passed through small communities and sped up in the sparsely populated areas, where we left a trail of dust behind us. Way to the west somewhere was the Paraguay River, and to the east was the Paraná River, both of which paralleled our route. We intermittently talked and listened to music on my tape recorder while traveling through the green, rolling countryside for the nine-hour trip to my new site.

As a Mexican American in Texas, Abel had grown up speaking Spanish. In Paraguay, he quickly became fluent in Guaraní and was often mistaken for a tall and lanky Paraguayan. Driving me to Ybycuí was like a homecoming for Abel, and he shared his experiences with me as he drove. Although I knew a good deal about my host country, Abel filled in some of the gaps in my knowledge.

The Guaraní word "Paraguay" literally means "water that comes from the sea" (*para* = sea; *gua* = comes from; *y* = water). The landlocked country borders with Bolivia on the northwest and Brazil on the northeast, while Argentina wraps around Paraguay from the southwest to the southeast. The country itself is divided into east and west sections separated by the Paraguay River. Flowing a southerly course from Brazil, the river creates the geographical split between the semi-arid and sparsely populated Gran Chaco area to the west and the lush, green-forested jungle areas with most of the country's inhabitants to the east. Most Volunteers during my service worked in sites in the eastern half of the country. The one exception I knew of was Burl/Reynaldo in the town of Villa Hayes on the eastern edge of the Chaco.

The Paraná River, forming Paraguay's eastern border with Brazil and Argentina, is a rich source of hydroelectric power. In 1973, Brazil and Paraguay signed a treaty for the development of an enormous dam. In 1975, the construction of the Itaipú Dam would begin on the Paraná as a Brazilian-Paraguayan project. It would generate power in 1984. (By 2020, it would be one of the top-producing hydroelectric power plants in the world. Unfortunately, the vast lake created by the dam would flood the massive Guairá (gwa-ee-RAH) Falls 135 miles upriver. In 1975, I would have the good fortune to visit the magnificent waterfall system before it was inundated in the name of progress. While electricity can improve the quality of lives, the loss of this natural wonder is a tragedy.)

Although Paraguay is far from the jungles of the Amazon River basin and the Andes Mountains, it does have remote jungle areas and some rolling, rugged hills as well as an occasional isolated *cerro* (hill) or two in relatively flat areas. Two such hills in the vicinity of the town of Ybycuí are the volcanic-looking *Cerro San José* and the Sleeping Lady of Acahay (A-kah-AYE), named as such because it looks like a woman in repose outside of the town of Acahay.

In rural areas throughout Paraguay, agriculture was the basis of the economy. Many rural families lived by subsistence farming. Most important were their plots of *mandioca*. Translated as manioc in English and *mandi-ó* (mahn-dee-OH) in Guaraní, it was the carbohydrate staple in the Paraguayan diet. This bland, starchy tuber is also used to make the spray that stiffens clothing when ironed. A derivative of the tuber is used to make the sweet tapioca pudding I remember eating as a child. Families also grew citrus and tropical fruit trees that contributed vitamins to their diet as well as corn. Chickens were ubiquitous, but people generally raised them for their eggs, serving the actual chicken only on special occasions. *Yerba mate* and sugar cane were also cultivated. The small coconuts growing on palm trees could be eaten or used for its oils.

If families had a cow or two, they had milk. Farmers who raised herds of cattle sold the animals to a local butcher for slaughter and subsequent sale to the populace. Meat was successfully exported, but Abel explained that the international beef prices were dropping, and the future of beef exports was unclear. (Paraguayan beef exports increased after the 1970s. According to worldexports.com, Paraguay ranked 15th in the world in the export of beef in 2019.) Cotton and tobacco were used within the country as well as exported. Tobacco use, in the form of cigars, was common by both men and women in rural areas. Its odor was earthy, acrid, and strong.

Agricultural extension programs in Paraguay involving Volunteers focused on crop and animal improvements, including the introduction of soybean for local consumption and exports. Abel explained that female Volunteers, like Mary Wirges in Ybycuí, organized 4-C clubs, similar to our rural agricultural 4-H clubs. The Cs were for *cerebro* (brain/head), *corazón* (heart), *cooperación* (cooperation), and *civismo* (civility), while the H stands for head, heart, hands, and health. At the 4-C clubs, teenaged girls were introduced to nutritious recipes using locally grown soybeans to boost their family's protein intake. In addition to her regular Volunteer activities, Mary was organizing a girls' volleyball tournament to encourage physical activity that wasn't work and provide an opportunity for rural girls to socialize. People in Ybycuí and Peace Corps fondly called her María-í, with the last accented "í" indicating "little" in Guaraní. That was to distinguish her from two other Volunteers named Mary: María Guazú (wah-SU, big Mary) and María Guai-guí (why-WEE, old Mary). Abel knew the people in and around Ybycuí, and he spoke fondly of the Feltes family in whose home he had lived. Mary was currently living with them.

Abel didn't know much about the special hookworm eradication project, but he confirmed that Martina had arranged for me to stay with a family who had hosted two North American male high school volunteers from the vaccination program called Amigos de las Américas (Friends of the Americas) for a short period of time the previous year. Being an independent person, I was apprehensive about living with a family but thought it would help me adapt to life in the town.

Upon approaching the town after dusk, Abel slowed the truck. The headlights shed some light on the small Paraguayan homes behind gated fences of wood or bamboo. Most of the houses had whitewashed adobe walls. Soon we were on the tree-lined main avenue of Ybycuí, made of hard-packed reddish dirt, and I noticed that the storefronts and homes generally lacked front yards. The buildings had tall, flat façades and large wooden doors shut tight for the night. Some buildings had a series of columns supporting the overhanging eaves of the roofs.

Abel turned off the main avenue and pulled up to an attractive house with a tiled roof, rather than the thatched roofs of more modest homes. The fenced-in front yard had a neatly manicured flower garden with a rainbow of colors visible by the light of the front door and the vehicle's headlights. Exiting the truck, Abel loudly clapped his hands at the front gate and introduced me to the family members who came out the front door. He then unloaded my belongings and left for the Feltes' home for the night.

The family's mother, Ña Elisa, was known as a good cook and had the hefty physique to prove it. She was about 5'4", only two inches taller than I, and had dark wavy hair and eyes that constantly scanned her environment. Her husband Don Angel, also large, was a kind-looking man with a pencil-thin mustache and straight dark hair. He owned and manned a pharmacy two blocks from the house. There were still three children at home—two teenage boys (José and Luis) and an overweight pre-teen girl (Teresa), as well as a large, mean-looking dog named Johnny, who growled at me. The younger son, Luis, had friendly brown eyes like his father. An older daughter, Mabel, was married and living in the States with her husband, a Paraguayan pediatrician.

Ña Elisa proudly showed me her house. I followed her into a small pink-walled living room with a black & white television. Only one channel was available in the country in 1974. The kitchen had a gas stove with an oven and shiny white electric refrigerator, which she had purchased the year before when the town received electricity through the national system. The large fenced-in backyard contained the well, the shower (for bucket baths, as there was no running water), a laundry tub, more manicured gardens, fruit trees (papaya, mango, orange, grapefruit, guava, and avocado), and finally the latrine at the far end near the property line fence. This rural Paraguayan house had many physical comforts.

Although it was late and the family had already eaten, Ña Elisa fed me dinner and then took me to my room. My belongings had already been moved in. I closed the door and collapsed on the bed, exhausted from the long trip after saying goodbye to my friends in Itacurubí del Rosario.

In the morning, I awoke refreshed and ready to face the day. First, I had breakfast, immediately realizing that becoming part of a family would be different than living with Kate and eating at her house or at a small restaurant. Ña Elisa showed me my designated place at the table where I would sit for each meal, allowing me to use the same edge of the cotton tablecloth hanging over the side as my personal napkin. Tablecloths, which were changed a couple of times a week, also provided a place to cut one's *mandioca*.

Every midday and evening meal we had *mandioca*. Peeling off the dark brown husk containing cyanide before boiling the tuber avoids poisoning. It is served plain on a platter. As Pat explained to us in Ponce, we should stab a piece of the tuber on the serving platter with a fork and plunk it down on the tablecloth next to our plates. After cutting a bite-sized piece with a knife, we'd then pierce it with our fork and eat it. *Mandioca* is also used to make flour, which can be mixed with wheat flour for baking. Leftover fried and salted *mandioca* is called *mandi-ó xyryry* (shuh-ruh-RUH), an onomatopoeic word meaning "frying."

For breakfast, Ña Elisa served me coffee, made from Instant Nescafé and milk, and hard Paraguayan bread made with *mandioca* and wheat flour, served with a fruit jam. Rather than coffee on some mornings, I would enjoy *cocido* (ko-SEE-do), a brew of *yerba mate*, hot milk, and caramelized sugar sipped from a mug that was also served to the children in the family. Ña Elisa served Don Angel hot *yerba mate* using a *mate* and *bombilla* in the morning and frequently drank it by herself during the day, but she never invited me to partake with her. That first morning, she told me that Martina would be by the house shortly to take me to the health center. Sitting down across from me, Ña Elisa talked while I ate. She assured me that I would eat well in her house.

Ña Elisa told me that I could take a shower every day, clearly insinuating that I should. She bluntly stated that the two North American teenaged boys who had lived in her house the previous winter had not bathed frequently, and many days they smelled bad. I was taken aback by her critical tone. Her talk was interrupted by hand clapping outside the front fence. Ña Elisa opened the front door and invited Martina into the house. They greeted each other in the Paraguayan way between two women, touching cheeks on both sides and exchanging pleasantries in Guaraní. I finished my breakfast and gently dabbed my mouth with the tablecloth hanging over the table's edge in front of me. Martina and I left on foot for the health center on the other side of town.

After leaving the house, we turned right at the first corner and walked west on a road parallel to the main avenue, passing house after modest house and an occasional person. According to custom, we exchanged a pleasant *adiós* with the people we passed. The word literally means "to God," and it is a way to wish people a good day or say goodbye. As in most rural Paraguayan towns, there were occasional cows, chickens, and pigs roaming freely, rooting and eating the garbage thrown out into the road. I began thinking of these domesticated animals as sanitation workers.

Martina, a determined young woman with a self-confident demeanor, lamented that her service in Paraguay was ending. She had grown to love Ybycuí, Paraguayans, and her work, but she admitted her readiness to return to the States. Inspired by her work at the health center with Dr. Orihuela, she was hoping to pursue a career in medicine. Martina spoke extensively of her positive relationship with Dr. Orihuela and his wife, Ña Irma. She was excited about the special hookworm eradication project in town. I silently admired her enthusiasm, hoping it boded well for my own service.

We passed a general store that was just opening its doors for business. I glanced in and saw some bolts of fabric, buckets, mops, soap, detergent, and an array of food items on display. Martina commented that the store belonged to Don Blasito. A few blocks later, we approached a small meat market in a grassy plaza. Martina indicated that Dave and Steve were living in the old gray building on the right with an elderly couple. Passing the semi-open market, I detected the smell of unrefrigerated meat. A small line of customers waited patiently to order cuts from the freshly butchered slabs hanging from large black hooks attached to the store's ceiling. I noticed flies in abundance swarming around and also attached to the beef.

Martina and I continued walking. We passed a wooden ox cart rambling down the dirt road with a family traveling in it. The lumbering oxen plodded along, pulling their heavy load and causing the cart's enormous wheels to squeak and moan as they rotated. We cut across the plaza and continued west.

Roughly twenty minutes after leaving Ña Elisa's house, we went through a gate and up a tree-shaded lane to the entrance of the health center. It was a tall one-story building with two wings, typical wooden doors, and windows with wooden shutters but no screens. The exterior was painted white except for the first yard up from the ground, which was a dark brownish red, the color of dried blood. Leaning up against a tree to the right of the entrance was a stack of large gray latrine floors. Called *losas* (LOH-sas), these sturdy and easily cleaned cement slabs were critical for the success of eradicating hookworms. Inside the entryway, we faced an open-air interior yard containing the well with an elevated tank for running water. Some latrines were located at the far end of the yard, a safe distance from the well to avoid contaminating the water. To the right and left of the entryway were covered, open-air corridors that ran along the two wings of rooms and offices. Wooden benches, where patients could sit while waiting for a consultation, lined up along the walls facing the interior yard.

There were two large multi-bed inpatient rooms for people staying overnight, one for men and the other for women. Because the health center did not have the capacity to provide food, relatives of the patients brought it in. Each painted metal bed frame held a thin mattress. At each bedside was a small wooden nightstand painted the same color as the bed frame. Between the beds were large wooden frames, each of which had a hanging cotton curtain to provide a modicum of privacy. In addition to the inpatient rooms, the health center had an office for the doctor, a dental office with a foot-powered drill, a laboratory, and rooms for examinations, delivering babies, conducting simple surgeries, and for the environmental sanitation staff. The laboratory had a large table upon which sat shelves holding racks of test tubes and an array of dark brown, light green, and clear bottles containing chemicals, all reminiscent of an old apothecary's stock of medicines. It also housed a kerosene refrigerator, although the health center had electricity. Either the doctor felt that kerosene was more reliable during times of electrical outages or there was not yet money to replace it with an electric appliance. The interior rooms had walls painted a dark color the first yard or so up from the floor and a pastel upper color. I took in the facility's environment, wanting to feel inspired by new challenges but fighting back the feeling of being overwhelmed and intimidated by the special project.

Passing the patients waiting on benches, I could sense their eyes on me, causing me to feel like a curiosity. I knew that this feeling would fade in the coming weeks as I became used to my environment, as had happened in Itacurubí del Rosario. While I was introduced to the staff, I concentrated on remembering names and faces. Almost all of the staff members wore white lab coats over their street clothes, as I would be expected to do while giving health talks.

Miriam, the curly-haired receptionist, was a tall, attractive woman about 20 years old. She took down the names of patients wanting to be seen by the doctor, midwife, or dentist and located their small paper medical folders. She collected a nominal fee for each consultation, as allowed by the Ministry of Health. Miriam also handled the sale of small ampoules of Novocain for patients facing painful dental extractions or the foot-powered drill, but not all those needing numbing could afford the small fee. I grimaced at the thought of dental pain.

Short and smiling María Luisa was one of the handful of staff nurses trained by the doctor. Nimia, the lab tech and older sister of Miriam, was working in the laboratory and wore a white cap on her head as well as her white coat. After I met the graying midwife, Ña Carmen, who attempted to put on a semi-friendly face, Martina discreetly told me in English that her disposition was usually not sunny.

Respectfully and timidly, I shook hands with Dr. Orihuela, whom I had met briefly during my first visit with Martina. The white-coated doctor was a 40-ish-year-old man of medium height and straight dark hair that always looked oiled. He had a short mustache, wore glasses, and displayed a somewhat stiff professional demeanor. He explained things in a technical fashion, making me feel like I should sit down and take notes while he lectured. His residency training had been at the Baptist Hospital in Asunción where a number of North American physicians were on staff. Dr. Orihuela was proud of the respect he had earned from Chuck, who had told the Volunteers in Ybycuí that it was okay for him to treat our medical problems in a pinch. Volunteers in other towns understood that under no circumstances should they seek local medical care. Rather, they should go to the Peace Corps office in Asunción when the need arose.

Obviously fond of Martina, Dr. Orihuela frankly told me that he hoped I would be as hardworking as she was. He expected me to be at the health center every morning during weekdays from 7 a.m. to noon giving health talks and helping out as needed. Although there could be exceptions, for the most part he wanted my work on the intensive sanitation project to be done in the afternoons. In each elementary school, there were three different sessions of students—morning, afternoon, and evening. I silently wondered about the morning classes we were expected to teach and whether Steve had any restrictions put upon him by the doctor.

Ña Irma, the doctor's wife, was frequently at the health center to help out however she could. In contrast to Dr. Orihuela, she seemed warm and approachable. She was a matronly woman with softly curled dark hair, glasses, and a quick smile. On many occasions during my time in Ybycuí, I sought out Ña Irma for cultural explanations about people's medical beliefs. For example, one time she explained how some people would often withhold water from their children with vomiting and diarrhea because they believed that giving liquids would simply cause more of the same problem. On another occasion, Ña Irma discussed cultural beliefs about avoiding the consumption of foods with inherent "hot" qualities at the same time as those having "cold" qualities. Hot and cold have nothing to do with temperature or spice; rather, they are culturally defined qualities. She gave the example that watermelon and wine are items of opposite qualities (I don't recall which is hot and which is cold), and both should not be consumed within a short period of time. If these parameters are violated, a person can become ill, with the watermelon turning into hard stone-like pieces in the stomach. Because meat is considered a "hot" item, while *yerba mate* (*tereré* as well as hot *mate*) is "cold," meat and *yerba mate* should not be consumed together. Therefore, a polite way to avoid drinking *mate* would be to say, "Thanks, but I just ate some meat." Ña Irma's stories, along with the compassion in her voice, were captivating.

Martina and I concluded our tour in the environmental sanitation room, where we found Steve and Dave sorting through their census forms. Setting the papers aside, the young men pulled up chairs for all of us. Steve maintained a quiet calmness about him. Dave, a thin individual with wavy blonde hair and blue eyes, showed steady energy that perhaps covered up a sense of fatigue. I glanced around at the large map of Ybycuí on the wall and the graphic of the hookworm life cycle, the only decorations in the room.

The three Volunteers brought me up to date on the status of the special project. It was easy to follow because of the information Steve had provided during our guitar shopping trip to Luque. Since then, they had almost completed the sanitation census. When I volunteered to tally the forms, they quickly took me up on my offer. They showed me the two educational pieces Steve had told me about—*Barefoot Pepe and the Hookworm* and the one-page form about a sanitary latrine consisting of a drawing and a checklist of its essential items. Martina had lead the development of these materials, and she typed stencils of them so that the Volunteers could produce a copy for each elementary school child to take home. The children were to read the story with their parents and use the form to inspect their own latrines.

Hookworms, sanitary latrines, roundworms, and hand washing now consumed my attention as a health educator. Peace Corps training had covered the essentials. I recalled from Chuck's sessions that hookworm infestation used to be prevalent in our rural south. It was common enough to be mentioned in the first chapter of Harper Lee's *To Kill a Mockingbird*, published in 1960:

"Walter Cunningham's face told everybody in the first grade he had hookworms. His absence of shoes told us how he got them. People got hookworms going barefooted in barnyards and hog wallows. If Walter had owned any shoes he would have worn them the first day of school and then discarded them until mid-winter. He did have on a clean shirt and neatly mended overalls."

During the mid-1970s, it was incorrectly accepted by medical and public health professionals that hookworm had disappeared in the U.S. by the mid-20th century. Unfortunately, unsanitary conditions in warm climates anywhere can cause hookworm infestation. (Even now, in the 21st century in the United States, there are people suffering from this parasite in areas that have inadequate waste water disposal. However, in the 2020 book *Waste: One Woman's Fight Against America's Dirty Secret*, author and advocate Catherine Coleman Flowers describes the open sewage problems caused by failing or nonexistent septic systems found today in Lowndes County, Alabama. She participated in and cites the 2017 study by the Baylor College of Medicine published in *The American Journal of Tropical Medicine and Hygiene*. Of the 24 households studied in Lowndes County, 42.4% reported a problem with raw sewage inside their homes. Researchers took 55 stool samples and found evidence of hookworms in 19 people, a rate of 34.5%. Flowers maintains that raw sewage disposal is a problem that can still be found not just in parts of Alabama but also in other southern states, California, the Midwest, and generally where poverty exists. According to the 2019 American Community Survey of the U.S. Census, 0.4% of the estimated 121,000,000 occupied housing units in the United States lacked complete plumbing facilities. Although 0.4% might not sound high, it represents almost 470,000 occupied units.)

    In Paraguay's rural areas in 1974, where many people went barefoot, sanitary latrines were often a scarcity, and running water for easy hand washing was almost non-existent. Scrutiny of Chuck's special project proposal, written in Spanish, provided a background of the public health need. It also detailed the lengthy work laid out for us.

Skilled at typing, I volunteered to produce additional stencils for the educational component of the project when the old ones wore out. We Volunteers had to pay for the stencils and other basic supplies with our living allowances, but we had access to mimeograph machines at the Peace Corps office. Creating stencils and producing copies with them took me back to my school years of the 1950s and 1960s, when my teachers commonly used them. I would become a pro with them in Paraguay. Each stencil, either letter- or legal-sized, had two layers. When the stencil was inserted into a typewriter, each typed letter would cut through the flimsy top layer but not through the waxy one underneath. When an error was made, the typist used a rounded paperclip edge to fill in the cut and a correcting liquid to patch the stencil before typing the correct letter. Once the page was completed and removed from the typewriter, the two layers were separated. The cut stencil was then placed on the mimeograph machine's round cylindrical stencil drum that turned manually by a handle. With each turn, the drum pulled through a piece of paper that, when making contact with the ink-laden drum, produced one paper copy of the stenciled letters and images. The ink used in Paraguay had the same distinct odor I remembered from my childhood.

Although a song about hookworm was not in the formal proposal, Martina suggested we write one in Guaraní. She and I did so during the next few days, and we called it "La *Canción de Cevo-i*" ("The Hookworm Song"). The word *cevo-i* (seh-voh-EE) means "worm" in Guaraní, and it can be spelled beginning with a "c" or an "s." Specifically, *py cevo-i* (PUH seh-voh-EE) refers to hookworm because *py* means "foot" in Guaraní, which is how the parasite generally enters the body. Roundworm in Guaraní is *cevo-i pytâ* (puh-TÁH), which means red worm, as it is usually red-tinged with blood when it exits the human body.

Martina's fluency in the language was impressive, but I was able to pitch in because the health words were some of the first I learned in the language. We put it to the tune of some North American folk song until Gloria, a local teacher and musician, came up with a catchy Paraguayan polka melody for us. (According to Wikipedia, the Paraguayan polka has a lively beat, combining a two- and three-beat rhythm. It differs from the two-beat rhythm of Czech and other European polkas.) How helpful that Steve and I both had guitars! Here's what Martina and I came up with:

La canción de cevo-í
Cevo-í, cevo-í, oipyté tuguy
Cevo-í, cevo-í, ñande mo-kangy
Oike-mi xe pype aikorô py-nandí
Ajhata ospital-pe xe pojhâ-no-mi
Oike-mi xe pype aikorô py-nandí
Ajhata ospital-pe xe pojhâ-no-mi.

Cevo-í, cevo-í, jajuká kená
Cevo-í, cevo-í, omanó jha jho-a-pá
Eipurú la sapatú, nê-resâi jhaguâ
Eguereko letrina i-potî porâ
Eipurú la sapatú, nê-resâi jhaguâ
Eguereko letrina, recacá jhaguâ.

The Hookworm Song
Hookworm, hookworm, sucks blood.
Hookworm, hookworm, makes me weak.
It enters into my foot when I go barefoot.
I will go to the hospital for some medicine.
It enters into my foot when I go barefoot.
I will go to the hospital for some medicine.

Hookworm, hookworm, let's kill it all now.
Hookworm, hookworm, it dies and all falls out.
Use shoes to be healthy,
Have a very clean latrine.
Use shoes to be healthy,
Have a latrine to poop in.

To address hand washing, we would explain the connection of roundworm acquisition with poor hand washing or food hygiene. When roundworms live in the intestines of a person, they lay eggs that fall out in the fecal material. If that person doesn't wash hands after using the latrine or if flies have access to human feces, an individual can ingest roundworm eggs from contaminated hands or food that flies have walked on. We also had a few specimens of roundworm in a jar of formaldehyde that Dr. Orihuela had given us for instructional purposes.

After using the handouts and teaching the song in each classroom, we planned to wrap up the educational program with a contest. This would involve the children completing a parasite or latrine mini-project at home and bringing it to school. A project could be a drawing or a little model that would reflect what they had learned. We planned to have prizes for all of the students. First prize in each class would be a color photo of the student with his/her family. Runner-up prizes were educational comic books in Spanish that we had acquired from USAID. The prize every child would win was a piece of candy—not very healthy but certainly popular and within our budget.

Steve, Dave, and Martina were also in the process of organizing a meeting to update town leaders about the project. Because the master plan called for a committee to provide us with advice and support, we hoped that such a group would be derived from the attendees. With advice from Dr. Orihuela and Ña Irma, the three Volunteers had scheduled it for August 23rd and were inviting the mayor, chief of police, municipality president, school directors, and a few others, including Mary and Ña Lali, her counterpart. (Peace Corps often assigned a Volunteer to work with a host country employee, and the two were referred to as "counterparts.") Although Steve was tapped to be the lead Volunteer at the meeting, I would attend, of course. Since Martina and Dave would soon be leaving Paraguay, they would be present to provide moral support. Dr. Orihuela agreed to introduce Steve.

∞∞∞

On August 9, 1974, Richard Nixon resigned from the presidency of the United States. The news reached us in Ybycuí via the Paraguayan newspaper *ABC Color*. The White House tapes Nixon was forced to give to Congress two weeks earlier had proved Nixon's participation in covering up the Watergate scandal during the 1972 presidential election. Burglars working for the Committee to Re-elect the President (CRP, or CREEP, as some adversaries preferred) broke into the Democratic Party's national headquarters at the Watergate complex in Washington, D.C., on May 28, 1972 and wiretapped at least one telephone. When they returned on June 17th to repair a wiretapping, they were caught and arrested. The ensuing process of investigation, including work done by *The Washington Post* reporters Bob Woodward and Carl Bernstein, compiled evidence of the crime and Nixon's complicity in the coverup. When Richard Nixon realized he faced certain impeachment by the U.S. House of Representative and conviction by the Senate, he opted to leave office before the ultimate disgrace of his impending removal.

Dave, Steve, Martina, and I gathered together to review the news of the president's resignation. President Nixon had not been a friend of the Peace Corps, which was founded by his adversary John F. Kennedy, who had defeated Nixon in the 1960 presidential election. While the Peace Corps had weathered the first term of Nixon's presidency that began in 1968, many advocates feared what might become of the program during his second term. Although there was no guarantee that Gerald Ford, the new president, would support the Peace Corps, we felt a sense of reprieve from attacks because Ford would have bigger challenges requiring his attention. We collectively breathed a sigh of relief and vowed to diligently continue our work at the local level of Ybycuí.

∞∞∞

Steve and Dave completed the sanitation census in mid-August. I compiled the results, including a breakdown by barrio (neighborhood) and rating the facilities as either sanitary or unsanitary. None of us was surprised by the results, which we shared with Dr. Orihuela. Of the 662 homes in Ybycuí, only 321 (48%) had sanitary facilities. There were 25 homes (4%) with no latrine at all. That meant more than half of the town needed a new sanitary latrine. There was work to be done.

On the morning of August 23rd, I awoke with a stomachache. Steve had been fretting about public speaking at our town meeting for three days, and I hoped he didn't have a stomachache as well. As the diarrhea and vomiting began, I knew I wasn't going any farther than the latrine that day. With a highly sensitive gag reflex to bad odors, I had developed the habit of breathing through my mouth when approaching a latrine. Unfortunately, these violent symptoms wouldn't let me do that. I spasmodically retched over the hole, inhaling fecal fumes with each breath. When I felt lower abdominal cramping, I changed to a squatting position over the floor opening, which left me in a weakened, pathetic state of existence.

By late morning, I agreed that Ña Elisa should send for the doctor. He came to the house almost immediately and gave me two injections, one for the vomiting and the other for the diarrhea. He also prescribed an oral antibiotic and told me to boil my water before drinking it for a few days as a precaution. After the town meeting, the Volunteers came to visit me. Dave and Martina said Steve did a great job with his presentation.

A few days later, I was well enough to get on a bus and visit the Peace Corps physician. When Chuck heard that Dr. Orihuela had put me on the antibiotic chloramphenicol, he told me to discontinue it immediately, as one of the side effects can be aplastic anemia, a condition in which there is damage to the bone marrow. It can result in a deficiency of all three kinds of blood cells—red and white blood cells as well as platelets—and aplastic anemia can be fatal. Due to its potential serious side effects, chloramphenicol was used only in rare situations in the United States. After that experience, I relied only on the Peace Corps medical staff for diagnoses and medications. I don't know if Chuck discussed avoiding chloramphenicol with Dr. Orihuela, but I never mentioned it to him.

∞∞∞∞∞

On my way home from the health center at noon on my first full day back in Ybycuí, I walked alone to Ña Elisa's house via the main avenue, smiling and saying *adios* to people I saw. Each side of the road was lined with bare-branched trees not yet showing springtime buds, as August was still mid-winter in the southern hemisphere. I passed the statue of General Bernardino Caballero in the middle of the intersection where Dr. Orihuela and Ña Irma lived. Ybycuí was the birthplace of General Caballero, President of Paraguay from 1881 to 1886 and the founder of the Colorado Party. I had heard that the town often received generous financial resources from the government of dictator Alfredo Stroessner because his party's founder was born there. Further along the way, I took note of the Municipality building and the pink façade of the *Seccional*, which housed the Colorado political party. I wondered what went on behind the scenes in Ybycuí, but thought it best to follow Peace Corps' caution to avoid discussing Paraguay's politics with local people.

Approaching my turnoff from the main road, I spotted Mary, the agricultural extension Volunteer, waving at me. I had met her briefly on my first visit to town. She now greeted me with a warm hug. Walking and talking in English, we discovered commonalities beyond our first name. We were both secondary education and Spanish majors in college, along with a minor in history. And we were both born on October 8, 1950. Mary blurted out, "We must have a big party on our upcoming birthday!" Vivacious, extroverted Mary immediately began throwing out ideas and planning in earnest for the event to be held in two months.

I resumed the hectic work pace. *Tranquilo* (tranquil) was commonly used to describe life in rural Paraguay. It was usually pronounced with a long, accented second syllable—trahn-KEEEE-lo. Life involved hard work, but people didn't rush around. They took time to drink *yerba mate* and talk with friends and neighbors. In Itacurubí del Rosario, I had been *tranquila*, without pressure or stress about timelines or project goals. However, beginning with the first day in Ybycuí, I was part of an effort that was far from *tranquilo*. We had North American deadlines with no time to spare. Although the sanitation census and the data analysis had been completed, the special project called for more elementary school teaching, the contest, and taking and distributing photographs of the winners. Chuck expected us to finish these tasks before the school year ended in November. Then we would conduct the stool sample study before proceeding into the phase of systematically encouraging families without sanitary latrines to build them.

Transition time would soon leave Steve and me with the project that had called for five Volunteers. Martina packed up her belongings, said her "good-byes" to everyone, and left on August 29th. Because Chuck was scheduled to leave his position in late September, the new Peace Corps physicians, a married couple who had previously served in Peace Corps Malaysia, arrived in late August to allow for some overlap. Bron was a pediatrician who would provide primary medical care for Volunteers. Her husband Eric, a psychiatrist, would be the health program officer. Dave began preparing for his departure in early October and was spending most of his time in Asunción. On the personal level, Mary and I had our birthday party to plan, and I was still struggling to adjust socially and financially to my new site. In addition, Steve and I faced a week away from Ybycuí to attend in-service training in Asunción.

As Volunteers in a rural area living on a tight budget, Steve and I also had the additional expenses of the educational materials and contest prizes for the special project. Fortunately, the project's budget covered resources for medications and laboratory expenses. Steve and I agreed to evenly split the cost of the materials and prizes needed for our jobs. During these busy days, Steve decided to save some money by renting a house on his own while continuing to eat meals with Ña Conchita, the elderly woman in whose home he had been living. He found an old three-room house with a large backyard but no electricity for about $8 a month. It was across the road from Don Blasito's general store and still an easy bicycle ride from the health center. Ña Elisa was charging me about $55 a month for room, board, and laundry.

Peace Corps also gave us a one-time transportation allowance of about $100 ($542 in 2021 dollars) to purchase a bicycle or horse. Motorcycles were allowed but were considered dangerous. Several months before we arrived in the country, a Volunteer had broken his pelvis in a motorcycle accident. Although he survived, he suffered greatly while laid out on the floor of a bus during the eight hours of being transported to Asunción. In addition to the safety concerns, a motorcycle cost about $350. Steve had recently purchased a bicycle locally, using all of his $100 transportation allowance for a one-speed purple bicycle. I was contemplating a bicycle as well, thinking that it would save me time and energy, both of which were limited. I planned on pricing them in the capital when I had an opportunity.

At the end of August, Steve and I went to Asunción for the week of in-service training involving more Guaraní classes and first aid instruction. We also had the opportunity to socialize with the others in our group. Some of us would lunch at the San Roque Restaurant a few blocks away or eat at the counter of the Bolsi near the main downtown plaza. We had to catch a red trolley car to the Bolsi, but it was worth it to enjoy a delightful dessert they always had on display—*dulce de leche,* a smooth caramelized milk spread, sandwiched between two round pieces of baked merengue made with sweetened egg whites.

In spite of the loud noises, diesel exhaust, and traffic congestion, the city seemed more *tranquilo* emotionally for Steve and me than Ybycuí, and we relaxed with the lack of project pressure. Others in our group talked about the laid-back atmospheres in their towns, contrasted with bustling Asunción.

When I asked other Volunteers for tips on purchasing a bicycle, Burl offered to help me buy one when I had the time. I tentatively arranged to meet him in his town of Village Hayes the following month. After finishing our training, Steve and I headed back to our town to resume project activities.

Mornings in Ybycuí seemed to come too early. I awoke to the loud chirping sounds of birds at the break of dawn. I don't know what kind of birds acted as my alarm clock, but Paraguay had feathered creatures from the ordinary (blackbirds, sparrows, swallows, finches, pigeons, woodpeckers, and parakeets) to the majestic (falcons, hawks, herons, and toucans with large bright-orange beaks). There were also tiny hummingbirds, including the iridescent glittering-bellied emerald, that flitted and zig-zagged with their almost-invisible delicate-looking wings. Red-breasted robins were nowhere to be seen.

An audio backdrop to the chirping was rooster-crowing, a penetrating sound that reminded me of a story I heard in Ponce during training. The cacophony of crowing roosters beginning before sunrise drove one sleep-deprived male trainee to come up with his own solution. He sought out the noise-makers in his immediate vicinity and slaughtered all he could find. Needless to say, he was terminated from his training group. Whether true or not, the story is an example of challenges we Volunteers can face under new circumstances and how not to cope with them. Having grown up in an urban area devoid of loud early-morning choruses of birds, I could appreciate the novelty of them.

On my trips to the health center, I avoided fresh cow pies emanating their pungent odor while walking at high speed so as not to be late for my expected 7 a.m. arrival. Sometimes I gave health talks in Guaraní to patients waiting to see the doctor. Other days, Steve and I prepared materials or taught in the schools. Toward the evening as I walked home feeling exhausted, I passed by houses with their doors open, allowing me to glimpse at the sparsely furnished front rooms illuminated by a single light bulb hanging from the tall ceiling. I smelled the aromas of the evening meal being prepared—fried mandioca, grilled meat, and perhaps the sweet smell of a cake baked for a special occasion—wafting from the outdoor or semi-enclosed kitchens that were common in rural Paraguay. I heard the occasional radio music or a live guitar accompanying a mellow voice singing traditional Paraguayan songs.

∞∞∞∞

In mid-September, I left town for a few days to run errands in Asunción before visiting Burl, A.K.A. Reynaldo, in Villa Hayes. While in the Peace Corps office, the Volunteers I encountered were buzzing with the news that on September 8th, President Ford had pardoned Richard Nixon for his Watergate scandal coverup. Ford said that he wanted to end the national divisions that the scandal had caused. The general opinion in the office, including my own, was one of betrayal. We wanted Nixon to be held accountable for his actions. However, as I headed toward Burl's town, the whole Watergate scandal seemed distant and surreal. My reality was Paraguay.

Villa Hayes was across the river to the west of Asunción and north of Clorinda, Argentina. In Clorinda, on the other side of the Pilcomayo River, bicycles and other items could be purchased at much lower prices than in Paraguay. Argentina was experiencing a period of hyperinflation, a situation that favored the buyer with foreign currency of any sort. However, Paraguayan officials at the border watched for items of value in order to tax them and/or collect bribes.

Burl said he frequently went back and forth across the border to buy goods. On occasion, he opted to smuggle items. Never before in my life had I smuggled anything. Burl assured me, "I do it all the time. It's easy, and everybody does it." Paraguay had a long history of corruption, including smuggling, bribery, cronyism, nepotism, and international drug running. Rumor had it that illegal drugs were filtered through Paraguay and left the country on jet planes for Europe and North America. When the planes returned, they were filled with Scotch whiskey and U.S. cigarettes, items readily sold on the streets for very low prices. In short, smuggling seemed to be a fact of life. I surmised that if I were caught smuggling a mere bicycle, I'd just have to pay a bribe. If I weren't caught, I'd have extra money for work supplies. I tried to justify it in my mind as a cultural experience. In the back of my mind, I heard my mother saying, "Just because everybody else does something doesn't mean you should."

Upon my arrival in Villa Hayes, I was readily directed to Burl's house—everybody knew where the Volunteers lived. Burl gave me a tour of his small house and explained in detail his methods of conserving water. At only 20 miles west of Asunción but located in the Chaco, Villa Hayes definitely had a scarcity of water. Unlike green and humid eastern Paraguay, the Chaco was arid and known for having deep wells go dry. Burl conserved water. He caught the occasional rainwater off the roof and stored it in an above-ground, covered cistern. He recycled dish and bath water to irrigate his small garden. Listening to him explain how he conserved water made me thirsty. However, having a mission to accomplish, a short time later we took a bus ride of an hour or so to the Pilcomayo River, stopping frequently to pick up passengers. At the river, we left the bus and walked across the small international bridge and into Clorinda.

Soon after arriving, I was the proud owner of a shiny new red bicycle for the price of about $50, half of what I would have paid in Paraguay. Burl purchased a few packages of foodstuffs and small household goods that we carried in tote bags. Before returning to Paraguay, we dodged off the road onto a dirt path leading to the edge the Pilcomayo River. About a hundred yards down the path, Burl pointed out some men drinking *mate* while lazing by canoes tied to trees on the bank. We approached them, and Burl deftly did some negotiating, finally nudging me to turn my new bicycle over to one of the men. I gulped but did so. As it was loaded onto the canoe, Burl and I took an about-face and returned to the border crossing. Presenting our passports and vaccination cards, we briskly walked over the bridge back to Paraguay. Once across, we again found a path along the Pilcomayo but this time on the Paraguayan side. A short distance away, we spotted the canoe with my shiny red bike, paid the previously negotiated fee of less than $7, and I had my one-speed bicycle! So I smuggled once. Successfully. Yes, it was an interesting cultural experience. I never did it again.

∞∞∞∞

Back in Ybycuí, I paid a small fee for a miniature license plate for my red bicycle, and then I rode it everywhere. I learned to dodge the free range chickens that would tend to dart directly in front of my bike with panicky yellow eyes in an illogical attempt to avoid getting run over. The question, "Why did the chicken cross the road?" became "Why did that stupid chicken dart right in front of me?"

With input from the principals, Martina, Dave, and Steve had developed a schedule for teaching in the three elementary schools in town. A few classes had already taken place, including the ones using the film in Spanish about hookworms (the one that Dave translated into Guaraní). Steve and I together continued the teaching, using the *Barefoot Pepe and the Hookworm* pamphlet and the latrine form. We repeatedly sang "The Hookworm Song" until the children learned it, and we introduced the idea of the contest. According to the plan, Steve and I had to complete the education component before the school year ended in November. Our bicycles made us more efficient, but we still had to hurry and scurry to keep the program from falling further behind Chuck's schedule.

Prior to his departure in late September, Chuck directed Steve, Dave, and me to organize a luncheon in Ybycuí to encourage involvement and support from the Ministry of Health and SENASA, as well as to boost local participation. We dealt with this task while continuing to teach the elementary school classes. Dr. Orihuela, the project director, and his wife Ña Irma would be present. Peace Corps physicians Chuck and Eric were invited, as were a married couple from USAID, Margarita from SENASA, a representative from the Ministry, the mayor, and the Catholic priest, whose support was considered important by all of us.

All but two of the invitees attended the pleasant luncheon in a private home with delicious food. Not appearing was the priest. We were told later that it might have been because the man and woman in whose home the luncheon took place were not married. The mayor was also a no-show. I feared we were moving too fast and pushing along without doing adequate prep work to avoid cultural mistakes. I can't recall who suggested the private home, but I remember that the reason for its selection was because the woman in the household was an excellent cook.

We didn't seem to accomplish much at the event with those who attended. Steve and I did receive some general statements of support, varied congratulations on our work to date, and subtle pressure and inquiries by Chuck as to when we would initiate the collection of stool samples from a randomized list of 10% of the town's inhabitants. In fact, Chuck had brought the randomized list, a centrifuge, laboratory slides, and other materials toward this end. Steve and I didn't have an answer for him because we first had to complete our teaching in the schools and the contest. The luncheon and site visit concluded with a group photograph in front of General Caballero's monument on the main road. A few days after the meeting, Chuck returned to the U.S., replaced by Eric as the health program director. Dave would soon be gone as well.

∞∞∞∞

Mary and I had our party scheduled for October 6, 1974, two days before our actual birthday. She came up with the ideas for the event and did most of the organizing. I was agreeable to whatever she suggested. Mary thought that we'd invite about a hundred people, and most would probably come. She estimated that it would cost about 30,000 guaraníes, or roughly $250. I told her I didn't have much money available, but neither did she. She assured me that people would gift us much of what we needed.

Ña Niní Cáceres de Feltes, Mary's Paraguayan mother, provided the venue, her small dairy farm called Posito, located just outside of town. ("Niní" was her nickname; Haydee was her given one.) It was a secluded place encircled by tall trees, bamboo plantings, and lush greenery, with cattle grazing in the distance. Posito had nice amenities for a large party, including a cookout pit for meat. Two small buildings, which housed the caretaker family and equipment for the farm, provided a place for food storage.

Abel came through as our hero. Not only did he provide the meat—beef and chicken—he also got up at 5 a.m. on the morning of the party to purchase it and begin preparing it. In addition, he provided four bottles of whiskey. Don Lalo Feltes, Mary's Paraguayan father, and Don Angel helped Abel cook the meat. Ña Elisa prepared a birthday cake. Peace Corps Director Jerry and Agricultural Program Officer Bob brought two kegs of beer. In addition to letting us use Posito, Ña Niní also baked a birthday cake and brought *mandioca* as well as some salads. Due to such generosity, Mary and I had little trouble covering the remaining costs.

Because this was a special occasion, Ña Niní also prepared the traditional *sopa paraguaya*, which literally translates as "Paraguayan soup." However, it is not a soup; rather, it is a tasty bread made with cornmeal, cheese, onion, eggs, and milk. It is traditionally baked in a clay oven called a *tata-kuá* (ta-ta-KWAH, hole of fire). According to legend, the dish came about in the mid-1800s when the cook for President/Dictator Carlos Antonio López made a mistake and added too much cornmeal to the soup, which was favored by López. Lacking time to start over, the cook placed the mixture in a pan and baked it. The president thought it was delicious and called it *sopa paraguaya*. It is a serious and steadfast tradition to serve *sopa paraguaya* at parties, during Easter week, and other notable occasions. It is particularly important to serve it at weddings, which is the origin of the forward question to people who are dating, *"¿Cuándo comemos la sopa?"* ("When are we going to eat the '*sopa*'?") Recipes for this typical dish are easily found on the internet, with variations using cream and lard. I prefer this one, adapted from a cookbook I no longer have:

Sopa Paraguaya (Paraguayan Corn Bread)
¼ cup canola oil
1 large onion, finely chopped
½ cup wheat flour
2 ¼ cups corn flour
1 tablespoon sugar
1 ½ teaspoon salt
1 ½ teaspoon baking powder
2 eggs
1 ½ cups milk
2 ½ cups grated or cubed cheese (Monterey Jack or Muenster)

1. Preheat oven to 375° F.
2. Sauté the chopped onion in the oil until it softens; allow it to cool slightly.
3. Beat the eggs and milk in a small bowl.
4. Gently mix the eggs & milk, the onions, and the dry ingredients together.
5. Fold in the cheese.
6. Place in an oiled and dusted 9" x 12" Pyrex.
7. Bake for about 45 minutes, until a toothpick comes out clean.

The party was a super success! Our Paraguayan families, friends, and co-workers attended, as did a number of Peace Corps people—Jerry and Bob with the kegs of beer, as well as the doctors, Bron and Eric, and their two little girls, Abby and Becky. Of course, Steve and Dave were there. Wyn and Larry from my training group joined us, too. Musically gifted Miguel Angel and Gloria, close friends of Mary, led the Paraguayan birthday serenade of *"Felicidades"* (Happiness). Although we had made it clear that birthday gifts were not expected, Mary and I received some that I still have, over 44 years later. Dr. Orihuela and Ña Irma gave us each typical embroidered fabric for a blouse. Mine was red, with multi-colored embroidery. A local seamstress made it into a blouse which I have worn during many

Christmas holidays. Bron and Eric gave us each a woven Paraguayan cotton blanket. Wyn presented me with a straw hat with a large brim that served as protection against the hot Paraguayan sun during my years in the Peace Corps. All in all, our guests, Mary, and I had a lovely, memorable day.

On October 8th, our real birthday, Ña Niní had a special dinner celebration for Mary and me at her home. Steve and Abel joined us, but Dave had already left town to prepare for his departure from Paraguay. Ña Niní prepared hamburgers, French fries, and another birthday cake. I felt drawn to this stout, lovable woman with wavy graying hair, glasses, and a competent air about her. Her home and the people occupying it, including Mary, had felt like a place of refuge since the very first time I visited them after moving to Ybycuí.

I clearly remember entering the large, one-story structure through a small pharmacy storefront stocked with bovine vaccines and medicines. Ña Niní and Don Lalo had been the first people in Ybycuí to use vaccines on their cattle after having read about them in veterinary magazines. After seeing the benefits of vaccines, they set up the veterinarian pharmacy in a room of their home to sell them to others. When I entered the pharmacy that first time, I immediately noticed a framed black and white photograph of President John F. Kennedy displayed on the wall. Next, I noticed Ña Niní sitting behind the counter with a warm smile and twinkling eyes welcoming me. After a big bear hug and kisses on both cheeks from her, I intuitively felt safe with her, unlike I had felt thus far with any Paraguayan.

Over time, I would come to understand why that was so. Ña Niní opened her home and her heart to Volunteers assigned to Ybycuí. Before Abel and Mary, there had been at least four others. Not only had Ña Niní adored Peace Corps founder President Kennedy and his goodwill toward Latin America, but also her son Antonio (Tonio) was a neurosurgical resident in Little Rock, Arkansas. She treated Volunteers as she hoped people would treat Tonio in the States.

Others in her household also welcomed me with their kindness. Ña Niní's other son, 16-year-old Carlitos, was an accomplished guitarist and became a younger brother to the local Volunteers. Amalia, a kind young woman from the countryside who lived in the household, helped Ña Niní with sewing and other domestic chores. Epí, a live-in single woman with a young son, did the heavy cleaning. Tomasa, who lived on the opposite side of the intersection, was another young woman who visited every day to drink *yerba mate*. Little did I know at the time that Ña Niní would become my guardian angel and Paraguayan mother, I would lovingly call Carlitos *"mi hermanito"* (my little brother), and Tomasa would be a life-long friend.

∞∞∞∞

Before and during the days of the birthday celebrations, Steve and I forged ahead with the elementary school program. Our approach to teaching the children was different than the usual rote form of education practiced in Paraguay. Education under Stroessner's regime was conducted all in Spanish, primarily because there were not many written materials in Guaraní, other than song lyrics and a few books. Also, independent thinking and discussions were discouraged. Students spent their time copying information into notebooks from the black slate chalkboards filled by their teachers. The students memorized the material and recited it. Our sessions were a mixture of Spanish and Guaraní, and we encouraged the children to interact with us. Over time, we completed two visits to each class.

Every time we entered a classroom, we felt the eyes of the students, seated at their desks, directly on us. The boys wore pants, and the girls had on skirts. These articles of clothing, as well as sweaters or jackets, could be of any color or pattern. Their blouses and shirts were always white. Some wore shoes, but most did not. Similar to the health center staff, teachers wore white lab coats over their street clothes.

After the teacher introduced us, we made the effort to actively engage the children in the hookworm and latrine discussions. "What should a sanitary latrine have?" asked Steve with a glint of humor in his eyes. In the course of our school visits, the children in each classroom listened intently, raised their hands to answer questions, and laughed with us, two North Americans talking about latrines, feces, parasites, and hand washing. They cringed at the roundworm sample and my graphic description of what worms can do inside of a person. Many of them had seen roundworms before because they or someone in the family had suffered from bouts with them. The students smiled with pleasure upon getting their own copies of the Sanitary Latrine form and *Barefoot Pepe and the Hookworm*. We told them they would be honorary sanitation inspectors if they inspected their family's latrine. "*Cevo-í, cevo-í,*" we had the children singing as we played our guitars. Guaranteed giggling always happened when we finished the last line, "Have a latrine to poop in!"

It took us about six weeks to complete the teaching and introduce the contest to the 42 elementary classrooms, with the number of students ranging from 25 to 35 in each class. Although a few teachers took the opportunity of our presence to leave for a break, those that remained in the classroom with us were as attentive as the students. The idea of a contest seemed foreign to the children, but prizes piqued their interest. We told the teachers and students that we would be back the second week of October to see their projects and determine the winners.

The education part of the project clipped along smoothly after a few adjustments. Chuck's proposal specified the viewing of parasite eggs and larvae under a microscope. Steve and I dropped this activity because we didn't have any microscopic slides available at the time. A second contest specified in the grant was discarded. If we pulled off one contest, we would be doing just fine. We also canned the idea of a puppet show because of the unpleasant prospect of writing another story, making puppets and a stage, and performing the same show over and over again. With only two of the five Volunteers specified in the project's proposal, there simply wasn't time. Steve and I proceeded with what we had.

Contest judging began on October 11th. Neither Steve nor I had wanted to take on the task of picking just one first-place project in each class. After Chuck's departure, we consulted Dr. Orihuela about this, but he responded that no one would want to have anything to do with an "infantile" contest like this, least of all himself. He would not even suggest that people from the health center help us out. This unfortunate rejection from the director of the project was noticed by one of the principals. She felt it was a snub not only of the Volunteers' work but also of hers as well. In the end, we were extraordinarily grateful to Mary and Ña Lali for judging in the 42 classrooms. They did a wonderful job and managed to pick a first-place winner in all but one class, where they decided on a tie for first. Once our judges declared the winner in a classroom from the model latrines, clay roundworms, Pepe drawings, and other entries, Steve was assigned to divvy out the educational comic books to runners-up and a piece of candy to each child. I sought out information needed to take a photograph in each winning student's home—name, parents' names, and a description of where the winner lived. This proved to be as challenging as understanding a song in Guaraní without a dictionary.

First of all, the dirt roads in town didn't have any name signs because the roads didn't have names. There were no house numbers either. If the family lived in the town itself, I asked the name of the barrio and then inquired about known landmarks, such as the church, the health center, the police station, the small telephone building, or the bus terminal. As I narrowed down the location, I asked how close they lived to certain people I knew, like Ña Niní, Dr. Orihuela, or the Ledezmas, a welcoming low-income family in the Sanja León barrio of town that Steve enjoyed visiting. Then I'd ask for a description of the property—the color of the house, the kind of roof it had, or any identifiers that would help us find the right place.

It was even more challenging for me if the family lived outside of town. I'd first ask which road out of town we should take. Was it the road towards the communities of Mbuyapey (mboo-jah-peh-UH) and Quyquyhó (kuh-kuh-OH)? (I just love saying those names aloud.) Or was it the road to Sanja León that went towards the hill known as Cerro San José? I took detailed directions from the student, occasionally with the help of the teacher. Fortunately, Steve and I both had our bicycles to make the ventures possible.

Enthusiasm among the teachers and principals was high. In addition, Peace Corps Director Jerry drove out for a day to observe the judging, and he was revved up about the program and our hard work. At the contest conclusion in each school, the teachers treated us to snacks and a private celebration that they referred to as a *clausura* (closure). It's the same word used when a road closes because of rain. Steve and I felt accomplished and happy. After the education program, whenever we pedaled around town, either together or individually, kids would wave at us and shout "*cevo-í, cevo-í.*" Maybe, just maybe, we were getting through to them. Hopefully, they weren't referring to us personally as worms or parasites!

As the 43 first-place winners were proclaimed and the locations of their homes more or less identified, I clustered the winners' names and addresses in order to develop a calendar of half-day photo-taking schedules. Next, I typed up notes in Spanish for the winners to take home, informing their families of the prize and the approximate date and time we would show up to take the photograph. Once these notes were delivered to the winners in the schools, we hoped for good weather for the rest of the month. We began taking photos on October 18th.

Using my second-hand Pentax camera loaded with Kodak film, we methodically worked through our winners. Some families were totally surprised to see us, perhaps because they couldn't read the note I had sent. Others seemed simply happy when we arrived. While Steve's steady hands took the photographs, I meticulously kept track of which frame on the roll pertained to which child and family. During each visit, we talked about avoiding parasites by using sanitary latrines. We planned to do the same when we revisited each family with the developed photo.

By early November, we received the photos from the roll of film developed in Asunción. Unfortunately, the other roll was Kodak II film, a relatively new product. Because Kodak had not yet sold the formula for developing it, we had to mail it to the States. An advantage was that Kodak returned the photographs and negatives along with a free roll of film. However, once word spread that some of the photo prizes were available, winners began asking for their photos. On November 10th, I wrote my parents:

"Yesterday we thought we'd give out part of the pictures [the ones developed in Asunción]. That was a mistake. Word gets around too fast. One little kid followed us to the outskirts of town on horse, asking us for his photo. And just can't you hear ME trying to explain in Guaraní about two different kinds of photos & one kind we had to send to North America, and his photo just hasn't come back from North America yet. People have really liked the photos. Some families have never had their pictures taken before, and those who have, they are usually in black & white. The color photos are something special."

We eventually delivered all of the photos. For Steve and me, taking and delivering these photographs was the most rewarding phase of the job, especially when the winner was from a very poor family. Sadly, the blistering heat of December and January damaged the negatives before we could make any prints for ourselves.

Although Chuck's educational plan had not included classes for older students, Steve and I designed and delivered a presentation on the special project targeted for teenagers. We taught grade by grade in the National High School in September and in the Catholic Niño Jesús High School in October. We felt reaching out to them made sense and would complete the school program in town.

After Chuck's departure in late September, Steve and I had looked to Dr. Orihuela as the true project director. With the education component and the contest completed, we attempted to talk to him about planning a big push for stool samples. USAID had given us a random sample list of town residents to determine the approximate parasite infestation in the population. Our plan was to conduct a barrio-by-barrio series of meetings to talk about hookworm, show the hookworm movie, and slip in the fact that we would be showing up at some of the homes asking for a stool sample. Steve and I both felt strongly that someone respected in the community and knowledgeable about the project should participate in these meetings. We felt Dr. Orihuela, as director of the project, was the most appropriate person for this role. When we approached him, the doctor responded that Steve and I should carry out the stool study by ourselves. He bluntly stated, "Just offer them a free analysis and free medicine sometime in the future, and **YOU** [emphasis added] will have no problem." In retrospect, I thought I saw Dr. Orihuela cringe at the prospect of participating in our proposed meetings. Another area of concern was who would perform the lab work, once the stool specimens were obtained. Steve and I were not trained in this area. Someone from the health center, either Dr. Orihuela or Nimia, would have to perform the lab work or teach us how to do it.

In spite of the seeming success of the education program, something wasn't right with Dr. Orihuela. His attitude toward me became blatantly cold. If I missed a few days giving talks in the health center, he let me know that he wasn't happy by comparing me unfavorably with Martina. He displayed no interest in the project work that we were doing. Steve wrote in his journal on October 16th:

"The Doctor's attitude has changed markedly in these past few days and we really don't know why. Ña Elisa is pissed at him because she was told he is referring people to [the mayor's] pharmacy [rather than to her husband's]… Miguel Angel's family is pissed at him because he diagnosed the face injury of the referee who was slugged by one of the family during a soccer game as serious. They say it's only a scratch but the brother is in jail and may be taken to Asunción. Aside from these factors, which may or may not be important, there may be other hidden forces at work… The gossip is rampant…This could possibly be affecting the doctor. He is absolutely essential in continuing the project and as of now he is reluctant and evasive and has yet to offer more than his backing from a distance."

Unsure where the project was headed, Steve and I sought advice from Health Program Officer Eric at the Peace Corps office in early November. A trip to Asunción was warranted because Peace

Corps had told us that the Ministry of Health was interested in putting "The Hookworm Song" on TV along with *Barefoot Pepe and the Hookworm*. The result of the trip was that Eric left any decisions about the project up to us, while the Ministry was very interested in putting us on a children's television program in Guaraní called ¿Mba-éi-xa-pa? (*How are you?*) When our contact at the Ministry asked if we would bring a small group of children from Ybycuí to sing "The Hookworm Song," Peace Corps Director Jerry offered to loan us his large carryall vehicle to make that possible. The program was scheduled for December 1st in Asunción at the studio Channel 9, the only channel in the entire country at that time. Steve and I were thrilled with the prospect of being on national television.

Back to Ybycuí we went, with the new task of recruiting a group of children to appear on television. Paraguay only had black and white programming in 1974, and TV sets were somewhat uncommon, particularly in rural areas. I knew of only a small number of families in Ybycuí who had a set, and Ña Elisa's was one of them. In the evenings, the family would gather in the front room to watch episodes dubbed into Spanish of *The Lone Ranger, Lassie, The Dick Van Dyke Show*, some Argentine soap operas, and *Peyton Place*, a popular drama in the U.S. from 1964 to 1969. I have never been much of a television watcher, but I did know most of the *Peyton Place* storyline. Ña Elisa wanted me to watch the program with her. She tried to pump me for information about upcoming episodes. Undoubtedly, she wanted to brag to her gossip network about the plotlines. Although I humored her to some extent, I was usually too exhausted to watch television. Neighborhood children, however, would flock into the front room, standing behind the family seated on the sofa and chairs, to view *Lassie* episodes. An overflow of children watched from the outside through a window.

Knowing the general fascination with television, Steve and I feared it would be tough to keep our recruiting effort under reasonable control. Channel 9 personnel had told us to bring a small group to sing the song, and we had limited space in the vehicle. We asked Dr. Orihuela for advice. Unsurprisingly, he had no time for us nor suggestions to offer. He shrugged us off by explaining that the onset of hot weather meant increasing cases of diarrhea and a busy health center schedule.

Steve and I discussed ways to assemble a group for the TV program and quickly opted for working with one of the school principals. We approached Ña Coquita, the director of one of the elementary schools, who was pleased to help. In fact, she handled the entire assemblage, which included her husband Don Ortiz, her daughter, and a handful of students from her school. She even approached the parents of the students she had selected for the event. Her proactive and enthusiastic involvement was refreshing.

As the planning proceeded for our television debut, Thanksgiving was fast approaching. I wondered how I could get through this special U.S. holiday without severe homesickness. But Mary came to the rescue! Ever the extrovert, Mary knew a USAID employee named Lee, who had served in Peace Corps Colombia. Mary managed to get Thanksgiving dinner invitations for Steve and me at Lee's house in Asunción. I so very much looked forward to the event!

Turkeys are not common in Paraguay. Mary, charged with the task of providing the turkey, was fortunate to find one on a farm outside of Ybycuí through her agricultural extension contacts. A live turkey was delivered to her the weekend before Thanksgiving, and she asked for my help in butchering it. When I arrived at Ña Niní's house to assist Mary, the bird was already dead and dangling upside down by its legs with its feet tied to a tree. Relieved that I hadn't seen Epí cause its demise by wringing its neck, I helped Mary pluck the feathers. Our task was made easier by pouring boiling water over the carcass before yanking on the plumes. I then excused myself from the degutting process. Mary and

Epí handled it.

Mary was able to leave Ybycuí at the beginning of the week before the rain arrived. Obliged to give talks at the health center, I couldn't leave until the day before Thanksgiving. Panic set in when I heard that the road had a *clausura* (not the celebratory kind). Steve and I were rained into town. Alone in my room, I fought back tears. But then it occurred to me that I might find someone to take me to the paved road on a motorcycle. I packed a small overnight bag, emerged from my room, and asked Don Angel for suggestions. He helped me find someone, and I left within a couple of hours. Covered with my rain poncho and hanging on for dear life, I rode behind my motorcyclist, who safely delivered me to the bus stop on the paved road in Carapeguá for about $8. It was worth it! Steve opted to stay in Ybycuí, but Mary and I brought him a large plate of leftovers—turkey, dressing, yams, mashed potatoes and gravy, salad, green beans, cauliflower, beets, and generous slices of apple and pumpkin pie—delivered as soon as the road opened. We were unable to manage delivery of the beer, wine, or homemade vanilla ice cream that we had enjoyed in Asunción, but we heard no complaint from Steve.

With Thanksgiving over and the television program quickly approaching, Steve took a bus into Asunción to borrow Jerry's large carryall vehicle. Early on the morning of December 1st, we met at Ña Coquita's house. Some of the children were already there waiting for us, and we picked up the others on the way out of town. We were as ready as we would ever be. Our guitars were packed into the back of the vehicle, along with snacks and everyone's belongings. The faces of the children beamed with excitement.

Nearing Asunción, Ña Coquita and I reviewed with the children what they could anticipate at the TV studio. Our drawings from *Barefoot Pepe and the Hookworm* had been transferred to pieces of poster board by station staff. One of the regulars on the show would relate the story in Guaraní and elaborate on it as the poster boards were shown. Then, our group would sing the song, accompanied by Steve and me on our guitars.

The day of our live televised performance was scorching hot, with temperature and humidity both close to 100 degrees Fahrenheit. Arriving at the studio, we found a parking place and unloaded the children and our gear. As we entered the building, I was stunned to realize that it had no air conditioning. In Asunción, the Peace Corps office, four movie theaters, and the more expensive restaurants were air conditioned, but not the only TV studio in the country. Already uncomfortably hot and sweaty, I could see the perspiration dripping off Steve. Under television lights, we were likely to become completely soaked in sweat.

We waited in a crowded, stifling room until our program time. Finally, we were herded to a place just off-stage to listen to *Barefoot Pepe and the Hookworm*. Our sweating increased. My clothing clung to my skin. Steve looked for something with which to wipe his face. All I had to offer him was part of a wad of toilet paper. I always carried some in a pocket in Paraguay, since many latrines and toilets had none. Taking it with a look of gratitude, he mopped his brow the moment before we were motioned onto the set. At the last second, he turned at me and asked with panic in his eyes, "Are there any pieces of toilet paper on my face?" Assuring him that there weren't, I stifled my giggling and followed him onto the sweltering stage, guitar in hand and children parading behind us.

It all came off surprisingly well. There were no blunders. Nobody fainted from the heat. Immediately after finishing, we were ushered out of the studio and into the December summer sun, heat, and humidity. Relief flooded over me as overwhelmingly as the sweat. It was over! It was Steve's first-ever television appearance and my first since participating in the children's show, "Sagebrush Shorty and his

Circle 2 Theater," as part of its live Detroit audience in the late 1950s.

Observing the children's grinning faces and basking in our glory, I looked at Steve and asked, "What now?" It would have been fun to see ourselves performing, but the program was live and unrecorded. He and I wanted to pile back into the vehicle and return to Ybycuí. Ña Coquita and Don Ortiz had another idea, however. We could take the children to the small zoo on the capital's outskirts and then look for something to drink.

Feeling the need for a celebration, Steve and I went along with the suggestion. Sadly, the zoo was depressing. Wild animals with sorrowful eyes were locked up in cages with barely enough space for turning around. The children gawked at the feral felines, monkeys, a pair of bears, and captive birds.

A short time later, as I felt my eyes tearing up with compassion for the animals, I proposed that we gather under the shade of a nearby tree to sing "The Hookworm Song" again with the children while posing for a photograph. Steve fetched my guitar and camera from Jerry's vehicle and took a photo of the children and me as I played the guitar and we all sang "*Cevo-i*" with gusto. We piled back into Jerry's vehicle to look for cold refreshments. In spite of having little money in our pockets because we hadn't yet received our December stipend, Steve and I pooled our meager funds to buy sodas for everyone at a restaurant on the road out of Asunción. Somewhat revitalized, we piled back into the vehicle just in time to escape the first late afternoon raindrops. The peels of thunder, the tingly smell of ozone, and the ominous dark gray horizon indicated that it wasn't a passing shower.

As we proceeded on the paved road toward Carapeguá, where we would turn left onto the unpaved road to Ybycuí, it rained with increasing fury. I silently worried what we would do if the dirt road closed. We had barely had money to pay for the sodas. I laughed off the thought of finding motorcyclists to take all 13 of us to Ybycuí in the dark as logistically absurd, expensive, and downright dangerous. Anxiety about a road *clausura* made me more uncomfortable than the heat had earlier. Riding in the front seat beside Steve, I asked what he was thinking. He shook his head slightly. The worry on his face told me everything. I futilely attempted to initiate a discussion with Ña Coquita and her husband about possible options if the road were closed. The two of them assured us that it would remain open.

They were wrong. As we approached the turnoff from Carapeguá to Ybycuí, the barrier was down, blocking access to the dirt road. We had a *clausura*. Steve pulled the vehicle over as the rain continued to beat down *a cántaros* (by the buckets). The two Paraguayan adults delved into a hushed, rapid conversation in Guaraní, after which Don Ortiz abruptly left the vehicle and disappeared into the gray sheets of water. Ña Coquita stated that we would wait where we were while her husband got permission to drive on the closed road. Steve and I exchanged suspicious looks. We had heard rumors that Don Ortiz had political connections and was a spy in town, always watching, listening, and reporting any behaviors that might be against the Colorado Party or the Stroessner Regime. Some of the children were dozing, some were softly talking to each other. Steve and I silently waited in the increasing darkness.

About ten minutes later, Don Ortiz returned, soaked to the bone but not at all bothered by it. He claimed he had obtained permission. I wondered if he had a spy connection in the town or if he were lying. He immediately began barking orders to Steve—go down two blocks, turn left, proceed three blocks, turn left again. We arrived at a steep muddy bank a short distance beyond the roadblock. With a bit of a running start, Jerry's carryall bumped and jumped up the bank with some spinning of the tires and spitting of mud. I muttered, "Glad we have a vehicle with a winch, glad we didn't have to use it just now." Feeling the need to comfort him, I reached over and placed my hand on Steve's right knee as we began the muddy drive toward Ybycuí. He drove slowly on the slippery road illuminated by the headlights as the darkness of the night completely closed in on us from behind.

Approaching Acahay, the town before Ybycuí, Steve and I discussed the possibility of facing another barrier. Sure enough, through the pounding rain the headlights revealed a closed barrier, indicating the *clausura*. Don Ortiz directed Steve to drive around on the left side of it, which he did. We continued. I again put my hand on his right knee to reassure him and spoke softly in English, "We're getting close to home. We're almost there." While nightfall and the rain had caused the temperature to drop at least 15 degrees Fahrenheit, I realized that my heart still felt warm because I was with Steve. I wondered if he had similar feelings toward me. At least, he hadn't pushed my hand off his knee.

It was still raining hard as we entered Ybycuí. For some reason, the barrier into town was not closed. We deposited each child safely in his or her home. The last stop before my house was Ña Coquita's. Then Steve saw that I got into Ña Elisa's house safely before slowly driving away. I breathed a long sigh of relief. Johnny the dog growled at me briefly as Ña Elisa opened the door. Although I had awakened her, she mumbled that she had seen us on TV. I closed the door to my room, peeled off my sweat-soaked clothing, collapsed into bed, and tucked in the ends of my mosquito net before promptly falling asleep.

The next morning, the rain had stopped, the sun was out, and the birds were shrilly chirping. After breakfast, I bicycled over to Ña Niní's house under the bright blue sky to hear what Mary and Ña Niní had to say about our national television appearance. As I approached, I noticed that Jerry's vehicle was there. Gathered around it were Ña Niní, Steve, Don Ortiz, and the police chief. Nobody appeared happy. Steve looked like he was ready to lose the contents of his stomach. I heard the police chief harshly admonish Don Ortiz, "**He** (pointing to Steve) is just a naïve North American! **You**, however, should know better. I hold **you** responsible!" Turning to Steve, he continued with a softer voice, "I am sorry, but I have to give you a ticket and confiscate your driver's license."

In a panic, I hopped off my bicycle and cried out, "But I don't want to drive the Peace Corps vehicle back to Asunción—the traffic frightens me!" Heads turned to my voice. While Ña Niní and the police chief both suppressed smiles, the chief quickly assured me Steve could drive the vehicle back to the capital. We could leave as soon as the road reopened and proceed directly to the Peace Corps office with the chief's written explanation in lieu of a license. It confirmed our suspicion that Don Ortiz had lied about obtaining permission to drive on a closed road. We doubt any fine was given to him, but he had at least experienced shame.

The road opened early that afternoon. With the police chief's note in his pocket, glum-faced Steve and I left for Asunción in Jerry's vehicle. We made small talk as he retraced his tire tracks, visible from the previous night's journey. The television program had been a success, the children were returned to their homes safely, we hadn't skidded off the muddy road, Steve had not been arrested, and the police chief held Don Ortiz responsible for the crime of driving on a closed road. We wondered what Peace Corps Director Jerry would say.

Jerry, the Peace Corps staff, and some Volunteers greeted us with big smiles. They had all watched the program and thought we did very well. The kids were cute, the song was clear and catchy, and our guitar playing was rather good! "There's just one problem, Jerry," I said, and proceeded to relate the story. As Jerry listened, he became increasingly nervous, as was his way when something went awry. After I finished, he abruptly collected the keys from Steve and said that he would hand the problem over to Juan Carlos, one of the staff members. And that was it.

A couple of weeks later when Steve and I returned to the Peace Corps office to check for mail from home, Felicita, the kind and helpful receptionist, informed us that Juan Carlos had retrieved Steve's Paraguayan driver's license. Peace Corps would absorb the minor cost of the fine and the bribe. As she returned the license to him, she smiled broadly and told us that we had performed very well and assured us that Peace Corps was happy with the job we were doing.

∞∞∞∞

Due to summer vacation from school and the intense heat and humidity, the rest of December was slow. I returned to giving health talks each morning. Steve and I managed one last work-related activity—a photo display of our school program. Mary's agricultural extension clubs were having an annual exposition, and she encouraged us to participate. Although rain prohibited people from the countryside from attending, those in town who saw the display seemed to enjoy it, except for Dr. Orihuela. The fact that he did not look at all of the photos nor wish to discuss our work was a clear indication of his dissatisfaction with the project and us. The doctor never even mentioned the television program. Up to this point, the funds spent on the project for the school program had come from our monthly living stipends. Now we needed money for upcoming tasks that were specified in the budget. When we talked to Dr. Orihuela about signing for the AID money as the project's director, he made excuses and quickly changed the subject. Although the doctor now overtly impeded the project's progress, he at least was honest and didn't pocket the money as some people might have.

Steve and I retreated to Asunción for Christmas at Mary's invitation. She had started dating Lee, and the two of them were organizing a Mexican Christmas meal for about 15 people. Lee was getting canned enchilada sauce, corn tortillas, and chili peppers through the Embassy mail system, called the "pouch." I volunteered to make flour tortillas, a skill I learned while a VISTA member in Utah after college. The planning, cooking, eating, and celebrating with other North Americans were just what Steve and I needed. We had a feast of enchiladas, burritos with my homemade tortillas, salad, hot sauces, and an array of desserts. Steve and I talked, laughed, and enjoyed being with each other without discussing sanitary latrines and intestinal parasites. Perhaps it was the simple task of making tortillas together—I rolled them out, and he cooked them—or maybe it was the neck and shoulder massage he gave me after our work in the kitchen. Whatever it was, we both realized that we were more to each other than just co-workers and good friends. In Ybycuí, however, I wanted to hide our developing relationship in order to avoid the gossip that would inevitably ensue.

Early in January of 1975, Steve and I had another conversation concerning the project with Eric in the Peace Corps office. Prior to that meeting, we had separately reviewed the random list generated by USAID of people who were to provide stool samples. On the list were some prominent people in town, and I could not imagine clapping my hands outside their doors and begging for a specimen of feces. Steve concluded the same. When Steve and I met with Eric, the three of us concluded that Dr. Orihuela would not or could not direct the project. Lacking a SENASA counterpart and without any options for an alternative director, we could not proceed. We decided that the special project had no future in Ybycuí under the current circumstances.

Facing reality, Steve and I returned to Ybycuí to inform Dr. Orihuela that we would not be working on the project anymore. He asked no questions; rather, we saw only visible relief in his eyes. The first comment he made was, "Well, now you can both spend more time in the health center." He had once commented to me, "Your latrine project doesn't do anything for the health center." It finally hit us that it was never Dr. Orihuela's project. Steve and I figured that he had only played along because he liked Chuck and sought his approval. Paraguayans tend to be amenable and go along verbally with an idea because that is the proper and polite thing to do. But once Chuck left the country, Dr. Orihuela expected that the project would be discontinued.

Our Peace Corps service and our lives were about to undergo a big change. After running ourselves ragged for several months in a place that was supposed to be *tranquilo*, Steve and I now had little to do. We both felt at a loss for purpose and direction. For a sense of closure, Steve took it upon himself to draft a final report of the project in English for Peace Corps and USAID. I typed on stencils his ten-page explanation of what the project plan had been, what we had accomplished, and why we would not draw down any USAID funding. We hoped that it would help future Volunteers avoid mistakes similar to what had plagued us. We opted not to translate it into Spanish in order to avoid offending people in our host country. Being polite to people was preferred to telling the blunt truth.

Mainly, our project failed because it was "owned" by Peace Corps and not by Paraguayans. Dr. Orihuela never embraced the role as project director as Chuck had planned. Nor was there meaningful buy-in from SENASA and the Ministry of Health in Asunción. SENASA did not have a sanitation inspector in Ybycuí. Paraguayans perceived the project as a Peace Corps effort that they watched from the sidelines. As Steve wrote in the report:

"The written project gave verbal recognition to the importance of Paraguayan involvement, interest, and initiative. To this factor, perhaps more than any other, the outcome of the Ybycuí project can be attributed. This involvement is by far the most important and also the most difficult to discuss in general terms. The history of development programs is full of failures resulting from the imposition of a foreign plan on some local scene. It can be safely said that a project of the scope and complexity of the Ybycuí project is bound to fall short without very definite involvement and vested interest on the part of at least a few local people. While foreigners may provide a valuable perspective, resources, or initiatives, a local person is inevitably closer to the realities and problems at the local level. Advice and active participation with the day-to-day work as well as general guidance (in other words, how to reach the over-all goals most effectively in the given local situation) we feel are very important prerequisites. In our particular case there was only one passive approval, which later disappeared."

There were other factors involved. The original written proposal had looked fine on paper—Chuck had developed a logical, professional grant proposal. It included good ideas and approaches, including the sanitation census and the educational program in the schools and community. However, the original timeline was unreasonable. It lacked any wiggle room for setbacks or delays that almost always occur in community development projects. There was no indication that time had been budgeted based on any reality, such as how long the census of approximately 700 homes would take, the average time of a home visit, record-keeping requirements, and the number of people conducting it. The school program involved 42 elementary school classes and multiple visits to each classroom, but there is no evidence in the proposal that the time needed for the classes had been calculated. Bad weather, required in-service training in Asunción, and illness were not taken into account. The proposal specified that five Volunteers would be dedicated to the project, but the timeline was not amended when there were only two of us. The project was at least two months behind the official timeline when

Steve arrived in Ybycuí, and it only became worse as the weeks passed. But the project's death blow was mainly caused by the lack of Paraguayan ownership.

"Nothing ventured, nothing gained," goes the old adage. Chuck had put a lot of thought and effort into the Ybycuí project. It is good that he tried, and I am not sorry that I was an integral part of it. A complete sanitation census had been conducted. All of the school children in town and many of their parents had been educated about the perils of hookworms and roundworms. People knew the importance of having and using a sanitary latrine. Hand washing was stressed. Wearing shoes can break the hookworm cycle. Forty-three families had a photograph in color of themselves. We had appeared on national television with some school children. Steve and I had learned a lot about living and working in Paraguay. But now we pushed a "pause" button on our Peace Corps experience.

Ybycuí's main dirt-packed avenue in 1974

Some roaming domesticated animals

An ox cart rambling down a road in Ybycuí

Latrine cement floors (*losas*) at the entrance to Ybycuí's health center

Barefoot children in Ybycuí

September 1974 site visit group photo, taken at the Bernardino Caballero monument on the main avenue; left to right, back row: Dr. Orihuela, Ministry of Health representative, wife of the USAID representative, SENASA's Margarita, Dr. Orihuela's wife Irma, Mary, USAID representative, Peace Corps' Chuck, Mary Lou, and Peace Corps' Eric; front row: Ministry of Health representative, Dave, and SENASA representative (Photo taken by Steve)

Steve, Mary Lou, Dave, and Mary, in an Asunción restaurant prior to Dave's departure

Steve showing roundworms to elementary school children

A student reading the story of *Barefoot Pepe and the Hookworm*

On my bicycle, purchased in Argentina with Burl's help

A Peace Corp Memoir 61

Steve at the wheel of Jerry's vehicle, on the morning of the TV appearance

Mary Lou on the guitar with a group of schoolchildren,
after the appearance on national television singing the Hookworm Song

CHAPTER 3

An Interlude

In three words I can sum up everything I have learned about life: it goes on.
—Robert Frost

During the remainder of the scorching days of January, Steve and I adjusted to life without the project. Government employees frequently take vacation time during the first month of the year, and the volume at the health center significantly diminished. Activity in general slowed because it was simply too hot to do much. Midday, people languished indoors or under the shady trees in their backyard patios, drinking cold *tereré* tea to stay hydrated. When the humidity passed 90% and the temperature soared above 40° Celsius (104° Fahrenheit), I desperately sought ways to escape the heat.

Early one sweltering afternoon, I plopped myself down on the hard-packed reddish ground underneath a tree in Ña Elisa's backyard. Leaning my back against the tree trunk, I listened to the quiet—no leaves fluttering in a breeze, no birds chirping, not even Johnny stirred to growl at me. I pondered whether or not it was worth it to take a bath. I decided it wasn't. Pulling water from the well required expending energy that would make me hotter. Also, I would immediately begin sweating again once the bath was over. Propped up by the tree with my eyes closed, I thought of Michigan winters with snowfalls adequate for making snowmen, which we did before the soot from the nearby Ford Motor Company Dearborn plant turned the snow gray. I recalled the brisk early mornings in June, when I worked out with my Patton Pool teammates in unheated Olympic-sized pools, swimming as fast as I could so my lips wouldn't turn blue from the cold water. In Ybycuí that day, I lingered under the tree, imagining myself elsewhere, until my thirst compelled me to seek out *tereré*.

Somehow, I survived the heat of the Paraguayan summer. During that time, Ña Elisa told me an old Paraguayan saying, *"Pueblo chico, infierno grande"* (Small town, large hell). She explained that small town gossip is so rampant that it often creates a sort of inferno for some people. For me, it had a double meaning. I knew that people in Ybycuí gossiped about all of the Peace Corps Volunteers, past and present. I heard more than I ever wanted to know about the previous Volunteers, whom Mary, Steve, and I referred to as "ghosts of the past." I didn't want to imagine what was said about me, but I feared that Ña Elisa was a major member of the gossip network. Still, the other meaning to me personally was that in summer, this small town I lived in was as hot as hell.

There was more quiet down time for me now. Occasionally after the sun set, Mary, Steve, and I would sit outside in front of Miguel Angel's home and sing with him and Gloria. Both were accomplished guitarists and patiently taught us songs in Guaraní and Spanish. As a soft breeze cooled our sweaty skin, the stars appeared in the evening sky to soothe our souls.

I had become enamored with Paraguayan music during training. My favorite sessions during our first month in Asunción involved beautiful Paraguayan music. Nationally known Eladio Martínez, an older cigar-smoking guitarist and singer, taught us a few songs and performed many more. I still have the printed words to the songs we learned, as well as the spiral notebook with a red, white, and blue cover (the colors of the Paraguayan flag) in which I compiled the words and chords of additional songs in English, Spanish, and Guaraní. Playing the guitar and singing mostly in Guaraní, Don Eladio mesmerized us with the traditional *guaranias* (gwa-RAH-nee-ahs, slow songs) and polkas (fast songs). Only the tempo varies between the two music styles. The rhythm was the same (five beats and a rest) and had a distinct Paraguayan strum that I began to learn. I sang along with Don Eladio and the other trainees, trying to get the words to spill out of my mouth while feeling the music flow through me.

The Paraguayan harp is also part of the country's musical culture. Introduced to the South American continent by Jesuit priests in the 16th century, the harp is smaller than the orchestral instrument but has the same sweet celestial sounds, although with a distinct Paraguayan flavor. Some traditional music includes the accordion, but I preferred the sounds of just the two stringed instruments. I grew to love traditional songs like "*Pájaro Campana*" (Country Bird), which incorporates the sounds of birds chirping, and "*Tren Lechero*" (Milk Train), a piece of music that truly sounds like an early morning train lumbering along the tracks and occasionally whistling. "*La Llegada*" (The Arrival) and "*La Salida*" (The Departure) are two traditional songs played respectively at the beginning and end of all the dances I attended in rural towns.

Although the music in between the "arrival" and "departure" at rural dances was often rock-and-roll style from the English-speaking world, the Paraguayan songs were performed according to a law requiring that traditional music be performed at least once at every public musical event so that it would not be forgotten. A Paraguayan friend told me that this law was initiated by the Stroessner regime in the 1960s when foreign music, including rock and roll, became popular in Paraguay. The preservation of traditional music and culture continues today. According to an October 12, 2009 article in the Paraguayan newspaper *ABC Color,* a law passed in 1990 requires that at least 30% of what is aired on Paraguayan television and radio be dedicated to traditional music and national cultural programming.

One evening at a restaurant while we were still in training, we saw a dance performance with live music, the blend of the Paraguayan harp and guitar. Dressed in traditional embroidered *typoí* (tuh-poEE) blouses with crocheted sleeves and billowing skirts, the women performed the Bottle Dance to a brisk polka tune. Holding onto their skirt hems with arms extended to each side and making a half-circle with the colorful fabric, they twirled and flowed around the dance floor. With perfect posture and precision balance, one woman had empty champagne bottle after empty champagne bottle stacked on her head by an assistant on a ladder. She danced the polka step without missing a beat until 12 bottles extended upward.

Traditionally, Paraguayan women learned to skillfully transport things on their heads with erect posture and gracefulness. I once saw a six-foot layered stack of homemade brooms balanced on a woman's head. At frequented rural crossroads where buses stopped, some vendors commonly balanced on their heads a platter of oranges, each with the top sliced off and the rind neatly trimmed to allow for easy squeezing and sucking of the juice. Others would balance a platter of *chipá* (chee-PAH), a tasty type of corn bread. Singing out "*naranja*" (orange) or "*chipá, chipá*," the vendors gracefully walked along the sides of the buses, exchanging the item for its price through an open window. I tried picturing myself as a vendor but always ended up imagining the oranges and *chipá* spilled on the ground. Now, after many months in Paraguay, these sights, sounds, and smells were no longer novelties, but I still enjoyed them.

When I was alone in my room or out in the backyard under a tree trying to find relief from the heat, I read books, wrote letters, or strummed on the guitar. I read Agatha Christie novels, among other books, from Peace Corps' lending library. Steve's family sent him a copy of *All the President's Men*, the captivating true story about *The Washington Post* research by Woodward and Bernstein of the 1972 Watergate complex burglary that eventually led to the resignation of President Nixon. Steve loaned it to me as soon as he finished it. I re-read *One Hundred Years of Solitude* by Gabriel García Márquez, a fascinating multi-generational fictitious saga set in rural Colombia. It remains one of my all-time favorite novels. I began seeing quirky traits of some of the characters in the novel mirrored in a few Paraguayans. It helped me reflect on how much I had learned about my new environment, which I tried to express to my parents in a letter:

"I think now more than ever before, I'm beginning to grasp the cultural differences…A student staying a semester can barely start to see it. A tourist rarely can even start to scratch the surface. But believe me, living & trying to work in a small town out in the country—well, I'm beginning to appreciate the differences… but trying to explain what it's like is like trying to describe what fried mandioca tastes like."

I took time to notice the ubiquitous flowers, and I stopped to smell the roses. While I never saw tulips or lilacs, the Paraguayan flora was colorful and copious. Lapacho trees were dazzling when their deep pink blossoms opened. Oftentimes, sunflowers waved in the breeze, fluttering their yellow petals around the rich brown centers of seeds. Orchids in pinks, purples, and whites graced some yards, as did white lilies, purple and white chrysanthemums, and exotic flowers I had never seen before. Steve's yard had robust green bushes from which grew bright red hibiscus flowers. He also had an array of coleus plants of various shades and patterns of green, red, brown, orange, and yellow. The most delicate flower in Steve's yard was the passion flower, or *mbu-ru-ku-já* (bu-ru-ku-JAH) in Guaraní, a splendor of showy purples and whites that formed a corona or crown. One of my favorite flowers, the deep red poinsettia, bloomed in the hottest months and was plentiful around town by December in time for Christmas and lingered through the worst of the heat.

While riding my red bicycle around town or taking a bus to and from Asunción, I consciously tried to relax and take in the scenery and the smells, fighting the tendency of considering them routine and mundane in my mind. I watched the pigs, cows, and chickens roaming freely along the reddish dirt roads as they searched for edible garbage and bugs. I admired the passing scenery of undulating land covered by scrub brush and bushes, with grazing cattle chewing their cud among the cacti, dauntingly tall termite hills, and coconut palm trees. I peered at the rural homes made with bamboo strips for walls and topped by a grass roof, as well as those with more durable adobe walls and burnt-orange tiled roofs. I observed women draping wet laundry, just having had the dirt beaten out, onto bushes to dry in the hot Paraguayan sun. I saw social circles of people drinking *tereré* together in the shade. As they sipped the cold tea, I imagined the refreshing flavor passing through the silver straw to cool me inside. I marveled at the lush trees when the citrus and tropical fruits ripened and caused the branches to sag under the increasing weight. The plentiful fruit often fell unattended to the ground. I would not live here forever, and I wanted to remember the sights, smells, tastes, and sounds of Paraguay.

On one particularly blistering day, my mind drifted to thoughts about why I had joined the Peace Corps. I recalled my years growing up in Detroit and the influence of my parents and community. Five years before I was born, my father found himself 7,000 miles from home in the Pacific Ocean in an active war zone. Hank Shefsky didn't want to be there. He didn't want to be in the military at all, but he felt it was his duty. Hank had received his draft notice into the U.S. Army on Christmas Eve 1942, married my mother a week later on New Year's Eve, and was inducted early in 1943. After being trained in the new technology called radar, he was shipped to Oahu in the Hawaiian Islands. Several months later, he went by ship to the island of Saipan in the Mariana Islands to await his next assignment.

Dad was destined to serve on one of the bloodiest battlefields of World War II. He landed on the strategic volcanic island of Iwo Jima in the Pacific Ocean in late April 1945, ten weeks after the invasion when the island was supposedly "secured," but the Japanese military still occupied many of the miles of tunnels they had dug to defend the territory. The island smelled of death. In a letter to my mother shortly after they landed, my father wrote, "One of the fellows said he must have died and went to Hell, no place on earth could be this bad."

Dad was assigned as the sergeant in charge of installing the radar unit on the top of 554-foot Mt. Suribachi, site of the famous raising of the American flag during the first few days of the invasion. He and the men in his unit helped guide and protect the long-range B-29 bombers during their flights to bomb Japan. Living conditions on Iwo Jima were primitive. The dark volcanic ash irritated eyes and skin. Vegetation had wasted away. Food and water for survival had to be supplied by the U.S. Navy, and sanitation was less than basic. The Pacific Ocean offered the only bathing option during the early weeks, and latrines were quickly dug trenches with planks spanning them. My father was there until late November 1945, three months after the war ended.

I came of age in the 1960s to the music of Motown, rock and roll, and the Beatles. I swam competitively on the Patton Pool Swim Team and played water polo. At 13 years of age, I watched President Kennedy's funeral on black and white television. I saw his young son John-John salute his casket and his widow walk behind the caisson. I watched Jacqueline Kennedy light the eternal flame at his grave in Arlington Cemetery. Within the year, I read about the Watts race riots in Los Angeles in 1964, along with news about the escalating United States involvement in the war in Vietnam.

In my own hometown of Detroit, I witnessed the July 1967 riots, initiated when police raided an illegal after-hours club hosting a party for African-American military veterans. National Guard tanks rolled down Grand River Avenue in my city and camped out near Patton Pool where my swim team worked out during the school year. The black community repeatedly suffered from police brutality and social injustices, but these underlying causes of the riots were subsequently addressed at barely a snail's pace.

On April 4, 1968, Martin Luther King, Jr., was assassinated. The civil rights leader and advocate of non-violence was a victim of white hatred. Two months later, Senator Robert Kennedy, brother of the deceased president, was assassinated while he campaigned for the presidency of the United States.

In May 1970 during Richard Nixon's presidency and while I was studying abroad, I read about the National Guard shooting into an unarmed crowd of students at Kent State University protesting the Vietnam War. Four students died, and universities across the nation shut down because of the outrage and protestations. Still, that war raged. Years later, it would come to light that the U.S. government had repeatedly lied to its citizens about the Vietnam War. In 1972, Nixon was re-elected, but he was eventually brought down by the Watergate scandal and coverup.

Along with my father's World War II stories, these youth events and experiences shaped who I am. They helped me develop a direction in life. I wanted to contribute to peace and justice in the world, if only in small ways, by solving problems. After college, I first served in VISTA to learn more about poverty in the United States. Then it was my choice to work far from home as a health educator in the Peace Corps. I was in Paraguay in the name of peace to improve unsanitary conditions.

In contrast, Hank Shefsky had been drafted into the Army in World War II to face the challenges and dreadful conditions of that war. I had the opportunity to pursue peaceful pathways as a Volunteer. We each did our best in service far away from home, and our experiences helped us grow as individuals. As World War II would always remain a dominant factor in my father's life, I knew that Peace Corps Paraguay had already played a major role in mine. I simply needed to figure out some meaningful direction for the remainder of my time in Paraguay.

∞∞∞∞∞

A pleasant diversion in January of 1975 was the arrival of Ña Elisa and Don Angel's eldest daughter Mabel, her husband Ruben, and their baby. They were visiting from the United States, where pediatrician Ruben was on a five-year medical scholarship for advanced training. Their visit had been anticipated for months, allowing time for Steve and me to contact our families with requests for some late Christmas presents. Ruben and Mabel had graciously consented to be couriers. I was delighted with my new tape recorder and relieved that Mabel's father-in-law had connections that helped her avoid paying $40 for fees (or bribes?) for it. A few months later, their good deed was reciprocated when Steve's father, Chairman of Pediatrics at Yale Medical School, was able to help Ruben with a training opportunity at Yale.

While listening as Mabel described to her family the cultural and language challenges of living in the United States, I stifled my amusement, knowing all too well what it is like to live in a foreign culture. Mabel commented that people tended to keep her at more of a physical and emotional distance than she wanted, and the pace of life was too fast for her. The isolation of caring for an infant by herself while Ruben worked, along with her lack of English fluency, prompted her to seek the company of other Latinos. I reflected on the cheek-to-cheek greetings, the constant repetition of questions, and the rapid chatter in Guaraní that sometimes wore me down in Paraguay. I often sought the familiar companionship of other Volunteers, particularly Steve and Mary. Mabel and I were experiencing juxtaposed cross-cultural situations.

During weekends in the Paraguayan summertime, local rivers and ponds attracted people by the throngs. One of the best spots about 40 kilometers (25 miles) from Ybycuí was *Salto Cristal* (Crystal Waterfall), a lovely spot in green, hilly terrain. Mary and Lee invited Steve and me to spend a weekend there along with Lee's friend Tom. I wrote to my parents:

"It's what you might expect to find in a south seas paradise, a river running out of the hills, a 7- to 8-meter high waterfall dropping into a circular natural pool surrounded by big rocks & lots of lush green trees & plants…Lee & Tom brought the food (chicken, cheese quiche, steak, granola, salad, beer, wine, Bourbon, & chocolate chip cookies). It was so nice! After about 5 p.m. we had the whole place to ourselves! There was almost a full moon, too. It was a beautiful place, until people showed up around 10 a.m. Sunday morning."

I omitted writing to them about the sweetest part of the getaway. Steve had thoughtfully brought along his mosquito net to hang from a tree. With the edges tucked under our sleeping bags, it was a heavenly night with a brief interlude after midnight when we went skinny dipping in the waterfall's pool by the light of the moon under the star-studded sky.

On the return ride to Ybycuí on Sunday afternoon, Lee lost a small duffle bag containing a light jacket, some paperback books in English, and his prescription reading glasses. He discovered it missing when he dropped us off in town. We guessed it had fallen from the back of the jeep as we bounced along on the bumpy dirt road. Having been a Volunteer in Colombia, where personal items were routinely and aggressively stolen, Lee laughed when Mary told him that she'd get it back for him. But within two weeks, the duffel bag was in her hands. After Mary put out word through her agricultural extension service families, someone had found it on the road and sent it to her. Lee was stunned! He shared with us that when he served in Colombia, women had been told not to wear expensive earrings because they could be torn off their ears by thieves, pickpockets were everywhere, and items that went missing were never seen again.

∞∞∞∞

During the first weekend in February, Pauline and Larry invited everyone from our training group to their site, Mallorquín for a reunion. Pauline, who had studied in Spain, was preparing *paella*, the yummy Spanish rice and saffron dish with veggies along with pieces of chicken, sausage, or seafood. I, too, had lived in Spain while in college, and *paella* remains one of my favorite dishes to this day.

Mallorquín was located on the paved highway that travelled due east from Asunción to Puerto Presidente Stroessner (now called Ciudad del Este) and the Brazilian border. At Larry's invitation, Steve went a week early. I caught a bus out of Ybycuí late on Friday afternoon. Three hours later, I arrived at the bus terminal in Asunción. After buying some food for dinner, I sought out the buses going to the Brazilian border and learned that one left at 11 p.m. I calculated that the bus would arrive in Mallorquín in about seven or eight hours, after sunrise. Once aboard the bus, more comfortable than the ones to and from Ybycuí, I settled into a double-seat by myself. When the driver's assistant collected my fare, I asked him to advise me when we approached Mallorquín.

About five hours later, much sooner than I had calculated, the bus driver's assistant informed me we were arriving in Mallorquín. As the bus slowed, a feeling of dread crept up my spine because it was still pitch black outside. I glanced at my watch—it was 4:00 a.m. How could that be? Numbly gathering my belongings, I confirmed with the driver that this was Mallorquín. The only other passenger leaving the bus was a middle-aged drunk man who followed me down the aisle toward the exit. Fear for my safety washed over me and developed into full panic as I stepped onto the roadside. I took a few quick steps to remove myself from the light of the bus and into the darkness, hoping that the drunk man would not lunge after me. Holding my breath while mentally preparing to scream, I watched him stagger off in the opposite direction and disappear into the night.

As the red taillights of the bus faded down the highway, quiet set in. With my eyes adjusting to the darkness, I saw countless stars filling the sky. The night air was slightly brisk, and I began to shiver but not from the cold. Feeling foolish and afraid, I wondered how I could have miscalculated to this degree. Moving a little further from the pavement, I considered my options. One possibility was sitting down where I was and waiting until daylight. With thoughts of fire ants, spiders, snakes, and critters of the dark popping into my mind, I quickly crossed that one off my mental list. I recalled tarantulas tended to appear at night. Fire ants would frantically swarm if their nests were disturbed, and their bites usually got infected and caused painful itching.

I did not have clear directions to the homes of Larry and Pauline. Since most people in a rural town knew where Volunteers lived, I had planned on asking someone after getting off the bus. I did not even have a flashlight among my belongings. As I suppressed my panic, my eyes began to discern outlines of things in the environment, including some houses. Searching the houses for any glimmer of light, I finally spotted something—a dim light from under a doorway of a house. It looked to be about 100 yards away.

Proceeding slowly, feeling the ground with my foot before placing any weight on it, I inched my way toward the light. Soon finding myself at the gate of the house, I paused to think of what I might say, and I felt my face flush with embarrassment at my carelessness. I clapped my hands, calling out with a trembling voice in Spanish that I needed help. Nothing stirred from within. I clapped and called out again. This time I heard noises that disturbed the silence all around me.

As the front door cracked open, I saw the outline of a woman. I repeated my need for help, saying that I was looking for one of the Peace Corps Volunteers in town. The woman muttered something in Guaraní, and opened the door wider. I began a quivering explanation that I had miscalculated my arrival time, thinking that I would arrive at daybreak, rambling fast with a nervous voice. The first words out of the woman's mouth were kind and reassuring. "Come in, come in." She had comprehended enough of my blathering and sensed my anxiety to welcome me into her home. I stood in the front room waiting to be told what to do while she closed and bolted the front door. After awakening one of her daughters, the two of them quickly prepared a bed for me in a corner of one of the rooms. With kind eyes, she assured me that the sunrise would soon come. I collapsed into the bed, fully clothed.

As the sun rose in the eastern sky a couple of hours later, I awakened in a strange place. It took a few moments for me to recall the emotional trauma that I had experienced a short time before. Everyone in the household was already buzzing about. The *señora* came to my bedside as soon as she realized I was awake. She directed me to the latrine, a place to wash up, and then the breakfast table. I obeyed with a grateful heart. Over breakfast she assured me that she knew both Volunteers, Lorenzo (Larry) and Paulina. When I was ready, her daughter would walk me over to one of their houses. I felt like I was living in a dream world.

I belatedly learned from Larry and Pauline that the night buses stop infrequently, cruising along at top speeds with little traffic on the highway. I was accustomed to slower daytime travel on the dirt roads, and thus, I had grossly miscalculated travel time. The rest of the weekend is a blur in my memory. However, I will never forget the kind woman who took care of me in my time of distress. Although I don't remember her name, and I barely recall her face, for me she will always be My Mallorquín Angel.

During that Paraguayan summer, my appetite for food declined for two reasons—it was too hot to eat much, and I wanted to lose weight. I confess that I was falling in love and wanted to look better, but I didn't want to share that reason with anyone. Estimating that I was about 20 pounds too heavy for my 5'2" frame, I was determined to cut back on food quantity. When I told Ña Elisa of my desire to eat less, the look on her face indicated that she took it as a personal insult. I insisted she was a wonderful cook, but I simply didn't have a big appetite. She decided to ignore what I said and continued to pile too much food on my plate.

The dog Johnny had barely tolerated me all the months I had lived in the house. In spite of my efforts to be friendly toward him, he glared at me whenever I crossed his line of vision and growled menacingly when I came too close. With others in the family, Johnny was an obedient coward, slinking away when they kicked him, as if he were a pile of refuse that belonged in a corner. An idea came to mind. At the end of dinner one evening, I waited until others had left the room, leaving Johnny and me alone. I scooped a handful of food from my plate and passed the offering under the table, softly calling his name. His glare melted into a look of disbelief at what he saw and smelled. He quietly raised himself from the floor and cautiously approached me. After gingerly licking my hand clean of the tasty contents, Johnny turned around and promptly strode back to his spot in the corner. The dog played a perfect role as my sneaky co-conspirator, and he never glared or growled at me again.

Johnny knew better than to ever beg for table food—he knew his place in the household, and it was the lowest possible. He was there only to guard the house. I continued slipping him food underneath the table whenever a discrete opportunity presented itself. The clandestine bond between Johnny and me grew and flourished. Both of us were careful to hide our interactions, limiting our symbiotic friendship to eye contact and under-the-table fatty food transfers. We were never caught. At one point I made a casual comment to Ña Elisa that I was relieved Johnny no longer growled at me. That was it.

Months later, I was walking down the road when I saw Johnny for the first time after moving out of Ña Elisa's house. He was at the far end of the block when he spotted me. I was surprised to see him because the family usually kept him behind the gate. Running toward me with a passion, he locked his adoring eyes with mine. I bent down to his level. He was a mean-looking, rough mixed breed who smelled strongly of dog because he was never bathed. His fur was wiry and filthy. But Johnny was my friend. As I embraced him with both arms, his warm dusty body leaned into mine. While I gave him some loving pats and scratches, I spoke kind words into his ear telling him we would always be friends. I never saw him again, but when I think of Johnny, I remember a true friend who helped me to successfully lose weight.

Life became more routine and mundane—health talks in the morning, socializing in the afternoon, quiet time in my room after dinner, and an occasional evening out to play guitars and sing with friends. I read borrowed books from the Peace Corps library, wrote letters, and tried to speculate about the remainder of my Peace Corps service. I wondered if I could survive another year in this town. How could I, a single North American woman, develop a relationship with Steve in a rural Paraguayan town? In the heat and confines of Ybycuí, I felt lethargic and frustrated.

Occasionally, there was a dance in town. Steve, Mary, and I, along with friends, attended them. Although they were advertised to begin at 8:00 or 9:00 p.m., people never came at the designated time. Arrivals prior to 10 p.m. were rare, and things didn't get roaring until after 11:00, with successful dances lasting until after 2 a.m. I looked forward to when the traditional Paraguayan music played, typically *"La Llegada"* at the beginning and *"La Salida"* at the end. Some dances were mostly Paraguayan music, the beautiful melodic blend of guitars and harp, along with the accordion in some songs. Other dances had North American styled modern music played way too loudly and sung in incomprehensible English.

There were always plenty of older folks present at these dances, particularly gray-haired women dressed in black, sitting around the edges of the dance area to watch for any inappropriate touching among the young people. Sodas, beer, imported Scotch whiskey, and *Aristócrata* were available for purchase. *Aristócrata* was a crude form of rum made from sugar cane that, unless adequately aged, was joltingly harsh in the mouth. As it passed beyond the palate, the liquid caused a semi-pleasant burning sensation in the throat. Once in the stomach, it absorbed quickly to give an alcoholic buzz. If overindulged, *Aristócrata* caused misery in the morning.

A favorite drink of the young women at dances was beer mixed with orange soda. Perhaps this combination cut some of the beer's bitterness, or maybe it helped slow down the effect of the alcohol, but I found that mixture hard to swallow. Although Steve told me he really didn't care for dancing, he often asked me to dance. Because of cultural proprieties regarding single women, we didn't touch in public while in Ybycuí. He and I maintained the front that we were good friends and co-workers. Dancing was the one public venue permitting us close physical contact, gliding closely together to the thrum of the music under the Paraguayan night sky.

∞∞∞∞∞

As summer transitioned to fall, my energy level rose. During the last week of February and the first week in March, Steve and I were asked by Eric to conduct health training in Asunción for a new group of trainees. We welcomed the break from our rural rut in Ybycuí and appreciated the acknowledgement by Peace Corps that we were seasoned Volunteers. Like several other Volunteers, Steve and I stayed at a place dubbed "the Castle" while in the capital. It was an old cement building only a block from the Peace Corps office that did, in fact, resemble a castle. All who stayed there chipped in guaraníes for the rent and spread sleeping bags on the floor or on top of available beds. Later, when the Castle became unavailable, Steve, two others from our training group, and I found a two-room rental we referred to as "the Basement," a convenient place that saved us money and provided privacy from the watchful eyes and wagging tongues of Ybycuí.

In April, Steve and I vacationed in southern Brazil. Although initially interested, two others from our training group ended up not going. In retrospect, I realize how important this trip outside of Paraguay was in developing a more intimate relationship. On the long bus trips, Steve and I logged over 2,500 miles, most of them in Brazil. Early during the trip, as we watched the scenery through the bus window, Steve's hand sought mine. Sitting side by side, we rehashed the Ybycuí project, talked about our college years, and shared stories about our families. We occasionally played cribbage, an old English card game involving the accumulation of points through grouping cards, with score-keeping done by pegging on a cribbage board. Steve had learned the game from his father and had a compact cribbage board for traveling. My parents had taught me. We thumbed through guidebooks and planned activities for the upcoming destinations. With passing miles and hours, Steve and I became increasingly comforted by each other's constant company. When I dozed on the bus, I used his shoulder as a pillow without fear of being labeled a fallen woman.

Our first stop was at the Guairá waterfalls mentioned earlier. The rushing and falling of water over a precipice has something romantic about it. Perhaps that's why Niagara Falls has long been a honeymoon spot. Maybe witnessing the tumbling, free-falling water is a visual experience similar to the emotional process of falling in love, with emotions and hormones flowing faster and faster until there's a thrilling leap over the edge into the unknown, not knowing where we'll end up. After the initial plunge, we find ourselves in the foamy white water at the foot of the falls ready to gently float downriver in a warm and fuzzy emotional state. Being in the vicinity of such a wonder in South America caused me to reflect on how close I had become to my traveling companion.

During my first weeks in Ybycuí, Steve was an effective co-worker who became a friend. Teaching with him in the elementary school classrooms was fun and easy, like playing a relaxed game of tennis with the goal of keeping the ball in play as long as possible. We learned the other's strengths and challenges, achieving together more than we could separately. By the time we had reached the contest photo-taking, I genuinely liked Steve and trusted him. He was considerate, thoughtful, respectful, and hard-working.

Sometime before our appearance on national television, when we were sitting next to each other on a bus from Ybycuí to Asunción, I yearned for Steve to put his arm around my shoulders. That feeling seemed to come out of nowhere, or maybe it was from some part of my brain stem. That moment was the first flash of desire for a relationship beyond what we already had established. At that time, I wondered if Steve felt the same and thought it best to wait and see, not wanting to ruin a very positive platonic friendship. Then, on the return to Ybycuí after our successful TV appearance, I had placed my hand on his right knee to reassure Steve that I was with him on the potentially illegal act of driving on a closed road. He later told me that my gesture made him perceive our relationship differently. By Christmas that year, we were on a romantic pathway. The camping trip to *Salto Cristal* earlier in the year, had been a quiet, intimate interlude. A few months later, our vacation together was a bold emotional step.

These waterfalls that we visited, known as the *Saltos de Guairá* in Paraguay and *Sete Quedas* (Seven Waterfalls) in Portuguese-speaking Brazil, were located on the Paraná River between Paraguay and Brazil north of the cities of Puerto Presidente Stroessner, Paraguay, and Foz do Iguaçu, Brazil. Travelling the main east-west highway from Asunción, we crossed into Brazil and transferred to a bus heading north along the Paraná River. Other Volunteers had advised us that the wild, rustic six-hour ride on Brazil's dusty dirt road with only humble accommodations available at our destination was better than the more primitive road and lack of amenities offered on the Paraguayan side of the river. During our full day at the waterfalls, we meandered through thick tropical greenery by following the beaten dirt paths leading to thrilling views of water cascading and surging down the river. As the Brazilian name indicates, there were seven waterfalls, with each cascade wider and higher than the previous one. Reaching the last and most voluminous of the seven, we sat on a rock to rest. Steve put his arm around my shoulders and held me close as we gazed in awe at the wonder and beauty of the falling water.

The Paraná River is second in length on the continent, with only the Amazon River surpassing it. Its *Guairá/Sete Quedas* area accounted for the highest volume of water of any waterfall system in the world until the falls were flooded when the massive Itaipú Dam was completed in 1984. Paraguay has benefitted financially from the dam by selling most of its assigned electricity. In 2016, the Itaipú Dam was the highest energy-producing dam in the world and provided electricity to an extensive part of southern Brazil, including São Paulo and Río de Janeiro. However, when the dam treaty with Brazil expires in 2023, Paraguay hopes to renegotiate its terms with Brazil to reap what many Paraguayans feel would be a fairer share of the financial benefits. If the dam is ever removed and the area is restored, the largest section of the falls will remain destroyed—the Brazilians blasted away the rock that had formed this area so that navigation would be safer. (For photographs and more information, see various internet entries on the Itaipú Dam, including Wikipedia, Stanford, Atlas Obscura, Cannon & Cannon, and Britannica.)

Saddened by the knowledge that the Itaipú Dam would cause the waterfall system to disappear in the near future but grateful for the opportunity to see it, Steve and I proceeded that April of 1975 to Río de Janeiro via São Paulo, one of the most populous cities in the world. We only changed buses in São Paulo, fortunately not lingering. News about the deadly meningococcal meningitis outbreak in the city at that very time didn't reach us until Steve's dad wrote him about it after our return to Paraguay.

Río de Janeiro's tourist posters only begin to portray its beauty and majesty. From the beaches of Copacabana and Ipanema to Sugarloaf Mountain to the Christ the Redeemer statue atop Mount Corcovado, Steve and I took in the sites walking hand-in-hand. I felt anonymous, free, and happy. The only unfortunate moment was when a pickpocket on a bus stole Steve's wallet. Because we both carried our passports and the bulk of our money hidden in pouches underneath our clothing, he lost only a small amount of cash and some photos.

While in Río, Steve and I met up with vacationing Kate from Itacurubí del Rosario and Don, who had settled in Rio after completing his Peace Corps service in Paraguay. Don took us to the Cowboy Saloon, a gay bar and male striptease joint, for a rowdy evening of entertainment far from conservative Paraguayan culture. In a reverse situation, Steve clung to me for protection. As a man provocatively approached him, Steve whispered in my ear, "Put your arm around me. Show him that I belong to you." The ploy was successful in foiling the pick-up attempt and in helping us to laugh and relax together. On Easter Sunday morning, I awoke to the sound of Steve returning to the hotel room with his sweet smiling eyes, cups of rich Brazilian coffee in hand, and a bouquet of multi-colored roses for me.

∞∞∞∞∞

Returning from vacation, I realized the newness of Paraguay had long ago worn away. I wearied of living under the scrutiny of townspeople, and I was tired of the same questions asked of me in Guaraní on a daily basis: "Do you like it here?" "How do you like the food?" "Do you know [previous Volunteers] Jimmy, Wanda, Barbara, and Ricardo? No? Why not?" Rapid-fire Guaraní frequently followed the questions, and my energy for encounters in Guaraní was limited. Even though I participated in simple conversations and sang a number of songs in the language, I was far from fluent. People knew I couldn't follow a fast barrage.

Although relieved that Steve and I no longer had the responsibility of the hookworm eradication project, I felt a lack of purpose in my work and wondered how different it might be if we had a few dedicated Paraguayan counterparts or professionals trained in public health working with us. Sometimes Steve and I visited families together in the afternoon to talk about building latrines. We often gravitated to the neighborhood we knew as Sanja León, a poor area on the edge of town.

The Ledezma family was one of our favorites in that barrio. They were low-income, subsistence farmers with a plot of *mandioca* and corn as well as a flock of chickens in their yard. They primarily spoke Guaraní, but they were kind and patient with us in our communication attempts. Steve often went into that neighborhood alone in the mornings, doing what he could to encourage better sanitation. The days passed, and the cooler weather of late autumn was in the air. White lilies and crimson hibiscus bloomed, and the lush green was ever-present in dominating the environment.

Steve began helping local groups fundraise for particular projects, such as soccer activities or school events. One way to raise funds was to show movies, projecting them on the side of a building and charging each viewer a small entry fee. Local young people organized the movie events and arranged the seating, while Steve checked out a projector from the Peace Corps office and then borrowed or rented films. Some Asian action movies, either dubbed or with Spanish subtitles, were on loan for free. The local people watched them with rapt attention. One movie I did enjoy was a documentary about the construction of the Panama Canal, after which Steve shared with me that his father was born in the Panama Canal Zone. Whether a comedy, documentary, or thriller, the movies all had one thing in common—they frequently broke. When this happened, Steve was ready for it. He turned off the projector and whipped out the Scotch tape and scissors for a quick repair.

One fundraiser, held in an area outside of town lacking electricity, required the use of a generator. Unfortunately, the dubbed soundtrack was difficult to hear over the generator's noise. In addition, the seats were rickety wooden benches. My bench swayed precariously under the weight of four adults. Halfway through the movie, the opposite end of the wobbly structure suddenly collapsed to the ground. I escaped injury, but the others were bruised. Unfortunately for the injured, refunds were not given.

Another local project that Steve helped with was clearing some ground for a new soccer field. Soccer, called *fútbol* in Spanish, was the most popular sport in the southern hemisphere. North American football was thought to be a joke, something met with laughter and hooting, as we experienced in an Asunción movie theater showing a short on the U.S. sport.

For this particular project, Steve was asked to bring his machete on a Saturday to a designated location at the edge of town. The volunteer work crew was promised a free meal for a morning of hacking down the weeds. Luckily, the weather wasn't too hot, but the work was still hard manual labor. As noon approached, the organizers arrived with the free food. Steve was handed a bowl and spoon along with the advice, "Eat it fast, Esteban!" When asked what it was, he was told "*puchero avá*" (Indian stew). The contents quickly cooled, causing the stew, composed of animal innards, to begin congealing. Steve spooned a couple of bites, trying not to gag. Discretely edging toward an uncut area, he waited until nobody was looking to empty the bowl behind some standing weeds.

That wasn't Steve's only queasy-food experience in town. Late one Saturday morning, I was bicycling past his house when I saw him at Don Blasito's store across the road. The children in the family were taunting him as Steve made an attempt to eat some unidentified delicacy. I stopped to see what was happening. "Marilú, you have to try some of this!" they exclaimed.

"What is it?" I inquired in Spanish. Insisting that I eat some and only saying it was "*toro ra-yî*," I turned to Steve and asked him in English what it was. Out of courtesy, we generally refrained from speaking English when with Paraguayans, but hearing us talk in our native tongue always caused these particular children to laugh at the strange noises of our language.

With a half-smile, Steve responded in English, "Mountain oysters/bull testicles." They knew by the look on my face that he had told me. While the children still insisted I have a taste, Steve added, "But they don't taste like 'balls,'" first in English to me and then in Spanish to the kids. As they roared in laughter, I declined their offer of the delicacy.

∞∞∞

In early May, my parents wrote me that they were putting their Detroit home on the market in preparation for a move to a suburb. It was the house where I grew up, the only home I had ever known. The City of Detroit had experienced increasing violence since the 1967 Race Riots had rocked the foundation of our community, and my folks felt that it was time for a change. Within a short period of time, they relocated to Westland, Michigan. Burl heard from his family in Detroit that his father had been diagnosed with colon cancer. Times were changing for our families at home while we lived drastically different lives in South America.

∞∞∞

At the end of May as we reached the halfway point in our two-year service, Peace Corps called our group into Asunción for in-service training. It was a welcome reprieve from our work in Ybycuí and a good opportunity for everyone in our group to review the successes and the frustrations of our experiences to date. The females in our group were doing much the same as I was, giving talks in the health center on hookworm, anemia, tuberculosis, hand washing, vaccines, and other pertinent topics. They also felt the novelties of Paraguay had completely worn off. Frustration flourished.

Steve discovered the other males working in sanitation had about as much success as he in building latrines (not much), even though they had Paraguayan counterparts. The group was interested in hearing about our project and the underlying reasons for its demise. Steve and I shared our "final report" with them. Wyn lamented that people in her town persistently begged her, although to no avail, to help them immigrate into the United States. Most of the Volunteers in our group, attempting to work but facing myriad challenges, were trying to accept life at the slow Paraguayan pace.

The trainers assured us that our experiences and emotions were common for Volunteers mid-way through service. Together we mulled over what we might end up trying to accomplish during the second year. On one hand, I felt that the Ybycuí project had been a tremendous learning experience; on the other hand, I felt a sense of futility about making any kind of a positive difference as a Volunteer.

At this midpoint of our two years' service, we had our vaccination records reviewed and updated yet again. Back in Ponce, the Peace Corps nurse had poked us with needles and recorded the information on our yellow international vaccination cards. The process was repeated in Paraguay. Among the required vaccines were typhoid, yellow fever, tetanus, and rabies. The worst was the painful experimental rabies vaccine. Because rabies is so deadly, Peace Corps gave us the shot so that if we were exposed in the countryside, we would already have some antibody protection. "Get to the capital immediately if you might have been exposed to rabies," the nurse urged.

Although not a vaccine, gamma globulin was another painful shot we were given every four months throughout our service with the hope that it would protect us against disease, particularly hepatitis A. The injections were supposed to temporarily boost our immunity against diseases by giving us antibodies derived from pooled blood serum from large population numbers. The gamma globulin was given in the buttock, which then hurt for a few days when sitting. I repeatedly told myself that the temporary pain these shots caused was preferable to contracting a potentially deadly disease.

Before returning to Ybycuí, Steve and I met with Margarita at SENASA at her request. She was one of the top administrators at the sanitation agency who had participated in the special project's meeting in our town the previous September. Although approaching middle age, Margarita was not addressed using "Ña" because she wasn't married. She was a thin, wiry, intelligent woman with a determined air about her. We were fortunate to have her in Paraguay during our Peace Corps service.

Margarita spoke to us bluntly and boldly without sugarcoating her thoughts. SENASA officials had not been happy with the special project in Ybycuí because their inspectors were not involved. They were now planning a new effort in and around the town of Capiatá, about an hour from Asunción. Modeled after the Ybycuí plan, this would be better because SENASA would assign five Paraguayan inspectors to the project. When Margarita stated that she wanted us to be the co-directors of the project, Steve and I stiffened. We didn't have to verbalize it to each other that taking on such responsibility was out of the question. After an awkward silence, I smiled and responded, "We would be pleased to participate in your effort by conducting the educational component, but this project needs a Paraguayan director."

I felt the tension instantly release from Steve. He wisely added something that we had previously discussed between the two of us. He said, "Rather than teaching the children directly, we should train the elementary school teachers on the curriculum. In turn, they can use our materials and educate the children. This will be more efficient, can directly involve the teachers, and will likely have a more lasting effect in the communities."

A smile broke out on Margarita's face. From that moment, we looked to her as the project director. She accepted our offer and agreed to our request for reimbursement of our transportation costs. Our first focus would be in the Capiatá schools, scheduled for the week of June 23, with subsequent visits in four nearby communities. Returning to the Peace Corps office, we discussed the situation with Eric and requested per diem from the Peace Corps for the time we would spend in Capiatá. He agreed. Steve and I would split the cost of producing enough copies of *Barefoot Pepe and the Hookworm* and the latrine form to give to each child. When we returned to Ybycuí and informed Dr. Orihuela that we would be absent for about a week each month, the doctor didn't seem bothered by the news.

One day in late June when I noticed that Steve introduced himself in English as "Stephen," I asked him which name he preferred. From the moment he replied "Stephen," I stopped calling him "Steve." From then on, it was either "Stephen" or "Esteban," the Spanish translation of his name. The switch was obvious in a June letter to my family. My sister Cynthia commented to me later that they immediately noticed the change and suspected something was serious between us. Little did they know that "something serious" had begun several months previously.

Salto Cristal, a paradise in the hot summer

Johnny, after he stopped growling at me

Saltos de Guairá/Sete Quedas on the Paraná River between Paraguay and Brazil, 1975

"Courting in Paraguay," taken without our knowledge (Courtesy of Larry Hodgson)

CHAPTER 4

Fighting Intestinal Parasites in Capiatá

Education is the most powerful weapon you can use to change the world.
—Nelson Mandela

On June 22nd, we left Ybycuí for Asunción. The following morning, we met Margarita and Pedro, the lead sanitation inspector for the Capiatá project, at the SENASA office and piled into their van along with our guitars, materials, and a movie projector. Within the hour, we were in Capiatá. After rendezvousing at one of the schools with the other four inspectors assigned to the project, we huddled with our new team to discuss detailed plans for the week. Stephen and I followed the general approach we used in Ybycuí's elementary schools, covering what hookworm and roundworm look like, the damage they can do, how to break their cycles, the *Barefoot Pepe* story, our latrine form, and "The Hookworm Song." Our focus on the teachers rather than instructing children directly was already boosting our spirits because it had the potential of lasting well beyond our Peace Corps service.

Margarita and the inspectors were present to observe and to be introduced to the teachers prior to SENASA's push in the community to get latrines built. Pedro, however, was interested in actively participating in the classrooms. Stephen and I incorporated him into our routine from the start, and he proved to be a natural teacher with a good sense of humor.

Using a small latrine model with a curtain for a door, Pedro spoke bluntly in Guaraní to the teachers and included practicalities about having a wooden door rather than a curtain. "A curtain doesn't keep out animals, and we have all seen ugly brown smudges on the fabric," he stated, causing giggles and blushing faces among the teachers. We included a health talk on addressing the importance of hand washing, using the same story from the Peace Corps office with which I had made the filmstrip in Itacurubí del Rosario, "*Panchita Po-ky-â*" ("Francis Dirty Hands"). It was well received. Still, "The Hookworm Song" served as the highlight of our program. We soon had teachers belting out "*cevo-í, cevo-í*" with enthusiasm. The idea of a contest went over well, with SENASA taking responsibility for the judging, prizes, and planning a *clausura* (the celebratory kind) with the teachers. We called our teaching training *cevo-í cursillos* (hookworm workshops), but we referred to ourselves privately as "The Traveling Hookworm Show."

For each school, Stephen and I prepared a packet of materials that teachers could borrow from the principal to utilize in their classrooms. At the end of the *cevo-í cursillo*, we presented each teacher with a formal certificate of achievement, looking as dignified as a diploma, for having completed our workshop.

Through our *cursillos*, the SENASA program would reach over 1,000 children in Capiatá and another 1,700 in the surrounding communities. Although we had scheduling setbacks, Stephen and I managed to train teachers in all of the schools by the following March. After the teachers worked on the curriculum with their students, we returned to each community for the contest judging and *clausura*.

A number of SENASA officials and Peace Corps staff attended the *clausura* in the town of Capiatá, lending importance to the event. The children put on a dramatic skit based on *Barefoot Pepe and the Hookworm*, performed a Paraguayan dance in traditional costumes, and sang the song with Stephen and me playing our guitars—a chorus of hundreds of children, some on stage but most in the audience—that was followed by a roaring applause. The contest judging and announcement of winners preceded the teachers' private celebration with food and beverages for SENASA staff, Peace Corps officials, and us.

During the celebration, I humbly accepted a gift of two pieces of embroidery. One was a picture of a mean-looking worm saying, *"Chuparé tu sangre. Te volverás pálido…débil."* ("I will suck your blood. You will become pale…weak.") The other was of a stitched shoe and the wording, *"Yo te defenderé. Úsame."* ("I will defend you. Use me.") It was all a heartwarming success and brought us the satisfaction of having accomplished something that SENASA had requested and the Paraguayans appreciated. (Today, the embroidered pieces are framed and hanging on the wall in my home office.)

In the process of covering Capiatá and its nearby communities, Stephen and I wore out mimeograph stencils of our materials, which meant extra typing for me. As I was gearing up to cut new *Barefoot Pepe* stencils, someone suggested that we change "Pepe" to "Pedrito," a more common name in Paraguay. Smiling at the thought of honoring our lead SENASA inspector Pedro in this way, I made the change. Pedro, who made no objection to the edit, remained a steadfast worker and leader in Capiatá for several months until he was sent to supervise the sanitation program at the Itaipú Dam construction site. Stephen and I had confidence that Pedro would live up to his new challenges. In Capiatá, he helped make learning both interesting and entertaining. It was a privilege to work with him.

At one of the outlying schools, we spent a lively morning with the teachers before breaking at noon for lunch. I went out to the schoolyard to use the girls' latrine on that bright sunny day. As I approached it and automatically began breathing through my mouth, my eyes saw something I didn't want to believe. The latrine pit was completely filled, and the floor was overflowing with human fecal material. I gagged and furtively looked for bushes. Because I felt eyes watching my back, I forged ahead and tippy-toed into the latrine to limit the coating my shoes would get. To my dismay, the latrine had only a partial roof, allowing the noontime sun to cook the overflowing poop into a penetrating fetid stench. I was as quick as possible. With a queasy stomach and pale face, I returned to the classroom. Looking shameful and not knowing what to say, the teachers were quiet. I said nothing, but the afternoon session had a more serious undertone to it. Afterwards, in a private discussion with the SENASA inspectors, I shared my noontime experience and urged them to start their campaign to build latrines with the school. Stephen told me later that the boys' latrine wasn't any better.

During one of our weeks in Capiatá, we visited the town's small private museum of life-sized statues of creatures in Guaraní mythology. People in the countryside frequently talked about them. The best-known creature is the *Pombero*, also called *Karaí Pyharé* (kah-rah-EE puh-hah-REH, "Man of the

Night") in Guaraní. Described as short and ugly with hairy hands and feet, the *Pombero* is believed to steal things, scare horses, and cause pregnancy in single females. Leaving gifts of alcohol and cigars for the creature is thought to appease him. The *Pombero* was used by adults to frighten children into good behavior, similar to the Boogey Man in our country,.

Also short, hairy, and ugly was the creature known as *Kurupí* (ku-ru-PEE). Thought in olden days to be a spirit of fertility, *Kurupí* has a penis so long that it has to be wound around his body. He could be blamed for the disappearance of young women or for the pregnancy of an adulterous or single woman. Adults would use *Kurupí* to frighten girls into saving their virginity for marriage.

There are several other creatures in the folklore, including the couple *Tau* (pronounced like the Greek letter) and *Keraná* (keh-rah-NAH). According to mythology, they had seven cursed sons, one of whom is *Ao Ao* (AH-oh AH-oh), a cannibalistic creature who feeds on the flesh of disobedient, wandering children. The Capiatá museum brought to life the lore and mysteries of the Paraguayan culture based on its Guaraní heritage. This was particularly true of the *Pombero,* one of the most commonly mentioned creatures. I often heard parents tell children to go to sleep or the *Pombero* would get them, and others of these mythological creatures would occasionally appear in conversation.

While working in Capiatá, Stephen and I stayed at the Basement, our shared Volunteer space in Asunción. It was less expensive than several nights in a hotel, and we could cook modest meals in the tiny kitchen that had a sink and running water and a small stove. Because Lee had been a gracious host to us during holidays, we invited him and Mary for dinner at the Basement. After a workshop *clausura* celebration in one of Capiatá's schools, we stopped at the *Mercado del País*, still the only supermarket in the country, with a shopping list for dinner. Proceeding to our humble kitchen, we chopped vegetables and prepared meat for a stir-fry dinner. When Mary and Lee arrived, we served a tasty dinner with local beer (Pilsen Paraguay). After only a few bites of his food, Stephen excused himself and disappeared for the duration of the meal. He appeared only to say goodbye to our dinner guests. Unfortunately, he had spent the evening in the apartment's small bathroom violently emptying the contents of his stomach. We surmised that he had acquired food poisoning from eating the snacks prepared by the teachers for the *clausura*, maybe the mayonnaise or perhaps the canned horse meat, served on crackers. Luckily, I hadn't eaten them.

With the exception of the food poisoning, we had a successful time in Capiatá. SENASA administrators, especially Margarita, were pleased with our partnership. In the wake of the disappointing Ybycuí project, a more positive relationship between Peace Corps and SENASA was developing. The seeds that Chuck had sown were beginning to reap some profitable results.

∞∞∞∞

Whether in Capiatá or Ybycuí, we worked hard that winter, spending our downtime in Ybycuí preparing hookworm and latrine materials for the Capiatá communities. However, one of my most vivid memories about the winter of 1975 from June to August was the extreme, penetrating cold. In June, the temperature inched towards freezing, the winds blew, and bone-chilling rain fell. I piled on the clothes, with my old lime-green ski parka as the comfy-cozy top layer. My royal blue down sleeping bag helped at night, although crawling out of it on a cold morning took willpower. The Peace Corps loaned propane gas heaters to interested Volunteers. We had to pay for the tank refill, but it was worth it. Paraguayan homes did not have heat, and many Paraguayans lacked adequate clothing for a severe winter. There wasn't enough sun during those months, and I frequently thought of that Paraguayan adage, "The sun is the poor man's poncho."

One miserable, inclement winter morning with no patients waiting to be seen, I was asked to help with the tedious task of making cotton balls for use in the health center. A small group of us—Miriam, María Luisa, Nimia, and I—pulled chairs together and gathered around a large bag filled with picked cotton still containing the seeds and scratchy debris from the fields. Following the example of others, I grabbed a small handful from the bag, removed the seeds and debris with my fingers, untangled the cotton with a rustic wire comb, and rolled it into neat little balls for sterilization in an autoclave. This process was much less expensive for the health center than purchasing ready-made cotton balls. Eli Whitney had invented the cotton gin in 1793, but 182 years later, I was manually cleaning cotton.

Frosts were rare events in Paraguay, but the temperature plunged below freezing on the night of July 18th. The next morning, there was ice on the rim of the well in Ña Elisa's backyard. The frost in Paraguay extended east of the Paraná River into Brazil's coffee-growing area, killing half of the coffee crop and causing a steep rise in world coffee prices for a couple of years. Two more nights of frost caused additional damage. The freeze killed off some the tropical green growth around town, adversely affecting the economy of the subsistence farmers and the physical comfort of the population. On a personal level and most concerning to Stephen, the large banana-tree plant in front of his latrine that served as a door suffered. He described the problem in a cassette tape to his parents:

"The plants began to droop as if the life were draining out of them with each drip-drip of moisture falling off the leaves. By the end of the cold snap, the banana plant in front of my doorless latrine had gone from a thick and lush green mass that shielded the outhouse entrance from curious eyes to a sad drooping heap of vegetation. Fortunately, the angle of the latrine in a far corner of the backyard was such that someone would have to be physically within the property fence to see [into] the structure…It says something for the agricultural potential of Paraguay that the banana-plant-serving-as-a-latrine-door bounced back within a week or so to its previous state of a stout visual screen protecting the latrine user."

Fortunately, Stephen's risk of "getting caught with his pants down" was time-limited. The fact that he didn't have a secure door to keep animals from messing around in the latrine didn't bother him because his was not a squat latrine. Stephen had a wooden bench with a hole in it. Concerned about getting splinters while sitting after he rented the property, he had purchased a white plastic seat in Asunción to mount over the wood.

However, Stephen experienced a more potentially serious problem that July. We had borrowed a slide projector from the Peace Corps office to show some slides to friends. He plugged in the projector, but the light bulb didn't work. Stephen inserted a replacement bulb. When he turned on the machine, the glass bulb exploded in his face. Fearing pieces of glass had flown into his eyes, he immediately sought help from Dr. Orihuela. The doctor could not see any obvious damage but encouraged him to get to the Peace Corps office as soon as possible. I accompanied Stephen on the next bus. Eric was at the Peace Corps office when we arrived, and he dropped what he was doing to examine Stephen's eyes. Fortunately, Eric found no damage and gave him some eye ointment. Stephen applied the medicine several evenings in a row, carefully swabbing it from around his eyes each morning. The residual ointment felt gritty at first, and he used it until the grittiness passed.

While at Peace Corps, we learned that Burl, who had flown to Detroit to attend his father's funeral, was planning to return in August to complete his service. July was a difficult month for all of us, but another troubling situation was on the horizon.

∞∞∞∞

Throughout the year I had lived in Ña Elisa's house, I was acutely aware that she loved to talk, especially about other people. She periodically gossiped to me about the Volunteers who had previously served in Ybycuí, the two teenaged North American boys who at one time had lived in her house, and some Paraguayans as well. Much of what she said was not flattering to her subjects, often judgmental, and not necessarily completely true. She skillfully twisted the truth and elaborately presented her own interpretation of a situation. Rarely did I hear her praise anyone. I listened but never commented nor encouraged her. As time passed, I increasingly wondered how she portrayed me during her gossiping around town.

I made good-hearted efforts to give Ña Elisa the benefit of the doubt. However, I was cautious about what I said to her, and Stephen and I both made attempts to do good deeds. In addition to Stephen's father successfully helping her son-in-law obtain a pediatric training position at Yale, his dad had also helped Ruben and Mabel with a visa problem. When Ña Elisa's son Luis expressed interest in spending a year in the United States as a high school exchange student, I made inquiries and obtained an application for him in Asunción at the Paraguayan-American Cultural Center, a program facilitating exchanges between our two countries. I explained the process to him and the family. In spite of our efforts, however, I had a sinking feeling in my heart that my stay in Ña Elisa's house was not good for me.

One day in July, my eye caught something not right with my laundry drying on the clothesline in the backyard. While I had washed my own clothes in my first town, Ña Elisa insisted that she would oversee my laundry needs while I lived in her house. She assured me that there would be no additional monthly cost—she had included laundry in the monthly payment amount Martina had negotiated for me. Ña Elisa had flatly told me that I would not be allowed to do my own laundry because people in town would speak badly of her. I caved in, worrying about the wear and tear on my underwear but not wanting to risk a confrontation.

On that day in July, I noticed that two of my bras were missing. I had given Ña Elisa three to wash, and only one hung on the clothesline. I immediately returned to my room and reviewed my underwear inventory. Yes, two of my six bras were missing. (I had brought enough with me to last two years of vigorous laundering.) When my clean clothing was returned to me neatly ironed, folded, and piled, only one bra was included. At a loss as to what to do or say, I did nothing. A week later, the mystery was solved. Ña Elisa proudly showed me "her" two new bras, claiming she had acquired them through the Catholic Charities clothing distribution. I instantly recognized them—my brand, my color, my size (prior to the elastic expansion). My two missing bras each had a broad band of elastic sewn into the torso girth to expand it for Ña Elisa's large size. Speechless, I retreated to my room.

In early August, Ña Elisa informed me that she would be raising my rent/food/laundry fee by a third. She was adamant about charging me a fixed price per month, whether I was present in her house or not. I was spending an average of one week a month in Capiatá, but I said nothing. It was time for me to look for another place to live. I left the house to search out Mary. Finding her at Ña Niní's house,

I told her my predicament—I worried about gossip, and I couldn't afford what she wanted to charge me. Mary confirmed my suspicion. "Mary Lou, she *has* been gossiping about you, and she's *mean-spirited*. Ña Elisa apparently doesn't like your relationship with Stephen, whatever she thinks that is. You must move out of that house!" Mary explained that when Martina had originally made arrangements for me to live in Ña Elisa's house, Ña Niní had told Mary that my living there was a mistake because of Ña Elisa's "loose tongue." At the time, Mary thought it was too late to approach Martina about it. Mary's advice now, a year later, was that I confide in Ña Niní, whose guidance and protection I needed.

Mary and I found Ña Niní. Near tears, I bared my frustrations, sorrows, and fears to this kind, maternal woman. When I finished, warm hugs from both Mary and Ña Niní reassured me that such problems were solvable. Ña Niní strongly urged that I not talk to anyone else about this except for Stephen and that I not say anything negative about Ña Elisa or her family. In fact, she discouraged me from saying anything about them at all. Because Mary was occupying the accommodations in her household set aside for a Volunteer, Ña Niní thought it best to find a nearby arrangement for me. Until she did, she recommended that I immediately move into her household.

Mary walked me over to Stephen's house to explain the turn of events to him. The three of us returned to Ña Niní's house to borrow her pick-up truck, and Stephen drove us over to Ña Elisa's house. I found Ña Elisa in the kitchen and simply announced, "I'm moving out." I proceeded to my room, with Mary and Stephen on my heels.

As we were carrying my belongings to the truck, a red-faced and furious Ña Elisa blurted at me, "I know you have been saying bad things about me around town, and I demand that you stop telling such lies."

Taken aback at her outrageous outburst, I almost laughed in her face. Instead, catching myself, I stared at her and simply repeated, "I'm moving out."

Following Ña Niní's advice when people asked me why I moved, I only stated it was for economic reasons. Although Ña Niní remained in the background, the use of her vehicle for the move and the fact that I was temporarily staying in her home sent the message to gossipers, especially Ña Elisa, that I was now under Ña Niní's protection. Throughout this ordeal, Mary and Stephen were true friends indeed.

Within two weeks, Ña Niní had arranged for me to rent a small house a half block from her home. Again, Mary and Stephen helped with the move. Although I now had my own house, I was considered part of Ña Niní's extended family, and I felt safe. Even though I prepared most of my own food and ate alone in my little house, I was often invited to join the Feltes family to drink *yerba mate* or to eat dinner. Amalia, a relative near my age from the countryside who helped with sewing and light household chores, was among those whom I trusted.

Another frequent and trusted visitor at the Feltes home was Tomasa, who lived kitty-corner from Ña Niní's house. Tomasa Centurión was an attractive, soft-spoken, petite woman two years older than Mary and I. She usually joined us in the afternoon to drink hot *yerba mate* in the winter and cold *tereré* in the summer. Tomasa had systemic lupus erythematosus (SLE, or lupus), a chronic autoimmune disease in which the body's immune system attacks one's organs and tissues. Symptoms include fatigue, joint and muscle pain, and skin rashes. She occasionally became very ill and had to take steroids to reduce inflammation. Because of the lupus, her parents and siblings were quite protective of her. Tomasa was always welcomed in Ña Niní's house, and I observed that Feltes and Centurión families were good neighbors.

Following Mary's lead, I felt comfortable enough to begin asking questions about politics. While the Feltes family belonged to the Colorado Party, they did not believe it was okay to discriminate against those of other political affiliations. Ña Niní cautioned me to be careful what I said around Ña Coquita and her husband, which confirmed my suspicion that he was known to "spy" on people and report to politicians in Asunción. I learned that teachers in the public schools had to be card-carrying members of the Colorado Party, as did all government employees. The Centurión family belonged to the Liberal Party. They owned a business with outlets in Asunción, Ybycuí, and a few other towns where they sold imported washing machines, televisions, stoves, radios, and refrigerators. At times life was difficult for them because they were not Colorados, but they survived by paying bribes, an understood necessity in Paraguay.

Political differences were not of concern between the Feltes and Centurión families. There were close friendships between the two households, and good character was important and valued. Ña Niní privately guided me on people to be wary of because of their gossiping. At one point, Ña Niní softly commented that Don Angel never spoke ill of anyone, and her eyes silently told me we should feel sorry for him. My time in Ña Niní's home was a healing experience for me, and she never accepted any money from me for staying or eating in her house. She loved me like a daughter.

On very few occasions outside the Feltes household, a Paraguayan would try to engage Stephen or me in a political conversation. Stephen told me of one instance in which a poor, desperate-looking farmer pled with him for help. The man feared arrest and persecution from the government. Stephen apologized to the man that he could not become involved, but he promised he would never mention that the man had approached him. There were other times that we Volunteers would be accused of being CIA spies or communists. We denied the accusations and pointed out the work we were doing in health education and sanitation. For the most part, we were successful in avoiding unpleasant political confrontations.

Having studied world history, I knew that authoritarian governments in various stages of oppressive control have been the rule throughout humankind's history. It had crossed my mind that working in a country with an authoritarian regime, such as we had in Paraguay, might in some way aid and abet that government. However, I believed then, as I do now, that the presence of the Peace Corps does not condone violations of human rights in a developing country. The potential for power-grabbing, corruption, and oppression exists everywhere there are people. I had witnessed it in the United States—election meddling, hands in the till, distortion of truth and facts, and unfair to brutal treatment of African Americans, Latinos, Asians, immigrants in general, and women. Most governments appear authoritarian to at least some segments of their population. I knew that life wasn't fair. I could only hope to make small, positive contributions in improving the health and education of our fellow human beings either domestically or abroad, under an authoritarian government or a budding democracy, with empathy and humility. It was a relief knowing Stephen, Mary, Ña Niní, and Tomasa were available and safe for questions, discussions, and comments regarding complicated, confusing, or potentially touchy situations.

Soon, I was settled comfortably into my little pink house with its three rooms, which I used as a living room, kitchen, and bedroom. Ña Niní loaned me some wooden benches to use as seating in the living room. I purchased a wicker rocking chair that would be a soothing comfort for me. In my modest kitchen, I had a table and chair, a two-burner tabletop gas stove, and two wooden crates that I hung from the ceiling rafters with plastic rope, propping them away from the wall with wooden pegs.

I sprayed both the rope and the pegs with insecticide weekly, successfully keeping crawling bugs out of my dried food and utensils with this treatment. In my bedroom, I hung my mosquito net from the rafters above my bed and tucked a chamber pot underneath with a green Frisbee as a cover. With the chamber pot, I avoided going out in the middle of the night to visit the latrine located some 35 yards behind the house, a potentially dangerous nocturnal trip for a single foreign woman living alone. I purchased a broom, buckets, and other cleaning implements.

Although my house had electricity, installed after the last time the walls had been painted, I kept a good supply of batteries for my flashlight and a kerosene lamp for the electrical outages that occurred when bad storms swept through town. I secured the three wooden doors each evening when darkness came by placing heavy wooden bars into their wrought-iron holders. The sole window, located in the kitchen, had shutters secured by the same method.

When I discovered that small cockroaches lived in the wooden doors and window shutters, I made a deal with them. If I clunked on the wood and they quickly disappeared from my sight, I wouldn't attempt to eradicate them. We kept our bargain. Not counting the cockroaches, this was the first time in my life that I lived alone. With books, my tape recorder, music on cassettes, letter writing, and guitar playing to occupy my non-working time, I enjoyed my solitude, secure in the knowledge that I had caring friends nearby.

My new neighbors were attentive and curious about me. On my second evening in the house, my guitar music, as rudimentary and basic as I played, attracted nine neighbors and a dog. I sat strumming my guitar on the narrow front porch, enjoying the tranquility of the early evening. The neighbors approached and changed from spectators to singers as I played some of the Paraguayan songs we all knew. Even the dog seemed happy.

A few days later, a fierce storm moved into the area while I was sitting on my covered back porch writing a letter to my grandmother. The wind picked up and blew in threatening clouds. The impending bad weather would likely knock out the electricity, and it caused me to reflect on how close to the elements I lived. As the rain began pelting down, my neighbors to the west invited me to stay with them until the storm passed, even if it meant sleeping overnight with them. They were convinced that I would be frightened by the storm if I were alone in my house. I stayed with them a couple of hours until the downpour abated. From our conversation, I learned that the family had two daughters living near Washington, D.C., and heard about the barber shop business they had in their home next door to me. When I finally left, the electricity had not yet returned. I assured them I would barricade myself in the house and be fine with my flashlight, kerosene lamp, and candles. I survived in my cozy little home.

After settling into my house, I passed by the pharmacy of Ña Elisa's husband Don Angel, whom I had not seen since before moving out. Sitting in a chair at the doorway, he waved upon seeing me. I dismounted from my bicycle to say hello. He returned my greeting with sad, sorrowful eyes. There were no ill feelings harbored between us, and I sensed a feeling of embarrassment and regret on his part. He gently wished me well as we briefly hugged. I told him that his son Luis needed to submit his papers for the exchange program within the next month and that I would gladly meet Luis at the pharmacy to help him. A soft jolt of surprise flashed in his damp eyes, his large body shook slightly, and his face reddened. Pretending not to notice, I commented that it would be such a good experience for his son. I asked Don Angel to pass the word along to him. I was good to my word. With my assistance, Luis submitted his application on time. He would eventually spend a year as a high school exchange student in eastern Oregon, becoming a star field goal kicker on his high school football team and having a wonderful experience.

∞∞∞∞

Having first shed the Peace Corps latrine project and then gossipy Ña Elisa from my daily life, I settled into my own pleasant routine while in Ybycuí. In the morning after a quick breakfast of bread, jam, and coffee, I rode my red bicycle to the health center, arriving as close to 7 a.m. as possible. Along the way I waved and greeted people with the traditional "*adiós*" of the countryside. At the health center I gave health talks to the patients in the waiting area. Between talks I chatted with Stephen in the sanitation room or Miriam at the reception area. At noon, my work at the health center completed for the day, I retraced my path to my pink house on the other side of town, waving to friendly people along the way. Occasionally, I would have to dodge a chicken pecking for bugs, trying to anticipate if the bird would dart in front of my bicycle or turn the other way. The meandering pigs, cows, and animal droppings were easier to avoid as long as I paid attention.

After my dusty ride home, I pulled water from the well that was just outside my kitchen door, expertly making a neat loop of the rope onto the brick rim of the well. Next, I washed my hands, fixed and ate lunch, and cleaned up the dishes. Then I proceeded to my bathing ritual, following the procedure that Ellen of Itaguá taught me. Without a designated bathing spot in my pink house, I set up my water, shampoo, and soap in the kitchen and closed up the doors and window. After disrobing and dousing myself with a few cups of water, I quickly shampooed my hair and washed my body. The rest of the water was used, cup by cup, to rinse myself from head to toe. However, halfway through, I had to stop and sweep the water under the kitchen door to the outside. Otherwise, the water would seep into my living room. It wouldn't harm the brick flooring, but I preferred to keep my living room free of soapy water.

Along the path to my sanitary latrine was a fence demarcating my rental property from the neighbors' land. On their side of the fence were several trees that occasionally shed broken pieces of thorny branches. After learning that those thorns easily penetrated my rubber flip-flops, I always wore sturdy shoes for any trips to the latrine.

I took a *siesta* in the early afternoon and socialized afterward. Sometimes I met with Stephen to prepare materials for an upcoming hookworm workshop. Otherwise, I might drink *yerba mate* in the afternoons with Ña Niní, Mary, Amalia, and Tomasa. Occasionally, Don Lalo, Carlitos, Stephen, or a neighbor would join us.

Whether I ate with Ña Niní's family or by myself, I had access to unlimited fresh fruits as they ripened on the trees. I was invited to pick and take what I wanted for free from the Feltes yard, or I could buy fruit at a nominal cost from small stores scattered around town. Although filled with copious seeds, sweet oranges and tart grapefruits were ubiquitous and provided delicious freshly squeezed juice at breakfast and in the mid-afternoon. I never tired of the mangoes and papayas with a touch of lemon or lime juice. A perfectly ripened avocado just plucked from a tree, mashed, and lightly salted was as smooth as soft butter. Paraguayans added sugar to a pureed avocado for a dessert, but I preferred it salted. Guayaba, a fruit whose exterior is similar to a lemon or lime, has a seedy-looking interior the deep color of a wild salmon. In some countries, it is called guava or guanábana. In Paraguay, women often prepared jam or a jelly-like bar with it when the guayaba was in season, and the pattern of the guayaba fruit when cut in half is a common center woven into spiderweb lace, as mentioned earlier.

Whatever the seasonal fruit, I thoroughly enjoyed their fresh, robust flavors flooding my mouth within a couple of hours after they left the tree.

In my own humble kitchen, I prepared soups from packages of dried Knorr mixes sold at the supermarket in Asunción. Peanut butter (also from the supermarket) and marmalade sandwiches were a quick and easy lunch. I often stopped at Don Blasito's store on my way home from the health center to buy eggs to scramble, bread rolls, or other food items. My dessert was usually fresh fruit. Without a refrigerator, I purchased small amounts of fresh food on a daily basis. My cooking during those days was basic but sufficient.

Fresh milk was another culinary delight for me. Ña Niní's dairy herd at Posito on the outskirts of town (where Mary and I celebrated our 24th birthday) provided a daily milk supply. Although she routinely boiled it as soon as it was delivered, one weekend morning when I stopped at her house, Ña Niní asked me if I had ever tasted raw milk. When I shook my head, she smiled and offered me a small glass. Cautioning me that it's safer to pasteurize it by boiling, Ña Niní suggested that heating milk changes the taste. She reminded me that her cows were healthy and vaccinated. I took the chance and slowly sipped the milk, savoring every creamy ounce of it. I already had judged that her *dulce de leche*, the sweetened caramelized milk spread I loved, was the best I have ever eaten. I now realized that fresh milk from her herd was the special ingredient.

One memorable Saturday evening just after dusk while I was at Ña Niní's house, we heard clapping outside. I followed her to the door and strained to pick up the gist of the conversation in Guaraní. A man from an outlying area was asking for her husband, Don Lalo. The man needed help with his cow, standing in the road behind him. "Don Lalo's not here right now, but what's the problem with your cow? I can probably help," I heard her reply in Guaraní. He explained that the cow was seriously constipated, and he feared for her life. I observed that the animal looked uncomfortable and bloated. I also noticed that behind the man and his cow, a small crowd had begun to gather, possibly looking for some Saturday night entertainment.

The conversation in Guaraní escalated, with some men from the growing throng joining in. Ña Niní stepped back to explain details to me in Spanish. The cow's owner didn't have confidence that a woman could solve the problem, so Ña Niní refrained from giving advice. Instead, the cow's owner listened to vocal spectators regarding possible treatments. "The cow needs eggs! Someone bring some eggs!" one man loudly proclaimed. Money and instructions were given, and a boy promptly returned with a dozen eggs in a basket. The animal's owner maneuvered the cow to the ground and proceeded to crack open and deposit one egg after another into her mouth, held open by a teenaged boy. We watched and then waited for something to happen.

Close to a half-hour later as it grew increasingly dark, an older man in the crowd shouted, "Mineral oil! That's what she needs!" A short time later, a bottle of mineral oil appeared out of the darkness. Again, the cow's mouth was held open while the mineral oil was poured into it with a glub-glubbing sound. We all watched expectantly as the treatment was given by light shining from Ña Niní's doorway and waited again. A short time later, the cow began squirming and tried to stand up. Everyone cautiously moved back out of harm's way, forming a large circle so nobody would miss the show.

The agitated cow finally struggled to her feet, grunting and swaying. The circle grew larger to give her more space. And then, like a dam breaking, the manure began to plop out. "OOOH, AAAH," exclaimed the audience, backing up even further. Ña Niní and I slipped back into the house, closed the door, and broke into peals of laughter. A short time later, she saw me avoid the messy manure pile in front of her house and watched until I was safely back in my pink house. I intermittently chuckled late into the night, replaying the scene in my mind.

Some afternoons I'd find Ña Niní working on a sewing project. As I had always enjoyed sewing, I watched her with keen interest. Ña Niní and other seamstresses in Paraguay would have a client pick out an item of clothing from an old pattern book or magazine, take the person's measurements, and advise as to the amount of fabric needed. When the client returned with the fabric, the seamstress smoothed it out on a table and drew lines on it with a piece of chalk, guided by a tape measure. After cutting the fabric and basting the pieces together by hand, the seamstress had the client come in for a fitting. Any needed adjustments were made before the sewing machine was used for stitching.

Ña Niní had two sewing machines, one electric and the other an old, mint-condition Singer with a foot treadle. I watched Ña Niní work her magic with the fabric as expertly as she did with food in the kitchen without ever following a recipe. I had always relied on patterns and recipes. One day she asked if I would like to work the Singer sewing machine. Of course I would! She gave me a quick demonstration, showing me the fluid, steady rhythm of her feet on the treadle. Sitting down and putting my feet into position, I began the rhythm she had used. The sharp needle pumped up and down, whirring with a soothing sound, in and out of the scrap of fabric she had given me. The machine was as clean and oiled as it must have been on its first day of use. Passed down to Ña Niní from her mother, the Singer was a treasure and the tool of an artist, which is how I perceived Ña Niní when I saw her creations. She had the reputation of being the best and most expensive seamstress in town.

Having survived the trials and tribulations during the winter months, I looked optimistically on September and the coming springtime. I was maintaining my weight at an ideal 120 lbs. I felt happy, except for the fact that I wanted to spend more time with Stephen. In an attempt to protect my reputation, he never visited my house unless Mary joined us. Ña Niní understood our situation and frequently invited both of us to dinner, often entertaining us with stories about previous Volunteers trying to cope with the rampant gossip. Before long, she had us laughing at the absurdities of life in general and Volunteer struggles in particular.

∞∞∞

In an attempt to broaden my public health repertoire, I wrote and proposed a brief dental hygiene curriculum for the elementary schools and received permission from a school principal to try it out before the end of the school year in November. With a quantity of donated toothbrushes from my Aunt Helen in Michigan and my poem below, a mix of Spanish and Guaraní called *"Sara Sonriente"* ("Smiling Sara"), I taught oral hygiene outside in the schoolyard, brushing together, spitting, rinsing, smiling, and having fun. The message of the poem works well if the pulled tooth is a baby tooth. It was something different, and it felt rewarding to teach elementary school children again.

Sara Sonriente

Sara Sonriente tenía un dolor.
Le molestaba un diente, cada día fue peor.
Oky-jhy-jé ojhó dentista-pe oconsultá jhaguâ
Por fin ojhó dentista rendape porque la jhâi jhasy tuixá.

Él tiene que sacarlo pero después jhe-í xupe
Siempre tenés que cepillar los dientes recarú riré
Jha nde reúro la kamby nde rera Sara Sin Diente
Ocambiá-ta jha jha-é jevy Sarita Sonriente.

Smiling Sara

Smiling Sara had a pain.
A tooth was bothering her, each day it got worse.
She was afraid to go to the dentist for a consultation,
Finally she went to the dentist because the tooth was really hurting.

He had to pull it but afterwards he said to her,
"You have to always brush your teeth after you eat,
And if you drink milk, your name Sara Without a Tooth
Will change and will again be Smiling Sara."

∞∞∞∞

With slightly warmer weather on the way, Stephen decided to plant a garden. He had wanted to do this during his first year in town, but the demands of the Ybycuí project prohibited it. A garden would be a way to learn about history, acquire new vocabulary, discover local ways and traditions, and gain a new topic of conversation. I followed the garden's progress almost daily, stopping by Stephen's place on my way home from the health center before the midday meal. It was a process that took about twenty days from start to planting seeds.

Shortly after the July frost, he staked out a 30' x 10' area in his expansive backyard and began by hoeing weeds and turning over the sandy soil with a shovel. His neighbor Don Blasito loaned him the tools he needed. During his initial labors, Stephen discovered two things he hadn't seen before: 1) Some nests of the "ñandú cabayú" (nyahn-DU kah-bah-JU), directly translated from Guaraní as "horse spiders." In English, they are tarantulas. One nest was full of baby spiders, and another had a big hairy adult in it. 2) A round tuber with a white interior resembling a potato. According to his neighbors, it was considered a weed, but the Paraguayans ate it during the big war of the 1870s.

As Stephen's neighbors explained to him, the big war was the War of the Triple Alliance. Paraguayans often talked about it. When dictator Carlos Antonio López died in 1862, his son Francisco Solano López, *El Mariscal* (Marshall), took power. Mariscal López led Paraguay in the five-year desperate and disastrous struggle of Paraguay against Argentina, Brazil, and Uruguay. The war ended when López died on the battlefield of Cerro Corá in 1870. It took eight years of negotiations to arrive at a final peace treaty. U.S. President Rutherford B. Hayes served as the arbitrator during the negotiations, prompting Paraguay to name Burl's town across the river from Asunción in his honor. In spite of the estimates that Paraguay lost 70% of its male population in the war, Mariscal López remains one of Paraguay's greatest heroes today. It would take decades for Paraguay to recover from the war's devastation.

With the mini-history lesson behind him, Stephen proceeded to fertilize his garden. Using aged manure brought from a cow pen two blocks away by repeated trips with a borrowed wheelbarrow, he developed a rich dark soil begging for vegetable seeds to nurture. His neighbors and passersby, observing his manual labor, were openly amused. Some of them wondered aloud why he, a "rich gringo," didn't pay somebody to do this dirty work. They laughed and called him *guapo* (hard-working). The daily physical labor and social interactions, involving a topic other than latrines, were as satisfying to him as memories of hitting the winning run in the ninth inning and celebrating with teammates over pepperoni and cheese pizza.

Shortly after he moved into his house almost a year earlier, Stephen had noticed that livestock frequently invaded his yard. To prevent cows from entering through the gate to eat his ruby red hibiscus blossoms and drop fresh cow pies, he had laced the gate and latch with barbed wire. Stephen initially noticed cow hairs on the barbed wiring near the latch, but soon the animals learned that a few flowers weren't worth getting poked by sharp barbs. Although the grove of sour orange trees in his yard provided ammunition against chickens, they easily waddled away under the wooden split rail fence hemming the property when he hurled one in their direction.

For intruding pigs, entering as casually as the fowl, Stephen had a pile of broken bricks. A few months before starting the garden, he whacked an invading hog in the head with a piece of brick. It fell to the ground with the blow, and for a moment Stephen feared he had killed it. Thoughts briefly ran through his mind about being held accountable for killing someone's pig. However, it revived, slowly got to its feet, staggered a few steps, then picked up speed as it escaped from the yard. Slipping under the gate, the hog began oinking with increasing volume. A small group of pigs gathered in the road as the hurting porker told his tale of woe to his audience. The pig must have told a good story, as Stephen wasn't bothered with pigs in the yard for several weeks. Prior to the garden, invading animals had simply been a bother. Now the stakes were higher.

After observing fences around town, Stephen opted to build a *takuara* (bamboo) fence. He could have hired someone but decided to be *guapo* and build the fence himself. Stephen sought advice from some friends and neighbors about how much bamboo he would need, how to acquire it, and how to go about constructing the *takuara* fence. Acting on their advice, Stephen placed an order from the countryside for 20 round bamboo shoots, each with the diameter about the size of a medium can of Campbell's pork and beans. The shoots, varying in length from 15 to 20 feet, were delivered by ox cart.

The next step was to convert the shoots into 200 to 300 thin slats of bamboo of one to three inches in width and cut to the desired length. Stephen did this by first driving a stake very deeply into the ground. Then he took an axe and cut or split the bamboo at one end, leaving the axe in the cut. When Stephen pushed the long piece of bamboo towards the stake in the ground, the pressure widened the slit. Remarkably, the bamboo would split by this method. If one begins pulling the bamboo, using the stake as a wedge through the initial slit, one can split it lengthwise down the middle. Then it can split again in quarters, with the process repeated until the right width is achieved. This approach required dealing with the tough, tenacious, sharp fibers of the bamboo that run lengthwise and stick out along the split edges. If one is unlucky enough to slide a hand too hard across an edge, the bamboo can cut like a razor blade. Stephen had a neighbor help him with some of the initial splits and then proceeded alone. After splitting the next six bamboo shoots, his hands had little slices all over them.

When Stephen was working one afternoon, the man who sold him the bamboo walked by and began laughing. He said in Guaraní, "You're doing it wrong!" Entering the yard, he proceeded to show Stephen the right way. He used an axe to split the bamboo about two feet at one of the ends. Then, as if he were prying open an alligator's mouth, the man put his feet on the bottom part of the bamboo, placed his hands under the upper half, and jerked up quickly. The bamboo went "rrrRRR" and split right down the middle. (According to Stephen, it was really something to see.) The man said, "That's how you got to do it, Esteban." Stephen wasn't too sure about trying this technique, so he returned to the original method and slowly accumulated a pile of long, slender slats of *takuara*.

The following day the children from across the road came over to see how he was doing. While he was carefully removing some sharp little fibers, Stephen told them what the man had demonstrated to him the day before. They commented, "Oh, yeah? Show us." Stephen proceeded to do so, cutting the bamboo in about two feet like the man had shown him, putting his feet on the bottom, grabbing the top part, and jerking up. Unfortunately, he neglected to grip the bamboo tightly enough. As the shoot began to split, his hand slipped along the edge, causing a sharp fiber to almost cut off the tip of his right ring finger. The bamboo cut in deeply, close to the bone, slicing him like a razor blade. He immediately washed it with soap and water, covered it with gauze from the Peace Corps medical kit, and went to the health center. Dr. Orihuela, with almost a smile on his face, cleaned the wound with mercurochrome, sewed it up with one stitch, and bandaged it. And yes, Stephen was current with his tetanus shots.

Hoping to complete the fence as fast as possible following the accident, he hired two guys to finish the rest of the bamboo. By himself, Stephen had done six large bamboo shoots over five days. The hired men split the remaining 14 shoots in one morning. They also cut them into four-foot segments, the desired height of the fence.

In spite of his bandaged finger and working alone, Stephen managed to install the *takuara* fence, including a gate. He dug ten postholes, purchased the posts, and drove them into the ground. After stringing heavy wire between the posts, Stephen lined up the slats a few inches apart along the heavy wire and hammered each one a few inches into the ground with an axe head. To finish the fence, he looped thin wire first around the tops of the bamboo slats and finally around the bottoms.

With the garden area secured by his *takuara* fence and after hoeing weeds once again, Stephen prepared six raised areas of dirt, each about 8' x 3', to prevent plants from drowning when it rained. He used one raised area as a starter, planting seeds of tomatoes, green peppers, butternut squash, pumpkin, lettuce, cabbage, spinach, cucumbers, and carrots. He followed local advice about irrigating each morning and evening with a watering can. As the weather became hotter, Stephen asked Don Blasito about making artificial shade out of burlap sacks to prevent the lettuce from bolting and becoming bitter. Advised that it wouldn't help because of the severe heat of summer, he dropped that idea. (Over three decades later, a Paraguayan friend named Silvio would prove Don Blasito wrong by cultivating vast fields of thriving vegetables that he shaded from the intense sun.)

Stephen's gardened flourished. Within two months he was giving away produce. One day, I prepared a colorful, hearty soup a few hours after Stephen pulled the vegetables from his garden. He took some of his harvest to Ña Conchita, who still cooked for him. Although she was reluctant to prepare food with so much vegetable matter, Stephen insisted that she do so because he wanted to enjoy the influx of his own homegrown veggies into his diet. He encouraged her to eat the food as well, but Stephen dropped the subject after a few days when Ña Conchita complained to him that the high vegetable content was giving her diarrhea.

∞∞∞∞

The president and dictator of Paraguay, Alfredo Stroessner, came through Ybycuí on September 4, 1975, to inaugurate the new national monument of Minas Cué ("Place of the Mines"), also known as La Rosada. Located 15 miles from Ybycuí, this old iron foundry had been established in 1850. During the War of the Triple Alliance, the foundry made arms and military tools until it was discovered and destroyed in 1869 by Paraguay's enemies. The Stroessner Regime supported the reconstruction of the foundry, established a museum, and created the 12,300-acre National Park of Ybycuí that included the foundry and the Salto Cristal waterfall. (In the late 1970s and early 1980s, forestry Peace Corps Volunteers helped develop this area into a functional national park with rangers to maintain hiking trails and protect the flora and fauna, including monkeys, exotic birds, pig-like hoofed mammals called peccaries, and the South American coati, a member of the raccoon family.)

By 1975, adequate progress had been made on the foundry reconstruction to warrant its grand opening. Throngs of people attended the event that lovely spring day. Stephen and I went early with Ña Niní, Don Lalo, and others in the Feltes vehicle to set up our chairs in a place with a good view. Usually a quiet spot with only the sounds of the whistling wind and chirping birds, the area was buzzing with people, many of whom wore red bandanas or waved red banners signifying the Colorado Party. When someone gave me a red bandana, I wasn't sure what to do with it. I wasn't a Colorado, a dictatorship was not my choice of government, and Peace Corps had warned us to stay out of Paraguayan politics. I nervously twisted it until giving it back to its owner.

While waiting for Stroessner and other dignitaries, our small group feasted on picnic food prepared by Ña Niní and Epí. Soon the crowd's excitement grew as a small motorcade approached. Stroessner and his bodyguards emerged from the president's vehicle, a gold-colored Ford, and were greeted by Paraguayan music performed by a choir with harp and guitar accompaniments. Stroessner then casually walked through the awaiting crowd to the red ceremonial ribbon draped at the foundry's entrance. Without any speech, he cut the ribbon while the crowd cheered. Never before or since have I attended a political event in which there were no speeches! Stroessner, his bodyguards, and the dignitaries briefly walked around the foundry and then left without additional fanfare. As he departed, Stroessner walked within five feet of us, and I took some photos of him. Neither Stephen nor I were ever that close to a head of state before (or since). There were soldiers lining both sides of the entrance, but there had been no screening or frisking of attendees that day. Knowing the potential for violence in Latin America, I was puzzled about the apparent lack of security. Perhaps there was more going on behind the scene than what I observed.

Once Stroessner was gone, the crowd was allowed to roam the grounds and reconstructed foundry. We piled our chairs and picnic remains into the vehicle and joined hundreds of others weaving their way around the impressive stone reconstruction of Minas Cué, complete with waterworks, like it must have been in the days of yore. It was a proud day for the Paraguayans in attendance as they recalled the sacrifices their ancestors made for their nation 101 years earlier.

∞∞∞

The approaching summer brought hot and humid weather that came in cycles. As summer progressed, the heat and humidity would keep increasing until I didn't think I could bear it any longer, as if I were trapped in a damp and oppressively overheated terrarium. Finally, dark clouds would roll into the sky above me and let loose with rain to lower the temperature 15 to 20 degrees Fahrenheit, only to have the cycle repeat itself within a week or so.

Time seemed to drag until one November day, when Stephen and I were checking our mailboxes at the air conditioned Peace Corps office. Ellen, the education Volunteer coordinator, approached us with an interesting proposal. Not the Ellen who lived in Itaguá, this Ellen worked with teams of teachers around the country—a Volunteer and a Paraguayan on each team—to provide training to improve the quality of education. Several of her teams had requested assistance in sanitation education, and she thought we might be interested in helping out. Ellen had seen our performance on national television and was aware of our efforts in Ybycuí and Capiatá.

Stephen and I looked at each other with a glimmer of new hope. Perhaps this was the meaningful work we were meant to do for the remainder of our time in Paraguay. We told Ellen that we were definitely interested and would talk to Health Program Officer Eric.

We found Eric in his office. He listened attentively and seemed supportive, until we asked to move to Asunción to facilitate our traveling. His face changed. "Too many Volunteers have moved into the capital, and we have decided not to approve any new relocations at this point," Eric bluntly stated. Dejected but not defeated, we thought to wait a period of time before revisiting the idea with him. The school year ended at the end of November, and the next academic year didn't begin until February. The idea made too much sense to let it drop. Furthermore, we had some new materials to use. Stephen's father had recently sent us a set of microscopic slides of parasite eggs and larvae along with a second movie, *The Problem of Hookworm Infection*, containing real film footage of adult hookworms sucking blood in the intestine. We didn't think these acquisitions were appropriate for young children, but they could definitely be used with teachers.

∞∞∞

As the holiday season approached for the second time, Stephen and I took another serious step forward in our relationship. We were able to purchase airfare with our savings and some help from our parents in order to vacation at home, first visiting his family in Connecticut and then mine in Michigan. During our visit, we were prodded with countless questions about Paraguay, our work, and our relationship. Upon meeting his family, I wondered if some day they would be my in-laws. With my family, I felt more independent than ever before. While I always welcomed the advice of my parents, working abroad for well over a year had instilled in me the confidence that I could make my own life decisions. Overall, it was as special for our families as it was for Stephen and me, and the visit to our homes reenergized us.

Shopping occupied some of our time. Stephen and I had brought Paraguayan gifts for our families, and we wanted to return with U.S. gifts for friends in Paraguay. We loaded up with items unattainable in Paraguay, including Vermont maple syrup and scores of candy bars tucked into our suitcases. My mother suggested a Teflon non-stick pan for Ña Niní, who loved kitchen novelties. For Dr. Orihuela, Stephen's father obtained a two-volume Spanish version of *Nelson's Pediatrics*, the most popular pediatric textbook in use at the time. He had authored the chapter on hematology.

∞∞∞

Stephen and I arrived back in Ybycuí for a hot New Year's Eve in the middle of their sweltering summer. We had only five months left in our two-year commitment. Our friends were delighted with the gifts we had brought them, but most touching was the look on Dr. Orihuela's face when Stephen handed him the heavy pediatric volumes, spanking new and still wrapped in cellophane. It was one of utter disbelief. Stephen pointed out that his father was one of the authors. The usually verbose and stoic doctor was speechless and almost moved to tears. When he collected himself, he said it was the best gift possible for a doctor in solo practice. Stephen's dad later received a moving letter of thanks from Dr. Orihuela that we dutifully translated into English.

To start 1976 off with a new look, Stephen decided to grow a beard. At the time, beards were not common in Paraguay. In fact, they were associated with hippies and communists, particularly Fidel Castro and Che Guevarra. Luckily for Stephen, some Paraguayan heroes of old had been bearded. When anyone made negative remarks about his changed appearance, he whipped out some Paraguayan paper money and pointed to the historical heroes depicted on them. "No, no! Look at Mariscal López and Bernardino Caballero!" That brought chuckles and a reluctant acceptance of Stephen's facial hair.

As his beard grew, so did our determination to win over Peace Corps to the idea of a move to facilitate teacher training. Logistics would be considerably more expensive and time-consuming if we stayed in Ybycuí. A *clausura* of the dirt road to town would easily disrupt any planned work. Preparing for and conducting training would be full-time jobs for us, and we would risk awkward, conflicting situations with Dr. Orihuela if we stayed. We still had some Capiatá work to complete, and Stephen and I had four new proposed workshops. Ellen had identified three large communities for training: Villarrica east of Asunción, Encarnación in the southeast, and Concepción in the north. When Marty from our training group caught wind of the idea to train teachers, she invited us to train in her town in the north, Villa de San Pedro. Planning for a week in each of those communities plus preparation and travel time, we sketched out a schedule.

Stephen and I presented a formal proposal to Eric and the Peace Corps on January 7th to dedicate our time to teacher training workshops in sanitation education in conjunction with SENASA, the Ministry of Education, and the Peace Corps education program. Our proposal was approved, but we were informed we still would not be allowed to move to Asunción. Stephen and I persisted with our arguments.

Continuing to live in Ybycuí was not feasible, and pay level was also a problem. We were expected to cover all of our normal expenses on our monthly stipends, which varied according to site. Rural Ybycuí was in the lowest of the three tiers, and Stephen and I argued it would be a challenge to handle our expenses on the lowest tier. Preparing for and conducting the *cevo-í cursillos* required time in Asunción, and most travel connections had to be made in the capital.

At last, we arrived at a compromise with the Peace Corps staff—we would live on the outskirts of Asunción at the middle stipend level. The Ministry of Education would reimburse us for long-distance transportation to their sites, and the Peace Corps would support us with per diem while we conducted the workshops.

Back in Ybycuí, we informed Dr. Orihuela about our reassignment and properly thanked him for the opportunity to work with him. He and Ña Irma graciously invited us to a lovely dinner at their home before we left. Telling Ña Niní we were leaving was emotionally difficult. Mary had left Ybycuí a few months earlier for Asunción to become the agricultural extension coordinator for the women Volunteers, although she did visit often. I promised to visit as well. Stephen somewhat sadly said his good-byes and abandoned his garden. One of his last acts before moving was giving his white plastic toilet seat to his neighbor Don Blasito.

In spite of the Peace Corps' rule against unmarried, opposite-sex Volunteers cohabitating, Stephen and I moved in together. Our Peace Corps physician Bron and a few others knew, but nobody made any waves about it. I nervously told Ña Niní, Amalia, and Tomasa, but they were accepting and supportive. Stephen and I considered ourselves a committed, stable couple, and so did our close friends.

∞∞∞

Whether through a chance conversation in the Peace Corps office, a planned dinner in the capital, or a special celebration of some sort, we Volunteers naturally lent support to each other when a need arose. Near the end of January while looking for a new place to live, Stephen and I heard about a money-raising venture organized by some Volunteers. Proceeds were to go to the *manicomio*, Paraguay's psychiatric hospital. Although I never visited it, the Volunteers trying to help out described it as a disturbing, overcrowded institution with few resources. At that time in Paraguay, only people with severe mental illness were institutionalized. Most people with mental or physical disabilities remained in their communities, surviving as best they could with local help.

One such person was Leó, a young man in Ybycuí with dysmorphic facial features, an inability to talk, and likely a limited intellect. Stephen heard that he lived with family members. Leó, who would often beg for food around town, attended the community dances where young men provided him with alcoholic beverages. A drunk Leó, who never threatened nor harmed anyone, served as a sorry form of entertainment at these events. One day when Leó was wandering around town, Stephen invited him into his yard. Pulling up a small table and chair for him, Stephen offered him paper and pencil. Accepting the offer, Leó listened intently to the one-way conversation while doodling on the paper. When he lost interest in the activity, Stephen offered him some cookies on his way out.

The *manicomio* benefit took place one hot afternoon at the Paraguayan-American Cultural Center, a venue with an auditorium. Because of the law requiring the performance of traditional pieces at public musical functions, Stephen and I were called upon to fulfill the requirement. Most of the presentations were Volunteers performing comedy skits and songs in English for an audience of a couple of hundred people. Karen, Marty's housemate in Villa de San Pedro, volunteered to join us. With Karen singing, Bron playing the harp, and the two of us on our guitars, we performed two songs—"*Nde Rendape Ajú*," a love song translated as "I Come Close to You," and "The Hookworm Song." Bron brought daughters Becky and Abby onto the stage with us. We received a loud round of applause. The event raised $600 for the *manicomio*, a value of about $2,816 in 2021 dollars.

First-place winner in Capiatá

My rented pink house, with two front doors

A Peace Corp Memoir 97

Carvings of the mythological figures Pombero and Kurupí

Ña Niní at her sewing machine

A Peace Corp Memoir

Stephen by his partially fenced garden

Performing Paraguayan music at the benefit for the *manicomio*; from left to right, Karen, Stephen, Mary Lou, Abby, Becky, and Bron (Courtesy of Larry Hodgson)

CHAPTER 5

The Move to San Lorenzo and a New Assignment

Give a man a fish and you feed him for a day. Teach him how to fish and you feed him for a lifetime.
—Lao Tzu

Stephen and I found a small house to rent a couple of blocks off the main east-west highway in the outlying town of San Lorenzo, only eight miles from the center of Asunción. It was available as of February 1st, and we moved in that week. San Lorenzo used to be a rural town, but in 1976, the growing urban sprawl of Asunción made it difficult to tell where town boundaries were. It felt like we were living in a neighborhood of the capital, but it was still a 45-minute urban bus ride to the Peace Corps office. As we anticipated, San Lorenzo was much more convenient for us than Ybycuí, and the site was in Peace Corps' middle pay tier.

The house had a modest-sized room, with one end serving as a sleeping area and the other meant for the kitchen. The kitchen area had a sink, but the plastic pipe through which water was supposed to drain had been bent on purpose into an "L" shape to create an elbow. We were careful to allow only water down the drain. The small bathroom had a toilet, sink, and shower fixture, but there was no running water in the house. Water pipes were being laid a few blocks away, but the work was not advancing in our direction. Still, it was nice to have a more modern setup inside the house, an improvement from using a latrine. Stephen and I pulled water from the well to flush the toilet. The house, which had electricity, came with some furnishings—a large armoire, a double bed, vinyl sofa, kitchen table with chairs, and a small refrigerator.

While living in San Lorenzo, Stephen and I washed our own clothing most of the time. I was accustomed to the chore, but it was new to Stephen. He asked me to help him wash a quality down sleeping bag he had purchased from Burl, who was shunning all products made from anything of animal origin. I helped with the washing by hand, which wasn't a problem. Using rubbing and squeezing motions, we worked as a team to suds up the bulky item on a clean corner of our brick patio near the well. However, the process of rinsing it was prolonged and tedious. Stephen and I took turns pulling bucket after bucket of water from the well to rinse the sudsy mess. If the soap wasn't all rinsed out, an item developed an unpleasant sour smell. After a long afternoon of rinsing the sleeping bag, the two of us called it quits, hoping our labor had been adequate. It was, but we subsequently sent our heavy clothing and towels out to a laundress. I continued to wash lighter clothing in a basin, scrubbing with a soft brush to remove dirt while preserving the integrity of the fabric.

Before a trip, Stephen and I spent our time preparing materials. As we had done in Capiatá, for each school we assembled a packet of take-home copies of the *Barefoot Pedrito* story and latrine form for the students. We also included a set of health talks on poster boards, styled after the ones I had used in the health center. They covered the life cycles of hookworms and roundworms, sanitary latrines, and hand washing—we used "Francis Dirty Hands" for the last topic. Using carbon paper and lots of hand pressure, we traced our rough artwork on the front of each poster board piece, refined and colored the pictures, and glued a stenciled script onto the back for teachers to read as they held up each board. I typed stencils as the old ones wore out, and we continued mimeographing copies of our materials in the Peace Corps office. Stephen and I concluded our preparations by carefully packing our paraphernalia—films, the microscope we had acquired, slides, roundworm specimens, guitars, and packets—and made arrangements for a movie projector.

∞∞∞∞

On March 9th, Stephen and I boarded a riverboat to travel north on the Paraguay River to teach *cevo-í cursillos* in Villa de San Pedro, 100 miles away. Marty had traveled to Asunción to help us with our gear, and the three of us settled into a relaxing 14-hour overnight boat excursion against the river's current. To the west (on our left) was the semi-arid, sparsely populated Chaco. The landmass to the east was the more densely populated eastern Paraguay. While there was daylight, we took in the scenery of occasional soaring birds, plentiful palm trees and thick undergrowth on the banks, and the meandering flow of the river. The boat occasionally stopped to let off or take on passengers at a settlement on the river. Having spent a little extra money for a cabin, the three of us were able to get a good night's sleep with the gentle swaying of the boat.

The following morning, the boat docked at Marty's town. The sun had risen just above the tiled and grass roofs of the houses of Villa de San Pedro on the eastern horizon. Once on firm ground, Marty negotiated with a man to haul our equipment and bags to her house in a wooden cart for a modest fee. Stephen and I followed her up the riverbank and onto a hard dirt road. A small number of disembarked Paraguayans ambled along with their baggage.

Marty shared a house a short distance from the river with Karen, the agricultural extension Volunteer who had performed with us at the *manicomio* benefit. During the daytime, Stephen, Marty, and I taught the *cursillo* to teachers in and near the town. In the evenings, we relaxed with Marty and Karen, hearing stories about their work and lives in San Pedro. One evening, they arranged for us to attempt phone patches to our families by short wave radio, owned and operated by friends of theirs. We got lucky and connected with a man in Nebraska. The reception was good, and the radio operator was willing to make collect phone calls to our homes. What a pleasant surprise for both sets of parents! While letters and cassette tapes kept open the lines of communication, they can't compare with hearing the voices of loved ones in real time.

Marty had bragged to us that their house had a very nice latrine that didn't stink because of its water seal. It was a squat latrine with a large s-shaped white ceramic pipe in the hole. Picture an s-shape lying on its back. The top part of the "s" formed a small bowl filled with water, which sealed off the latrine hole, thus preventing the foul smells from escaping. On the walk to the latrine, one stopped at the well to draw a bucket of water for flushing out the s-bowl. It was a nice feature, but Marty warned us that the water in the seal did attract harmless little frogs, a small inconvenience to pay for an odor-free latrine.

My most vivid memory of our stay in San Pedro occurred late one afternoon while sitting out on the covered patio with Marty and Stephen after a day's work. While relaxing in a rattan rocking chair, I noticed out of the corner of my eye a hairy tarantula, almost the size of my hand, loping its way toward the three of us on eight creepy legs! I had never seen one in real life before, and it was like something out of a terrifying nightmare. I shrieked and pointed at it, causing the creature to stop in its tracks and stare at me with penetrating eyes. With my two legs shaking, I attempted to stand up on the rocking chair to get further away from the hairy spider. Stephen, my hero who doesn't like spiders any more than I do, took a broom and swung it down on the critter. In its last moment of life, the tarantula attacked the broom. We knew that tarantulas rarely come out during the day except in periods of drought when they need water. It had been dry in Villa de San Pedro.

I was still jumpy about an hour later when I had to use the latrine. Stopping by the well, I pulled up a bucket of water and proceeded to the odor-free outhouse. After setting the bucket on the floor, I squatted and… I shrieked for the second time that afternoon! This time it was only a harmless little frog that startled me by hitting my behind while jumping out of the ceramic latrine pipe. I heard peals of laughter from the two on the patio. Marty and Stephen needed no explanation for my scream.

Stephen and I easily incorporated Marty into our teacher training. She conducted the introductions and closures, and we divvied up the other segments of the workshop. Together, we taught and sang "The Hookworm Song." The teachers laughed at our jokes and antics, particularly Stephen's unbuttoning of the flannel shirt he was wearing to reveal a gift I had made for him—a pink t-shirt with purple embroidery of a bare foot and the rhyme, "*Si andas pynandí, tienes cevo-í.*" (If you walk barefoot, you have hookworm.) The teachers became serious when we discussed the implications of high loads of intestinal parasites in children. At the end of each *cursillo*, we gave the school principal a packet of our materials for teaching the sanitation curriculum. We received their heartfelt thanks in return.

Grateful for the hospitality of Marty, Karen, their friends, and local teachers, Stephen and I returned to Asunción by boat down the Paraguay River. Going with the current cut the travel time dramatically, with the scenery passing by in double-time, much like the pace of our Peace Corps service. Being busy and enjoying our work made the time fly.

∞∞∞∞

On March 24, 1976, we were at the Peace Corps office when we heard the news of a *coup d'état* in Argentina. A military junta seized power from President Isabel "Isabelita" Perón, who had taken the office after the death of her husband, Juan Perón, almost two years earlier. During Juan Perón's first presidency (1946-1955), which had also ended in a *coup*, his first wife Eva became a much beloved first lady in Argentina. In 1952, she succumbed to cancer and was immortalized in the musical *Evita*, made into a 1996 movie starring Madonna and Antonio Banderas. Isabelita never achieved the same degree of popularity in the chaotic mid-1970s that saw astronomical inflation, labor unrest, and political violence. General Jorge Rafael Videla took power at the end of March. (He ruled as dictator until 1981. The five years of his regime were dominated by his "Dirty War," during which up to 30,000 people, opponents and innocents alike, were "disappeared" or killed.) We heard rumors that many young Paraguayan adults, who had escaped persecution from Stroessner's Regime by fleeing to Argentina, began fearing Videla's repression and returned to Paraguay. Stroessner perceived them as a possible threat to his power. For the remainder of our time in Paraguay, we heard persistent rumors of young people being arrested and "disappeared" by the Stroessner Regime upon their return home.

Two weeks after the Argentine coup, a violent political incident took place close to home. In the early hours of April 5th in San Lorenzo, police raided the home of a suspected subversive. Shots were fired, and at least one person was wounded. Unaware of this activity, we innocently arrived at the Peace Corps office the following morning. Felicita, who also lived in San Lorenzo, greeted us with hugs and a huge sigh of relief. Peace Corps staff was aware that there had been doors knocked on and people arrested in our town during the night. Some homes in Asunción had also been raided. On another occasion, we heard from a reliable source that some of the young people who had returned from Argentina were pushed from small airplanes flying over the Chaco. They had not been given parachutes. Persistent rumors of arrests and torture by the regime continued.

Through the Peace Corps network, I was aware of two disturbing incidents directly involving Volunteers. Sometime in late 1973, a Volunteer in a town on the main paved highway to Brazil drank too much alcohol and began saying things against Stroessner. Local authorities arrested him. After the town's priest told Peace Corps about the jailed Volunteer, Peace Corps secured his release. The second incident took place sometime in 1975. A curly-haired Anglo Volunteer who had recently arrived in a rural area was detained at rifle-point by young soldiers "looking for communists." This young man looked "different" to them. The Volunteer kept repeating *"Cuerpo de Paz"* (Peace Corps) and blurting out names of other Volunteers to no avail. After spending a long, tense night locked up, he was released the following morning. While it was easy for Peace Corps to restrict our traveling to Argentina, we were still exposed to the repression and risks of living in Paraguay.

∞∞∞∞

During Easter week in 1976, Stephen and I went to one of the better movie theaters in Asunción with two other Volunteers to see *Blazing Saddles*, Mel Brooks' satirical Western comedy made two years earlier. The movie had Spanish subtitles, which made it doubly funny for us because the subtitles could not capture the numerous puns and ridiculous irony so skillfully portrayed. At one point, Mel Brooks' character, an Indian chief in full regalia, speaks Yiddish, a fact lost on Paraguayans. The four of us, seated in the middle of the movie theater, were the only ones laughing. But we laughed hard enough throughout the presentation to make up for the silence among the other movie-goers.

On the Saturday before Easter, Stephen and I went downtown to see *Jesus Christ Superstar*, the 1973 musical drama reviewed positively by critics but criticized by some religious groups. I loved the movie's soundtrack and looked forward to seeing the picture again. On arrival at the movie theater where it had been advertised, we were disappointed to find that it wouldn't be playing. It had apparently been banned in conservative, Catholic Paraguay.

∞∞∞∞

Our first *cevo-í cursillo* with a Ministry of Education and Peace Corps teacher team was during the week of April 19th in and around the city of Villarrica, located 100 miles east of Asunción near the rugged hills called Ybytyruzú (uh-buh-tuh-ru-SU). Villarrica was known for being a cultural center and for its cattle, sugar cane, and hardwood trees. The streets in the city center were lined with leafy green grapefruit trees. The large round yellow fruits on them were ripe, ready for picking, and emitted the aroma of pungent citrus. Our contact was John, a redheaded education Volunteer, who shared a large house with another Volunteer also named John. Temporarily staying with them while looking for a place of her own was newly arrived Volunteer Betsy. John and John had the reputation among Peace Corps circles of being outstanding cooks and big eaters. They welcomed us into their home for the duration of our stay.

Redheaded John had two Paraguayan counterparts but hadn't been well supported by them. One never showed up for anything; in fact, we didn't see him at all. John hoped our visit would motivate both him and the second counterpart. After being rained out on the first day, our luck changed for the remainder of our time in Villarrica. On the second day, we went to a rural school about 30 miles from the city. I wrote to my family:

> "We received a warm & open reception. [The teachers] seemed to understand our ideas, and they laughed at our jokes, liked our educational materials, and enjoyed our music. John's one counterpart and the three of us came back feeling tired but good about the day's work. The following day we worked with students studying to be teachers and then did teacher training in another school in an outlying area."

At another school, the local SENASA inspector, José, joined us for the day and showed interest and enthusiasm for our work. He and John set up the projector for our two movies and watched with intent interest, as did the teachers. With the movie projector a good distance from the wall onto which it projected, the images were much larger than life, making the real footage of hookworms sucking blood in the intestine appear like a horror scene. Not only were the parasites swelling with crimson red blood as they sucked away, but also, they wasted a lot of it as they gulped blood from the intestinal wall. Streams of excess blood spilled past the engorging hookworm bodies. John looked ill, but he made it to the end. After the teachers left and while we packed up our belongings, he urgently pumped us with questions. "Is that truly real film footage? Hookworms actually look like that? They suck blood in the intestine like that? And you can get hookworms from going barefoot around here?" The reality of what he had previously learned in Peace Corps training finally hit home with a vengeance. John confessed he had already been treated a couple of times for parasites, and he swore to us that he would never go barefoot in Paraguay again.

John and John's house had a large, closed-in yard, electricity, and running water, as well as a refrigerator and stove with an oven. What luxury! For us, the highlight of our visit was the food. One night they prepared delicious sweet and sour chicken on rice. Another dinner was a Mexican feast—beans, meat, cheese, and tomato on my homemade flour tortillas. I made 40 of them for the five of us, and there were no leftovers. We repeated the same dinner the following night with one of the Johns participating in the tortilla preparation. It was a dish they planned to repeat with my homemade recipe after we left.

One morning when no teaching was planned, Stephen and I took a bus to the friendly nearby town of Yataity (jah-tai-TUH), known for making hand-embroidered fabric called *aho-poí* (AH-oh poh-EE, fine clothing). The specialty of the town was *aho-poí-eté* (eh-TEH, the best). This "very best of the finest" *aho-poí* was cream-colored homespun cotton woven on a hand loom with thread spun by hand and then elaborately embroidered with typical traditional patterns. Mary had highly recommended a particular store in town where she purchased embroidered fabric. Ña Niní, who had designed and made Mary a long dress out of it, had promised to do the same for me.

The whitewashed walls of the houses in Yataity were gleaming on the mild sunny day of our trip. Stephen and I walked through the open doorways of a few of the shops, admiring the colorful designs on display. We soon found the one Mary had mentioned. Upon entering the impeccably clean front room, I knew we were in right place. A thin girl in her early teens greeted us and brought out piles of machine woven embroidered fabric, blouses, and shirts in vivid colors in addition to some lovely white tablecloths. Stephen and I set aside items we wanted to purchase. When I asked about the handwoven *aho-poí-eté*, the girl took us into an adjacent room containing more fabric on display and a handloom set up with a beautiful roll of homespun cotton in the works. The weave was even and pliable and of the highest quality I had ever seen in Paraguay.

I asked the young girl to show me some embroidery patterns and color options for *aho-poí-eté* fabric to be made into a long dress. From behind a counter, she pulled out a binder with designs and a box with silky threads of soft hues sorted by color. At that point, the girl excused herself from the room, leaving me to browse through the binder. She returned with a woman, who I surmised was her mother due to the close family resemblance. The woman, urging me to continue looking at the samples in the binder, offered to help if I had any questions. I took my time, page by page, admiring the intricate geometric designs and appreciating the skill required to create such beauty. I lingered on one page over halfway through the binder, deciding that I had found the right design. It was an intricate geometric pattern with circular swirls as well as sections with slipped stitches that gave it a lacy effect.

The woman returned to my side and smiled at my pattern selection. Next, I had to choose an embroidery color. I immediately gravitated to the blue shades, looking for a subdued tone. I opted for a soft baby blue with a silvery tinge to it. After eyeing my size and approximating the fabric needed for a long dress, the woman jotted down some notes and told me the price. It was expensive by Paraguayan standards, about $35 in 1976 ($164 in 2021 dollars). In most places it was appropriate to bargain on the price, but Mary had cautioned me about this store. It had the highest quality, and the prices were worth it. I smiled in agreement, gave her my name, and offered to pay a deposit. She declined any payment at that point but told me to return in two weeks for my completed order.

∞∞∞∞

"You won!" Stephen exclaimed, "You won the raffle!" He had returned to San Lorenzo from the Peace Corps office with what he thought was good news for me. In response to my puzzled look, he explained that he had purchased a raffle ticket from John and John, the Villarrica Volunteers, and signed my name to it. They had organized the raffle to benefit a remote rural school in their area, and a wealthy local rancher had donated the prize. But what had I won?

My prize was a *novillo*—a live steer! All I had to do was go to the rural community outside of Villarrica and claim it. I took a deep breath, looked at Stephen with a sweet smile, and challenged him,

"You purchased the ticket; you can take care of it!"

After mulling over his (our?) good fortune for a couple of days, he packed a few things and hopped a bus for the trip to Villarrica. Although redheaded John, John, and Betsy were disappointed one of them hadn't won the prize, they let Stephen stay at their house while he tried to figure out what to do. Stephen's first stop was to visit José, Villarrica's SENASA inspector. José had a *moto* (motorcycle). Yes, he was willing to take Stephen out to the ranch to see his prize. Hopefully, José would assist with the cultural challenges that would surely arise in the quest to claim the steer and sell it.

Stephen purchased gasoline for the *moto*. With directions from the Villarrica Volunteers, Stephen and José headed out to the ranch. The *moto* carried them both, although with a bit of effort, on the hard-packed dirt road. When the road inclined slightly, the *moto* struggled and protested, straining with the weight of two men. The road narrowed as the incline increased. The hard-packed dirt turned to crumbly loose dirt and then to dry sand, causing the *moto* to vehemently protest. It became impossible to proceed except on foot, pulling the *moto* like a stubborn burro unwilling to go any further. Eventually, the rugged road smoothed out, and they saw the ranch in the distance.

José parked his *moto* outside the gate to the front yard of the ranch while Stephen clapped his hands. A girl opened the door in response. As he attempted to explain the reason for the visit, she excused herself, asking him to wait. Shortly, a man appeared who seemed to be the ranch owner. Stephen and José introduced themselves, hands were shaken in greeting, and they were invited to pass through the gate and around to the backyard. While Stephen again attempted an explanation, the man pulled some chairs into a circle and the setup for drinking *yerba mate* appeared. A few more men joined them, listening attentively to Stephen's claim to a *novillo* won in the raffle. The first gentleman asked what Stephen wanted to do with the steer. "Well," he replied, "I'd like to see it first, and then I'd like to know what my options are." That set the men moving.

The tea was set aside, and horses were brought for the small group to ride out to the herd. Stephen paled as he faced the prospect of mounting a horse. He decided to decline, explaining he preferred to walk. Stephen didn't like to ride horses because, *"No tienen frenos"* ("They don't have brakes"). Humorous looks were exchanged among the Paraguayans, who proceeded to mount their horses. Stephen walked briskly to keep up. He dodged fresh and dry cow pies, fire ant hills, and the irregularities of the uneven ground that could cause a painful ankle sprain. After going a considerable distance, they spotted the herd. When the men on horseback and Stephen on foot closed the gap to about 30 head of cattle, the imposing animals took notice. The herd collectively turned and approached the humans and horses like predatory lions stalking their prey. "Why didn't I take a chance and ride?" thought Stephen.

One of the Paraguayans, looking down at the foreigner on foot from up high on his horse and observing the look of alarm on his face, calmly informed Stephen that the cattle were only looking for salt. The humans, horses, and herd mingled. While one rider threw out chunks of salt for the herd, Stephen asked which animal was his. The first gentleman looked the animals over like a woman selecting unwanted articles to sell at a garage sale and finally pointed at the smallest animal in the herd. The runt of the litter! Stephen took out his camera and snapped several photos while the Paraguayans chuckled at the spectacle.

With the photo opportunity over and the salt gone, the herd, including our steer, lost interest in the interlopers and returned to their grazing. The riders and Stephen retraced their steps to the ranch house, returned to their circle of chairs, and resumed sharing the *yerba mate*.

As the tea was passed around, the men bantered about Stephen's two options: 1) Sell the animal live, referred to as "on the hoof," or 2) Sell the animal once it is butchered, called "on the hook." For the first choice, he wouldn't have to pay a butcher to slaughter the steer. However, by selling it "on the hook," one could make more money. When Stephen had purchased the raffle ticket, he was told the steer was worth $100, a nice sum in 1976 ($469 in 2021 dollars). He decided to sell it "on the hook" to maximize the winnings. That decision prompted another round of questions by Stephen. "Where is the nearest butcher? How does the steer get to the butcher? How soon can all of this happen?" In response, the men raised additional problems—papers must be signed to transfer ownership of the steer, the nearest butcher only has permission to slaughter on Tuesdays (five days away), and by the way, his steer has never been off the range.

Stephen knew he was being teased. The men conversed in a mix of Spanish and Guaraní, bantering amongst themselves with occasional bits of information tossed at Stephen. It was obvious they were entertained by his struggles to follow the exchanges and grasp what he might have to do. What about transferring ownership? "Well," said the first gentleman, "I'm not the owner. My brother is, and he's in Asunción. I don't know when he'll return."

Someone else blurted, "Ah, don't worry about it, Esteban. They are twins, and they frequently sign papers for each other." Everyone laughed.

Then Stephen inquired about getting the steer off the range and to the butcher. One man responded, "Well, that's really no problem. You pay a couple of boys to do it. They'll pack it between two oxen and walk it off the range to the butcher." Sounds easy enough.

Stephen asked about the timing and why cattle were only slaughtered on Tuesdays. Another man said, "Well, that's the government's way of keeping control of things." Stephen told the group that he couldn't stay until next Tuesday because he had to get back to work. The group was unanimous in their advice that he must have a representative at the butchering and weighing because otherwise he would definitely be cheated. Stephen's friend José, who had been quiet up to this point, offered to represent him. The details were picked apart and figured out, papers were signed, hands were shaken, pleasantries were exchanged ("it has been a real pleasure"), and the *moto* was retrieved.

José and Stephen retraced the path to Villarrica, riding when possible and walking on the sandy semblance of a road when necessary. Upon their arrival, Stephen provided José with cash to cover the upcoming expenses. They made arrangements to meet in two weeks at the Peace Corps office to settle the matter. In the meantime, Stephen and I would travel to Encarnación for another series of *cursillos*.

The SENASA inspector was true to his word. The two of them met as planned, and José turned over the documentation and the "on the hook" sale proceeds. The steer had weighed in at 100.5 kilos (222 lbs.), and it was sold for about $70. It cost about $6.50 to legally transfer the ownership and $2.30 to walk it off the range and to the butcher's. Stephen had spent about $23 on his Villlarrica trip. For representing us, he gave José $7.60, a box of candy, and quality Scotch whiskey with a Kennedy half-dollar taped to the bottle. After calculating all of the costs, we evenly split the $24 ($113 in 2021 dollars) that we netted and spent a portion of it on a dinner at a nice restaurant. We both ordered chicken.

∞∞∞∞

During the second week in May, Stephen and I conducted *cursillos* in the city of Encarnación, on the border with Argentina southeast of Asunción and at the end of one of the paved highways. We stayed with one of the local Volunteers and repeated the training with groups of elementary school teachers. Everyone received us well. We returned a few weeks later for a *clausura* celebration with Peace Corps physicians Bron and Eric, who wanted to see the results of our work. They appeared to be duly impressed by the event.

In the Peace Corps vehicle on a paved road, the doctors, Stephen, and I were able to make it a one-day trip. About halfway back on the return, we were forced to stop at a military roadblock manned by young, nervous, rifle-toting Paraguayan soldiers. Their nervousness put me on edge. I sat in the back seat and reached out to hold Stephen's hand for reassurance. Bron and Eric patiently spoke to them, and we all surrendered our documents when asked. Young and fluent only in Guaraní, the soldiers carefully inspected our documents, comparing our photos with our faces while quietly conversing among themselves. They finally returned our papers and allowed us to continue on our journey. Stephen and I guessed that the roadblock was a direct result of the March coup by Videla and the Stroessner Regime's perceived need to screen for possible dissidents fleeing Argentina.

∞∞∞

After our Encarnación trip, we traveled back to Yataity for my *aho-poí-eté*. The same girl greeted us with a smile, immediately fetching the older woman who brought my order neatly folded and protected in a brown paper wrapper. Removing the fabric from its wrapping and unfolding it, I sighed with pleasure at the fine work, gently passing my hand over the intricate, silky embroidery on the soft homespun cotton. I paid the agreed-upon amount and thanked her profusely, and Stephen and I caught a bus back to San Lorenzo. The following day, we boarded another bus and headed to Ybycuí with my *aho po-í eté*. Upon seeing the fabric, Ña Niní nodded with approval and admiration at the fine work. She took my measurements again to make sure they were up-to-date. Ña Niní promised she would have the dress and some other items she was sewing for me (a wool suit and some short dresses) finished before our planned departure in July.

Between work trips, Stephen and I shopped for gifts and our own mementos and prepared for our end of service. We returned to Luque, where we had purchased our guitars, and bought hand-tooled leather cases for them. We both selected additional ñandutí in Itaguá. In Asunción, Stephen and I purchased some lovely woodcarvings, including an ox cart with two oxen and a male driver, a man drinking *yerba mate*, and a cigar-smoking woman breastfeeding an infant. As mentioned earlier, rural people cultivated tobacco and rolled their own cigars with it, and women often indulged in the smoking habit.

At the suggestion of another Volunteer, Stephen and I visited Señor Laterza in his home near Asunción to see his ceramics. The very elderly artisan was totally blind in one eye and had poor vision in the other, but he continued making elegant ceramics by hand with the help of his wife. Señor Laterza patiently explained the process to us as he provided a tour of his work area. First, he gathered the clay and made the individual items on a pottery wheel. Second, the pieces were fired in a kiln that he had made by hand. Next, his wife drew designs and painted them with paints mixed by Señor Laterza. The items were then returned to the kiln for a second firing.

From a large display of items for sale, Stephen picked out a set of six demitasse cups and saucers. I chose a sugar bowl and a couple of trivets. The elderly gentlemen lamented that there were no young people interested in learning his trade of making beautiful works of art. Sadly, his art would die with him. Today, Laterza pottery is difficult to find and pricey, if it's for sale.

∞∞∞∞

Our *cevo-í cursillos* were a popular hit with the Ministry of Education, Peace Corps, and SENASA. The three agencies had shown a good deal of support and enthusiasm for our work. Peace Corps asked us to train two newer Volunteers, Jeff and Ricardo (Richard), to take over our work once we completed our service. That idea pleased us. Stephen and I introduced them to our Traveling Hookworm Show by inviting them to San Lorenzo to help us prepare the packets for the schools. Both showed a sense of humor and had developed a fluency in Guaraní that surpassed ours. The four of us were soon singing "*Cevo-í, Cevo-í*" as Jeff and Ricardo traced pictures, glued scripts onto the back of poster boards, and completed the materials needed for our last trip.

Concepción was our third of three trips for the Ministry of Education and Peace Corps teams. Located 286 miles north of Asunción, Concepción was most easily accessed by airplane. For variety and to spare us traveling against the Paraguay River current, we decided to fly north and then return downstream by riverboat. At the end of May, loaded down like pack animals with our gear, we took a taxi to the airport, checked in at the desk of a small airline, and proceeded to walk out onto the tarmac toward the two-engine aircraft with six seats, including the pilot's.

The pilot himself stowed our gear, and we scrambled into the airplane along with two other passengers. As I settled into the seat directly behind the pilot, he turned to us and asked, "Who would like to be my copilot?" Stephen enthusiastically volunteered, leaving me with no one's hand to hold.

This was the smallest aircraft in which I had ever flown. The flight plan took us over the dry, desolate Chaco. It occurred to me that if the plane went down, we would never be found. I silently shivered at the thought of political thugs pushing young people accused of being dissidents out of airplanes over the Chaco. My personal worries were for naught, maybe due to the skill of the pilot and his copilot, and we finally bumped down on the small airstrip near Concepción.

Stephen and I spent five days working with elementary school teachers in and around this northern city. The teachers were all eager to learn and very interested in doing something about bettering the sanitation conditions. When Stephen and I asked the education team if there were any SENASA inspectors in the communities where we taught, we were told that there weren't. The teachers in each school confirmed this. Because an inspector could help promote latrine construction with families and gain access to inexpensive cement floors, we encouraged the teachers to request an inspector from SENASA. The *cursillos* were very well received, particularly the movies, microscope slides, and "The Hookworm Song." Stephen and I gave each school director a packet of our materials that the teachers could borrow for use in their classrooms. Feeling that we had done well, we returned to Asunción by riverboat, a more relaxing mode of transportation for me than the small airplane. I wrote in a letter to my family:

> "We had a great group of teachers in Concepción—probably the best group we've had, very responsive & aware of health problems. They have bad water problems (only 20% of the houses have potable water) as well as latrine problems (only 60% have sanitary latrines), and Concepción is the 3rd largest city in Paraguay. It's easy to understand why there was a typhoid epidemic in 1966 and a constant hepatitis problem in addition to the usual intestinal parasites."

The following week, Stephen went to SENASA to report on our activities. He was stunned to have Margarita come down hard on him, blaming him and me for a political problem in Concepción that arose because we neglected to involve the SENASA inspector. Stephen listened carefully and thought before responding. Finally, he suggested, "Perhaps as foreigners, we weren't understood when we inquired about a SENASA inspector. Now the important step would be for the inspector, with support and encouragement from the SENASA office, to begin working with the teachers." Stephen's diplomatic response allowed Margarita and SENASA to save face. In a letter home, I wrote:

> "We have started hearing repercussions…Teachers from two towns got together & wrote a letter to the director [of SENASA] asking for sanitary inspectors in their towns…And it sort of shook up some people in SENASA, for Stephen discovered that one of the towns already HAS a sanitary inspector (he's been there 15 years & obviously hasn't been doing a thing for probably that long because nobody in the teacher's group knew what SENASA is)."

Stephen and I clearly recalled that Chuck selected Ybycuí for the special project because it didn't have a SENASA inspector. Too many Volunteers had complained to Chuck that their SENASA counterparts didn't do any work. The Concepción inspector, like the SENASA counterparts that Volunteers complained about, was likely a political appointee who collected his pay without doing any sanitation work. Perhaps Chuck's reasoning had some degree of validity. In the end, the way Stephen handled the Concepción situation strengthened our relationship with SENASA, and we ended our Peace Corps service on a positive footing.

∞∞∞∞

In order to complete all of our work, we extended our Peace Corps service by six weeks, with a tentative departure date of July 12th. The month of June was occupied by last-minute shopping, packing, shipping boxes home, paperwork, and medical tests. We applied for new passports, special Bi-Centennial issues in celebration of the 200th anniversary of the signing of the Declaration of Independence. The medical tests included three stool samples to check for intestinal parasites. I had not gone barefoot except for one time when I was caught a short distance from home during a heavy downpour. I knew I would lose my flip-flops in the mud unless I took them off. After running all the way home, I quickly and thoroughly scrubbed my feet with soap and water, hoping to dislodge any hookworm larvae trying to enter through my skin. Thankfully, both Stephen and I would leave Paraguay without having contracted any *py-cevo*-í.

Stephen and I began our rounds of visiting favorite places for the last time. At the Hotel Guaraní on the main downtown plaza, we took the elevator to the top to enjoy the panoramic view of Asunción. Afterwards, we bought small cups of *granizado* (chocolate chip) ice cream on the ground floor of the hotel. We ate at our favorite restaurants, including the Bolsi in order to split our favorite dessert, the merengue pieces with *dulce de leche* between them. One of us would separate the two merengues by twisting them in opposite directions, attempting to give each piece the same quantity of the *dulce de leche*. We shopped at the Riojana, a small downtown department store, for mementos and gifts. Stephen purchased yards of a soft charcoal-gray pinstripe woolen fabric from Uruguay and had a Riojana tailor custom-sew a dress suit for him.

In late June, I had two impacted wisdom teeth extracted. For that ordeal, I returned to Dr. Riquelme, the U.S.-trained dentist who had done a root canal on one of my molars in January. Unlike the dentist in Ybycuí, Dr. Riquelme had modern equipment. I recovered quickly enough to return to Ybycuí for one more visit during the final three days of June. Stephen and I stayed at the Feltes' house. Mary was there for the occasion, and Ña Niní was ready for my dress fitting.

She took me into one of the bedrooms to reveal what she had created with the *aho-poí-eté* fabric from Yataity. It was a simple design taking full advantage of the silver-blue embroidered pattern. The slightly flared long sleeves each ended in a thick band of embroidery at the wrists. There was no collar, only a softly curved neckline, and down the front of the dress was a wide display of the embroidery. Ña Niní turned the dress around to show me the back, which had a slightly curved seam across the lower back from which flowed pleats of the fabric. This allowed a fullness in the skirt as well as an even border of wide embroidery at the hemline.

I stepped into the dress, gently pushing my arms through the sleeves and settling my shoulders into it. Ña Niní gingerly closed the zipper up the back. We walked together into an adjacent room to view the dress on me with a full-length mirror while Mary and Stephen chatted at the far end. I slowly pivoted around to admire what Ña Niní had designed and assembled for me. It fit perfectly. As I looked over my shoulder to see the pleats reflected in the mirror, she exclaimed to me in a voice loud enough for Stephen to hear, *"¡Te vas a casar en este vestido!"* ("You are going to get married in this dress!")

After celebrating July 4, 1976, at the U.S. Embassy, Stephen and I took a four-day trip to the Iguazú falls on the border between Argentina and Brazil, about 25 miles from the construction site of the Itaipú Dam. We first looked up Pedro, the SENASA inspector who had worked with us in Capiatá. It was a poignant moment for the three of us as we reflected on the work we had accomplished together in Capiatá. Pedro had enthusiastically embraced our work.

Stephen and I proceeded to the falls, spending a full day each on the Brazilian and Argentine sides. Walking on the wooden pathway structure to its very end on the Argentine side holding Stephen's hand, I peered down through the mist into the falling cascade called "The Devil's Throat," reflecting on the weeks and months of my South American adventure in the Peace Corps and how much it had changed my life. Joining the Peace Corps had been like diving into an unknown waterfall, not knowing what perils and pleasures were lurking but living the thrill of adventure and discovery. We still had our journey home ahead of us, which we estimated would take up to three months. I was ready to leave Peace Corps Paraguay, but I also knew it had become an important part of me.

Back in Asunción, we packed up and sent by airfreight seven boxes of belongings to Michigan, using the $100 shipping allowance Peace Corps gave each Volunteer upon completion of service. My brother-in-law Ray would retrieve the boxes for us at Detroit Metro Airport. We sent three boxes of books by ground and ship because it was less expensive. Peace Corps processed our request for the value of an airplane ticket home. It was money we could use for our traveling. Both of our families were helpful in supplementing our financial resources. Our readjustment allowance would wait for us in the States to tide us over until finding employment.

With a copy of *The South American Handbook*, an extraordinarily helpful travel guide for places on and off the beaten path, we planned our three-month itinerary through Latin America and compiled a list of American Express offices along the way where we could check for mail from home. Stephen and I looked forward to traveling together. Since our early days of the Ybycuí project when faced with illness, cultural, project, and Ña Elisa problems, our relationship had grown into a loving one of strong emotional support. After moving to San Lorenzo, we had spent almost all of our time together. Traveling for a prolonged period under a tight budget would be a different kind of compatibility test for us before the ultimate trial of readjustment together in the United States.

∞∞∞∞

"Would you two PLEASE travel to the Chaco with me?" pleaded Wyn with excitement in her voice. "Can't you postpone your departure by a week or so?" With only a few days left in Paraguay, Stephen and I were wrapping up our final affairs. We had sent our travel information, along with our bills of lading for the items we had shipped, to our two sets of parents via the Embassy pouch. The Paraguayan mail system had been notorious for lost letters and tapes to such an extent that the Embassy allowed Volunteers access to the pouch for important items.

Wyn explained her situation to us in the Peace Corps office. "I have the opportunity to return to the Chaco with a man from my town, but I **do not** want to travel alone with him. Gustavo has the time to take me and space for you two in his jeep. He has made arrangements to stay at the Kennedy Ranch, about eight hours northwest of Asunción, via short-wave radio with Don Tomás Kennedy." Gustavo and Don Tomás were short-wave radio hams and had talked frequently but had not yet met in person. It didn't take much arm-twisting from Wyn. Stephen and I postponed our departure from Paraguay until July 23rd.

Gustavo, Wyn, and Jim, a high school exchange student living in Wyn's town, were in the jeep when it stopped at our San Lorenzo house before daylight two days later. After stowing our bags in the rear and piling into the backseat with Jim, the five of us were off to the Paraguay River for a ferry crossing to the Chaco at sunrise.

We soon found ourselves bumping along on the main Chaco highway, a dusty dirt road. This highway extended northwest toward Filadelfia, the thriving Mennonite colony 290 miles from Asunción, and eventually ended at the Bolivian border. At Pozo Colorado, about halfway to Filadelfia, Gustavo turned left onto a poor semblance of a road leading to Rancho Kennedy. He periodically slowed down the jeep to make sure he was still on the right path. We crept along for about 40 miles through unpopulated, desolate brown terrain dotted with palm trees and wild ground covering as if we were passing through to the end of the world. It was in sharp contrast to the lush green scenery of eastern Paraguay. As dusk encroached, I wondered if we'd ever arrive at our destination. When the last remnants of glow in the sky faded and darkness enveloped us, Gustavo spotted the lights of the ranch.

We received a warm welcome from the Kennedy family. They rarely had people visit their cattle ranch due to its location—it really was out in the middle of nowhere. The house itself was lovely, with electricity and other amenities, including running water. Recalling what I had learned from Burl in Villa Hayes, I knew water was precious in the Chaco, and I carefully monitored my personal use of it. There were two children in the family, Roberto and Carolina, as well as a household staff, ranch hands, dogs, and a new litter of kittens. A feast of lamb was ready for us, and after dinner, the Kennedys showed us to our rooms.

After a hearty breakfast the following morning, we sat outside in a circle of chairs and chatted with the family while squeezing and sucking the juice out of peeled oranges freshly picked from the carefully irrigated Kennedy orchard. The thinly peeled orange rinds, casually dropped on the dry dirt at our feet, would later be fed to the animals. The custom of sitting in a circle and sucking on oranges or drinking *yerba mate* was one I knew I'd miss in the U.S. For over two years, I had enjoyed this kind of hospitality and acceptance from Paraguayans from all walks of life. Countless people had opened their homes and hearts to us Volunteer foreigners thousands of miles from our families. This trip to visit strangers in the Chaco was another opportunity for me to reflect on the goodness and decency of humankind.

The cattle ranch was a profitable one, but their isolation was extreme, even by Paraguayan standards. The ham radio was a lifeline for them, and they were delighted to finally meet Gustavo in person. The Kennedys suggested we visit their nearest neighbors, an indigenous tribe, and some nearby Chaco War relics during our two-day stay.

With Roberto as our guide, we briefly toured around the immediate area of the ranch and learned about their water management before driving to the indigenous settlement. I do not recall what tribe they belonged to, but the Indians spoke very few words in Spanish or in Guaraní. After Gustavo's futile attempts to make them understand by speaking louder, we resorted to a makeshift sign language. Gustavo offered one woman a cigarette, which she took with a smile. He lit it for her, and she puffed with pleasure. When Stephen and I conveyed to the children that we wanted to take photographs of them, they indicated we had to pay them something. A year before, the government had begun minting stainless steel coins because the lower denominations of the paper currency quickly wore out. We presented the children with some of the shiny new disks, but they did not believe the coins were real money. When Stephen pointed out the numbers on the coins, the children accepted them as money, running and grabbing them from each other. After things settled down and he distributed additional coins, Stephen and I photographed this isolated settlement of non-Guaraní Indians.

The following day, accompanied by Roberto and his father, we found the war relics. The War of the Chaco, from 1932 to 1935, was fought with Bolivia. The conflict is also known as *La Guerra de la Sed* (The War of Thirst) because scarcity of water in the Chaco likely caused more deaths than combat did. Since colonial times, landlocked Bolivia had wanted access to the Paraguay River, and thus to the Atlantic Ocean, and disputes over Chaco boundaries finally reached their peak in the 1930s. Fueling the fire were rumors of oil reserves in the Chaco. Led by Commander-in-Chief José Félix Estigarribia, the Paraguayans prevailed and obtained about two-thirds of the disputed territory in the peace settlement.

We gazed at rusty partial remains of a small tank, visited a modest white monument to the Paraguayan soldiers who fought on this land, and peered up at the bare-branched skeleton of a tall tree purportedly climbed by Estigarribia to observe troop movements in this remote, desolate piece of Paraguay. I breathed in the smells of dry, dusty air. The vastness and loneliness of the terrain enveloped me as I imagined what it might have been like for a young soldier at war.

Don Tomás explained how the battle was fought and won by Paraguay, that thirst was a major cause of death, and what happened in the aftermath of the war. The end of the war in 1935 was followed by 19 years of power struggles and strife. Estigarribia was elected as President in 1939 but died in a plane crash in 1940. The Paraguayan Civil War in 1947, also known as the Barefoot Revolution, was fought with veterans of the War of the Chaco playing an important role.

I recalled Ña Niní telling me that during those years, she was a young wife in Ybycuí, alone because Don Lalo was off fighting in the war. One day when soldiers approached her house, Ña Niní experienced some moments of fear until she realized they were on the same side as Don Lalo. In 1954, Alfredo Stroessner of the Colorado Party consolidated power in a *coup d'état* and established a dictatorship that would last for 35 years. It was 22 years into Stroessner's dictatorship when we completed our service as Volunteers in Paraguay.

After expressing our gratitude and saying good-bye to the Kennedy family, we retraced the dirt pathways of the Chaco to Asunción for our planned departure. During the hours of bumping along in the jeep, my life in Paraguay with the Peace Corps over the past two-plus years slowly replayed in my mind. I recalled struggling with Guaraní and my discomfort with politics. I remembered how cultural differences slowly disappeared as I adapted to a different way of daily living. I enjoyed learning the rich history and beautiful music of Paraguay. Our guitars were on their way to the U.S., and in three months' time, Stephen and I could continue to play and sing the music we both had grown to love. I relived the evolution of our work, from the Ybycuí project to teacher *cursillos*, including our frustrations, failures, and achievements.

Above all, I reflected on the people. I felt overwhelming gratitude for the friendships I had made with Paraguayans and other Volunteers, most significantly with Ña Niní and Stephen, who sat silently beside me in the jeep while holding my hand and watching the Chaco scenery through the dust kicked up by Gustavo's jeep. He and I had a three-month Latin American trip ahead of us and perhaps a life together for years to come. Time would tell.

Ña Niní and a small group of Volunteers bade us farewell at the airport on July 23, 1976. I fought back tears as she hugged me and whispered, "Write to me." I promised I would. The possibility that I might never see her again weighed heavily on me.

Stephen and I boarded a small Lloyd Boliviano jet to Santa Cruz, Bolivia. As the airplane lifted off the ground and gained elevation, we looked out the window at the Paraguayan vehicles, roads, houses, and palm trees shrinking in size. My mind swelled and swirled with emotions. I had successfully completed my Peace Corps service. I had deep friendships with some Paraguayans and Volunteers which I hoped would last for life. I had fallen in love with one of those Volunteers. I held Stephen's hand and looked forward to what the future held.

Detail of elaborately embroidered *aho-poí-eté* I purchased in Yataity

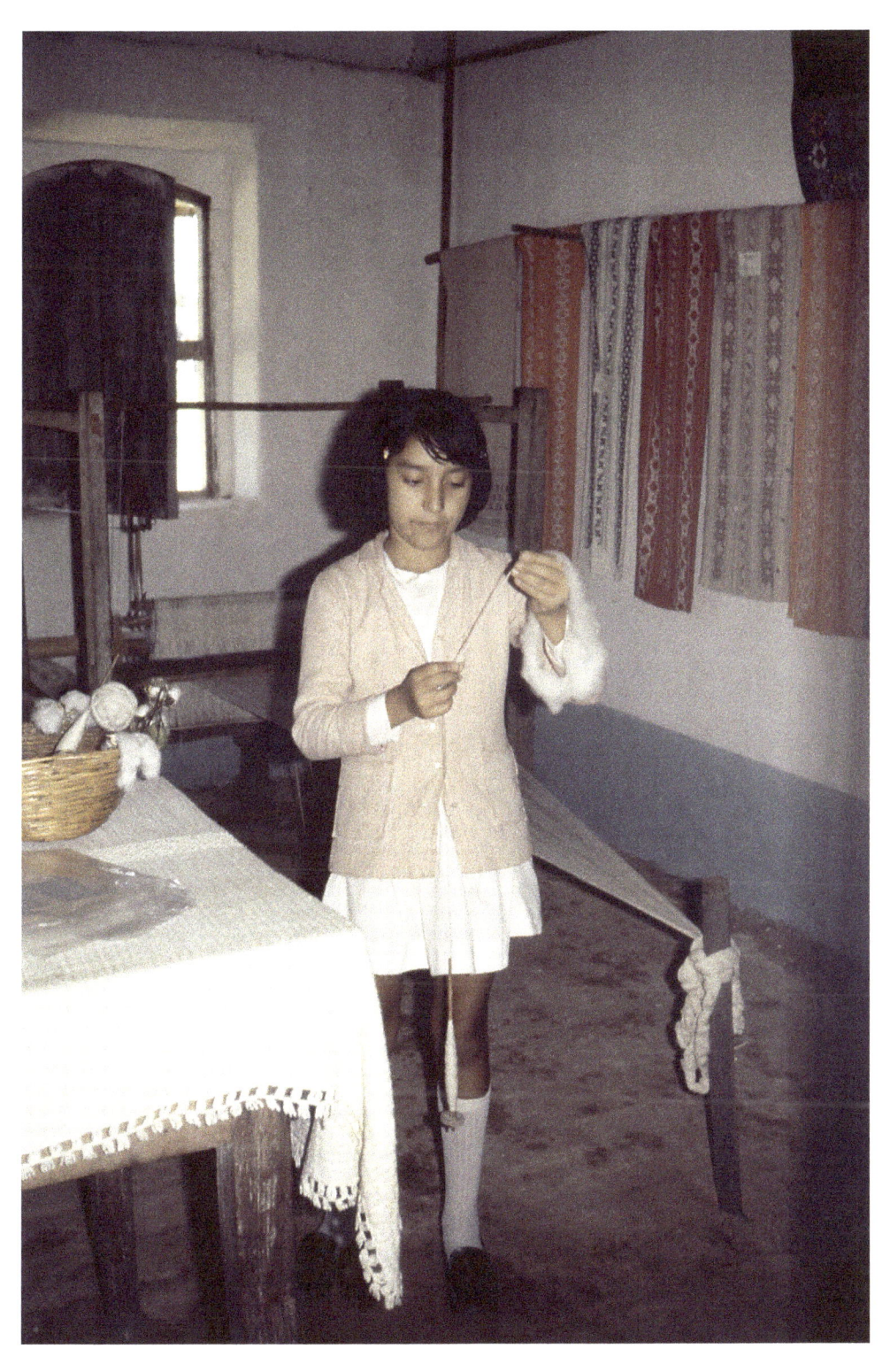

In Yataity, making cotton thread in front of the hand loom

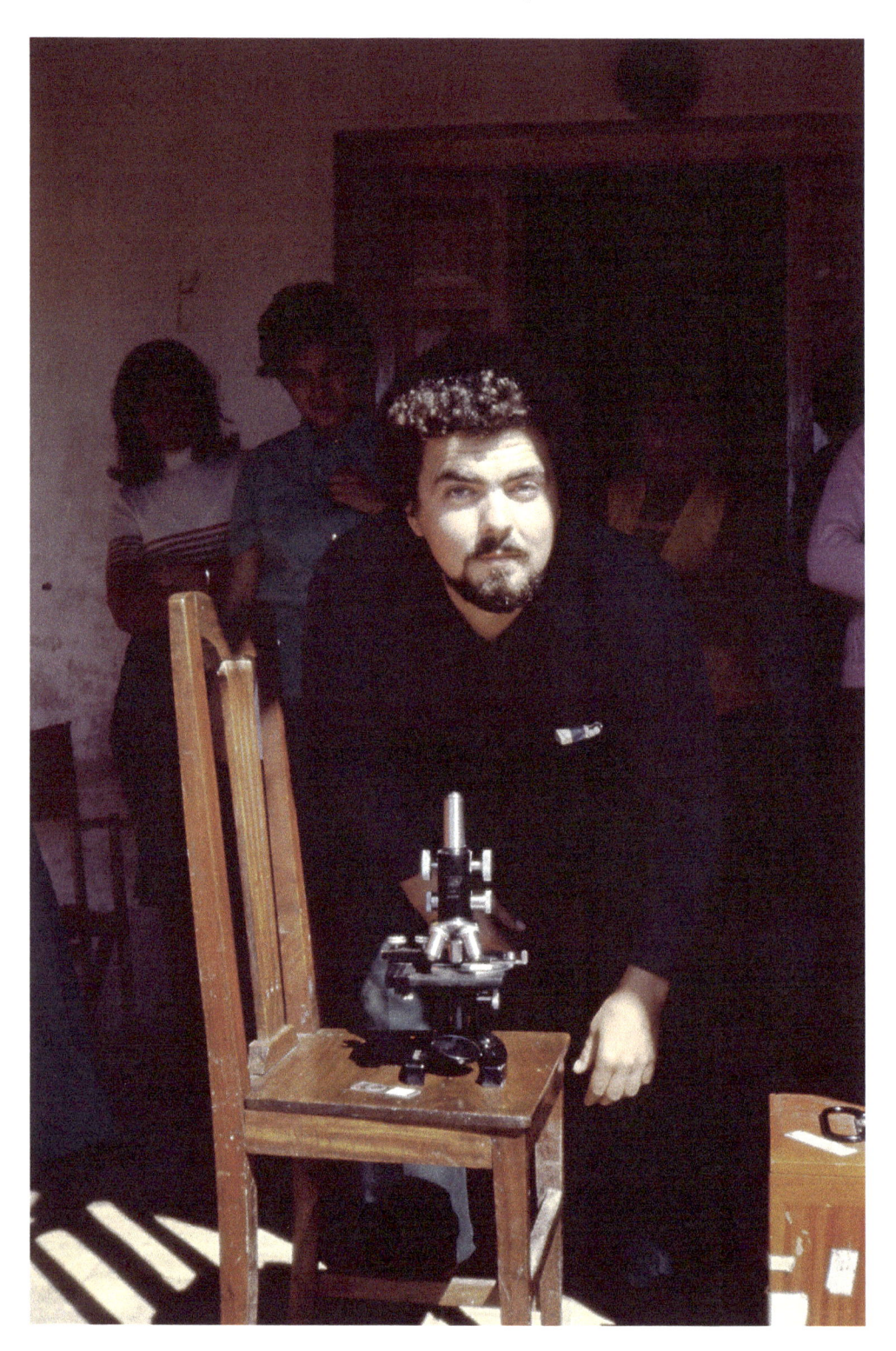

Stephen setting up the microscope for workshop participants
to view hookworm eggs and larvae

A Peace Corp Memoir

Ricardo and Jeff, preparing hookworm workshop materials

Iguazú Falls

Stephen at the Devil's Throat of Iguazú Falls

The Kennedy ranch in the Chaco

Viewing the remains of a tank from the Chaco War

Stephen and I cast our shadows while on a ride near Ybycuí,
with the San José hill in the upper left

CHAPTER 6

The Trip Home through Latin America

It isn't much good having anything exciting, if you can't share it with somebody.
–Winnie the Pooh

It was 10 hours after leaving Paraguay when the diarrhea hit me. Stephen and I had found an inexpensive *pensión* (boardinghouse) in Santa Cruz, dined, and unpacked a few things. Then the abdominal cramping started. I quickly disappeared into the communal bathroom. At least we had modern plumbing and a supply of Lomotil, an anti-diarrheal medication from our Peace Corps medical kit. Although the Lomotil helped, I still had mild symptoms a few days later when we traveled by train from Santa Cruz to Cochabamba. The train toilets, the kind that flushed directly onto the ground below, caused me distress as I imagined children playing on the stretch of tracks where we traveled.

I had probably picked up a germ on Lloyd Boliviano. As we were saying our last good-byes, someone had given Stephen a miniature bottle of scotch. Once we were airborne, he suggested I ask for some ice water, drink the water, and give him the ice for the scotch. I did. Lulled by the fairly clean water supply throughout Paraguay, I had forgotten the traveler's rule about drinking only boiled water. Stephen didn't get sick. Perhaps the alcohol in the scotch killed whatever germs were in the melting ice. My tourist activities in Santa Cruz and Cochabamba were limited by the need to stay near a bathroom.

By the time we traveled from Cochabamba to La Paz a few days later, the diarrhea had disappeared, allowing me to fixate on my shortness of breath, fatigue, and dizziness caused by the altitude. Over the course of a few days, my body began acclimating to the thin air at 12,000 feet, more than twice the elevation of Denver. Stephen's symptoms from the high altitude were milder than mine, and he considerately slowed his walking pace when I strained too much to keep up. Any inhibitions discussing bodily functions and disease with each other had long ago disappeared, and we easily tuned into the other's physical and emotional discomforts and needs.

While taking in the sites of La Paz, Stephen and I talked to locals and fellow travelers. Upon hearing Bolivians speaking either of the two major indigenous languages of the Andes Mountains (Aymara and Quechua), we laughed at our tendency to respond in Guaraní.

We felt the traditional Andean music pull us like magnets. It featured the guitar, the *charango* (a small stringed instrument), and pan flutes. The two of us were drawn to the doorways of stores and restaurants with strains of music emanating from them. Although the harp and guitar music of Paraguay remains my favorite, the echoing and mystical Andean flute sounds are a close second.

With my maladies behind me, I enjoyed trying new foods. Donuts were easily found in the city, a delicious treat after almost three years without them. Potatoes don't grow well in the tropics but they do in the Andes, where they are indigenous. Stephen and I ate spicy potato dishes and deep-fried mashed potato balls stuffed with vegetables. We tried one of the delicacies of the Andes called *cuy* (guinea pig), domesticated in the area for its meat. It tasted like chicken.

After a handful of days in and around La Paz, we boarded a bus and ascended out of the city's geographical bowl to the *altiplano* (high plain) where the altitude was 1,000 feet higher and the air thinner. Our destination was Tiahuanacu, an archaeological site that likely dates back to well over a thousand years ago, with evidence that people inhabited the area in the B.C. period. It definitely pre-dates the time of the Inca, who dominated the western part of South American beginning only about a hundred years before the arrival of the Spanish conquistadors in 1532. Stephen and I had briefly visited the Tiahuanacu Museum in La Paz but had found it wanting. The exhibits lacked labeling and adequate lighting, and no guidebooks were available. At the archaeological site, we had the *South American Handbook* for a general orientation, and it was pleasant to be outdoors in good weather. The site, over a square mile in size, has a sunken courtyard and massive walls of stones that neatly fit together. Looting over the centuries has taken its toll on the site, but the stone monument called the Gateway of the Sun still graces the area and stimulates the imagination to conjure up what Tiahuanacu might have been like years ago.

Tiahuanacu was the first ancient archaeological site that Stephen and I visited together. We had planned travels to include places that neither of us had previously visited and that we both wanted to see. In 1974 when I was entering the Peace Corps, I had the dream to take a boat down the length of Amazon River at the end of my service, but the heat and humidity of Paraguayan summers cured me of that idea. I was more than content to travel the western spine of the hemisphere with Stephen. Sadly, Paraguay does not have any obvious ancient ruins. The oldest ruins we heard about were those of the missions established in the 17th century by Jesuit missionaries. Located in southern Paraguay east of the city of Encarnación, the Santísima Trinidad del Paraná Mission is perhaps the most famous. When we taught in Encarnación toward the end of our service, we didn't have the time to visit the mission.

Our next destination in Bolivia was Copacabana, a town five hours away on the shore of Lake Titicaca, the highest navigable lake in the world. Even though the *altiplano* itself was flat, drab, and dismal, the daunting snow-capped mountains surging above it provided majestic vistas against a vivid blue sky. The passengers on the bus were colorfully dressed in hats and locally woven garments—men in shirts, pants, and ponchos and women in blouses and long skirts. These Bolivians in the Andes were short. Very short. While sitting on the bus, I could look eye-to-eye at adults standing in the aisle. They were barrel-chested to accommodate the large lungs developed to better cope with living at high altitudes.

The next day as tourists in Copacabana, we sought out the archeological ruins on the Island of the Sun in the middle of Lake Titicaca. In the process, we became intermediary tour guides for five Germans wanting to visit the same place. They spoke English but not Spanish. Stephen negotiated a tour price with a boatman for the seven of us, and off we went for a lovely day on the water and island, where we climbed Inca staircases and hiked ancient trails. According to legend, the island is the birthplace of the first Incas. I found the magnificent views, ruins, and climbing all breathtaking for their own reasons.

The following morning, Stephen and I attempted to buy bus tickets at the hotel desk for the return trip to La Paz. When told no seats were available for a couple of days due to a local festival ending, we began conversing in English about our options, of which we decided there was only one—stay in Copacabana until we could get on a bus. Two British men checking out of the hotel overheard us and offered us a ride in their Land Rover. The Brits had to stop at some of their work sites, but they would be back in La Paz by the end of the day. Stephen and I took them up on their offer. In addition to experiencing the breathtaking scenery of remote, ragged snow-capped Andes mountain peaks, I also found myself physically short of breath. The British men were installing microwave dishes for Bolivia's telephone system on the sides of mountains at altitudes of 16,000 and 17,000 feet. I gasped for air, inhaling as deeply as possible while sitting in the back of the Land Rover with a shooting pain up the back of my neck and head. Stephen left the jeep to enjoy the views but could only pace slowly around in the thin air. Once again in La Paz at only 12,000 feet, I felt okay.

The two of us left La Paz by bus and traveled the shoreline of Lake Titicaca before entering Puno, Perú in mid-August. In Puno, we hopped on a train for Cuzco, once the capital of the Inca Empire and now famous for its archeological ruins and Spanish colonial architecture. At an elevation of only 11,152 feet, I could actually walk at a decent pace up and down the streets of the historic city. We spent ten days in Peru, adequate time to tour Cuzco, the nearby archeological site of Sacsayhuamán (an ancient citadel to the north), and Machu Picchu. The Inca stonework was a marvel to see, with field stones so precisely cut and fitted together that a knife blade cannot be inserted between them.

This part of the continent, rich in Inca history and culture, had been high on our list of places to visit. We each had studied it in college, Stephen through his undergraduate minor in anthropology and I in my history studies. We purchased a copy of the renowned historian William Prescott's *A History of the Conquest of Perú* in a local bookstore and read it together to gain a deeper understanding of the Spanish invasion and its consequences. Published in 1847, it remains one of the classics in Latin American history.

While the walls of stonework were common throughout Cuzco, including one restaurant interior wall where we dined, the vast Sacsayhuamán fortress was a sight to behold. The main area had three terraced walls, each almost 20 feet high and a quarter of a mile long. The citadel had protected Cuzco from invaders until the Spanish, led by Francisco Pizarro, conquered the Inca in the 16th century.

It was a peaceful, sunny day during our visit, making it difficult to imagine the violence of the battles at the site when the Incas defended their capital. There were llamas grazing on the grounds and a wizened old man playing pan flutes for tips, his music drifting on the breeze as he blew his breath over the openings of the flutes' hollow reeds.

Machu Picchu is an impressive 15th century Inca citadel 50 miles northwest of Cuzco through rough terrain. Located on top of a mountain at an altitude of almost 8,000 feet, the Incas used the site for only 80 years or so. They abandoned it around the time of the Spanish Conquest. Its difficult access kept it hidden from Europeans until Hiram Bingham from Yale discovered its existence in 1911. Bingham's book, *Lost City of the Incas*, is a fascinating story, but Machu Picchu was never "lost" to local people.

Because it was a popular tourist destination in 1976 (it is even more so now), the night before our visit Stephen and I took the 3-½ hour train ride to the small town of Aguas Calientes, situated by the

Urubamba River near the base of the mountain. Up at the crack of dawn, we were eager to reach the top of Machu Picchu a half-day before the tourists would arrive by train from Cuzco. Stephen and I rode a bus traveling up the Hiram Bingham Highway, a rough, narrow dirt road 5-½ miles long that crisscrosses back and forth with 13 hairpin curves, all etched into the steep green mountainside and measuring an altitude gain of only 1,500 feet from bottom to top.

We congratulated ourselves on the foresight to have quiet time at Machu Picchu with only a few others before the tourist onslaught. The two of us marveled at close-up views of the stone structures with their trapezoidal windows, the residential section, an astronomic calendar, the Funerary Rock in the upper cemetery, and massive sections of terracing. With a few llamas grazing nearby, we rested at an elevated area at the far end of Machu Picchu, looking across the ruins with the mountain Huayna Picchu towering in the distance and other rugged mountains seen in every direction, providing an impressive, unforgettable panorama. Stephen took pictures of this classic vista. The black and white photos were superb, but the colored slides all had the tip of Huayna Picchu cut off.

Once the train deposited the day tourists, the site had hundreds of people clamoring and swarming around like ants. Stephen and I opted to take the early bus down the mountain to preserve our quiet, majestic memory of the place. However, the bus ride was anything but quiet. A handful of pre-pubescent boys raced the zig-zagging bus to the base of the mountain by going straight down, almost intersecting the bus in the middle of each road section and screeching at the top of their lungs to draw our attention. The boys won the race. As we stepped off the bus, they expected tips from their audience of passengers. Yes, they got them!

Stephen and I worked our way north through South America, and I relished in the anonymous role of tourist traveling with him. We explored new places and their unique sights, smells, and sounds. Also, the two of us respected the other's wishes and desires and took care of each other during times of colds and intestinal illnesses. Traveling with a male, I felt a degree of protection from being targeted by aggressive men. My single status wasn't an issue because we weren't trying to become part of a community; we were simply tourists passing through. For me, I felt a freedom and sense of relief from being under scrutiny as I had been in Ybycuí. I didn't feel judged poorly by being with Stephen without a wedding band on my hand. Still, I knew I would face judgment by some family members upon returning to the States. I pushed those thoughts from my mind with the hope that Stephen would want to marry me soon after arriving home.

Stephen and I flew from Cuzco to Guayaquil, Ecuador, deplaning into hot, muggy sea level air. While the adequate oxygen was nice, the climate and industrial city atmosphere weren't for us. Instead of lingering there, we opted to proceed by train on a day-long journey to central Ecuador on one of the most geographically impressive stretches of our travels. Starting off through a fertile coastal plain dotted with plantations of sugarcane, bananas, coffee, pineapple, and other tropical vegetation, our train gained elevation on the western edge of the Andes through an extensive switchback system, more massive than the Hiram Bingham Highway. The vegetation changed from tropical to Andean before our eyes as we ascended, arriving at an altitude of 9,035 feet at the city of Riobamba on the Pan American Highway, high in the central Andes and surrounded by snow-capped volcanoes. The distance as a crow flies was less than 150 miles, but rugged terrain and switchbacks had us traveling a much longer distance.

In Riobamba, Stephen and I boarded a late afternoon bus for the four-hour ride to Quito. As we traveled into Ecuador's capital, I noticed an amenity of which we had been deprived—laundromats.

We appreciated the reprieve from washing our clothes by hand for the duration of our stay in Ecuador.

A close second on our list of enjoyments was meeting Volunteers. During our travels through Bolivia and Perú, we had almost exclusively focused on each other. In Quito, Stephen and I emerged from our intense emotional involvement to actively interact with others. Kate's sister Ann, serving in her first year as a Volunteer, introduced us to a number of her friends. I had met Ann during her visit to Itacurubí del Rosario when she was considering joining the Peace Corps, and it was fun to catch up with her during her service. Stephen and I also spent three days with a Volunteer married couple at Rancho Donald, a Peace Corps project introducing Brahma cattle into the herds of Ecuador.

Time with Volunteers made us feel less like tourists and more like educated visitors because of our own service in Paraguay. Volunteers in Ecuador experienced challenges similar to what we had been through, including language acquisition, understanding cultural nuances, adapting to a slower pace of life, tolerating gossip, effectively working with counterparts, and suffering from health problems. However, unlike in Paraguay, Volunteers in Ecuador and locals alike were often plagued by amebic dysentery, which could cause serious diarrhea and dehydration. One Volunteer told us the ultimate treatment for it, when all others had failed, was a small quantity of arsenic. Stephen and I, having already suffered our fifth bout of diarrhea since leaving Paraguay, became especially cautious about avoiding uncooked vegetables and the local water unless it was in the form of hot tea or coffee. We felt gratitude for the quality of the water in most of Paraguay.

Stephen and I played the tourist role in Ecuador as well, visiting the *Ciudad Mitad del Mundo* (Half of the World City), where we posed for photographs as we straddled the equator with one foot in each hemisphere. The two of us roamed around the Andean highland town of Otavalo, known for its colorfully dressed indigenous population and its handmade woolen textiles. Similar to other towns and cities in the central Andes Mountains, the altitude was 8,300 feet, with the surrounding snow-tipped volcanic peaks soaring over 15,000 feet. Even at the equator, high elevations were cold year-round. Adequately accustomed to the thin air, we donned warm sweaters and meandered through the Otavalo marketplace, selecting some attractive wall hangings that in the future would remind us of our travels without burdening us with too much baggage in the present.

Our last two days in Ecuador were spent at a quiet, secluded beach on the Pacific Coast in the northern part of the country, well off the beaten tourist path. It was in the general area where Moritz Thomsen served as a Volunteer in the 1960s when he was in his forties, after which he wrote *Living Poor—A Peace Corps Chronicle*, one of the highly recommended books given to us in training. One Volunteer we met in Quito commented that Moritz, a talented writer and a Peace Corps legend, was still in Ecuador and occasionally appeared in the Peace Corps office. (According to Wikipedia's entry about him, Thomsen passed away from cholera in 1991 after living in Ecuador for 35 years.)

Next was Panama. Inspired by the movie on the Panama Canal that Stephen had shown as a fundraiser and knowing that his father was born in the Canal Zone (Stephen's grandfather had been a bookkeeper in the Zone), we both looked forward to a stop there. It was a quick one, due to riots in Panama City and our travel fatigue.

Stephen and I stayed one night in the Canal Zone with a toxicologist and his wife, a former Miss Panama. This was a suggestion from Stephen's dad, who had once treated the couple's son for a hematological condition. They were gracious hosts but abided by traditional standards regarding our unmarried status. We each were shown to separate rooms to stow our bags before our host and hostess segregated us for private conversations. Stephen chatted with the toxicologist in the living room while the former beauty queen took me into the kitchen for a girl-talk about when Stephen and I were going to get married. (I said, "Soon, I hope.") They fed us and took us to see ships pass through the canal at night, before returning us to the airport the following day for a flight to Guatemala. Someday, I'd like to take a cruise through the length of the canal. We didn't have the money or time to do that in 1976.

In Guatemala, we had on our list Antigua, Chichicastenango, the area around Lake Atitlán, and the Mayan ruins of Tikal in the Yucatán Peninsula. The small city of Antigua in the central highlands had some lovely, well-preserved Spanish colonial buildings in spite of frequent earthquakes since its founding in 1524. The most recent quake had hit eight months before our arrival, and the unstable façade of the church was still supported by massive braces.

Traveling to Chichicastenango and Lake Atitlán on public transportation found us amidst local people dressed in traditional woven clothing, such as the *huipiles* (blouses) richly embroidered in vivid colors on heavy cotton fabric worn by the women. In Chichicastenango, with its elevation slightly higher than Denver's and now easy for us to handle, Stephen and I sat on a bench to watch a passing religious procession, breathing in the smell of incense and witnessing the interesting blending of Catholic and indigenous rituals and icons. At the market, located next to the church of Santo Tomás, we walked down roads lined with vendors selling woven goods, live chickens, herbs and spices, religious idols, and arrays of daily household items while listening to a mix of Spanish and a Mayan dialect. The people around Lake Atitlán, also indigenous and colorful, had suffered greatly in recent years at the hand of the Guatemalan military and government. There was a continued heavy presence of soldiers.

Tikal, one of the largest archeological sites of the pre-Colombian Maya civilization, was our last stop. Our descending airplane provided us that iconic view of pyramid tops peeking out of the dense green jungle that would soon be immortalized in the 1977 *Star Wars* film, used to represent the Yavin IV Rebel Base. It was spine-tingling and beautiful. Stephen and I spent the next couple of days walking through acres of cleared jungle, climbing pyramids, descending them, and walking more, awed at the splendid remains of temples, ball courts, and the views from atop the pyramids. We saw countless stelae (stone shafts carved with hieroglyphs), altars, tombs, and lintels (elaborately carved wooden beams that have miraculously survived the jungle climate for centuries). During our meals at a small hotel, we enjoyed freshly made corn tortillas, scrambled eggs, and refried black beans, some of the simplest and tastiest food I have ever eaten.

During the hot 12-hour bus trip back to Guatemala City, Stephen and I agreed it was finally time to fly home and figure out what to do next. I wondered where "home" might be, hoping with all my heart that our relationship would evolve in positive ways in our own culture. We had individually taken a jump into the unknowns of being Peace Corps Volunteers in Paraguay, and we had emerged from the experience over two years later as a couple with a sense of optimism for a future together. After being constant companions in five Latin American countries since leaving Paraguay, it was time to return to the U.S.A. Our journey concluded on October 6, 1976, when Stephen and I landed in Washington, D.C. The next chapter of our lives began.

Machu Picchu in Perú

PART TWO

❁

LIFE AFTER
PEACE CORPS PARAGUAY

―◆―

The best and most beautiful things in the world
cannot be seen or even touched
— they must be felt with the heart.

–Helen Keller

CHAPTER 7

Returned Peace Corps Volunteers (RPCVs)

For the two of us, home isn't a place. It is a person. And we are finally home.
—Stephanie Perkins

Reverse culture shock was real. Back in my country of origin, I felt estranged for the first several weeks. My biggest fears at someone's home were automatically using the tablecloth edge in front of me to wipe my mouth and throwing used toilet paper in a little basket or on the bathroom floor. I'm proud to say that I quickly trained myself to U.S.A. habits in those regards.

The biggest irritation I felt was the wasteful, unnecessary commercial packaging of toys, foodstuffs, and merchandise. Items of all sizes were individually mounted onto a large piece of glossy cardboard and securely covered in molded plastic. Presumably, this was to make shoplifting more difficult, to keep the items clean, and to draw the consumer's attention with the cardboard's bold colors. The packaging was destined for the garbage and then a landfill. Sometimes it was discarded as litter. Purchased items were always placed in plastic or paper bags that also ended up as litter or landfill. I attempted to take my own reusable bags when I went shopping, but I received frowns. While the overt irritation that this waste caused me in 1976 has diminished, decades later I still prefer to reuse my own cloth or nylon woven shopping bags. Marketing prior to 1974 was likely much the same as it was in late 1976, but I didn't take notice of it until after my service. In Paraguay, I had become used to shopping with my own tote bags and displays of goods without special packaging.

Together, Stephen and I took initial necessary actions to readapt to life in our own country. First, we used our Peace Corps readjustment allowance to purchase a used car, and we visited our families. Next, with the help of my college roommate Lyn, we settled in Northern Virginia, south of the District of Columbia, in an apartment close to where she lived. Stephen landed a position in a laboratory on the campus of the National Institutes of Health, and I eventually found a job with Rural America/Rural Housing Alliance, a non-profit organization that developed decent housing around the country for migrant and seasonal farm workers. Kim, the man who hired me, had served in the Peace Corps in the Dominican Republic. My favorite housing developer became Kay, who had served in Colombia. With my approval and support, she was hired by an agency I monitored in Yakima, Washington.

We Volunteers returning from service don't call ourselves "former" Peace Corps Volunteers. Rather, we are "returned" Peace Corps Volunteers (RPCVs). For most of us who have served, the Peace Corps is a life turning-point, with the experience remaining indelibly deep within us. We look at the world differently than we did prior to our service. When news articles report events occurring in far-away places, some of the foreign-ness has disappeared. News items from our host country are meaningful, hitting close to home, because they are from a place we once called home. As the years pass, some memories may fade, but the Peace Corps was such a powerful growth time in our lives that we are forever changed by it. Undoubtedly, it's not quite the same for all returning Volunteers, particularly those who don't complete their two-year commitment for some reason. Many RPCVs, including us, choose careers and fields that serve others. These include the foreign service and other international programs, education, health and medicine, working to solve poverty, and generally attempting to make the world a better place.

∞∞∞∞

Old-timers in New England say that mid-January 1978 brought them one of the worst ice storms in their history. Reminiscent of winter scenes from the 1965 movie *Dr. Zhivago*, thick layers of ice covered the roads and coated tree limbs along the coast while heavy snow blanketed inland areas. Stephen and I married on January 14th in the middle of the storm. Due to the inclement weather, the small wedding we had planned became smaller yet, with only 31 people, including the organist and the reverend, in attendance. Fortunately, our relatives and close friends who braved the dangerous weather conditions arrived safely. We had wanted our four surviving grandparents to be our witnesses, but two of the four were unable to attend due to illness and bad weather. Our fathers stepped in to sign, along with our maternal grandmothers.

The ceremony was in Yale's Dwight Memorial Chapel, a towering stone structure built in the 1840s with multi-colored stained-glass windows and interior stone columns reaching the tall ceiling where they were joined by arches. As we gathered for the event, the chapel's massive pipe organ produced echoing music, including some J.S. Bach pieces and a moving rendition of "The Hookworm Song," a little surprise for my groom. Stephen wore the gray pinstripe suit made at the Riojana department store in Asunción, a white *aho-poí* shirt with white embroidery made by my college roommate Lyn with fabric we brought back, and a white *aho-poí* tie with silver embroidery. Of course, I wore my elegant *aho-poí-eté* dress as Ña Niní had directed. A heavy wooden table serving as an altar was covered with a white-on-white *aho-poí-eté* shawl. Reverend Duncomb, the chaplain at Yale Medical School and a friend of Stephen's dad, performed the brief ceremony we had written with his assistance. Neither of us changed our surnames, although we had joked about becoming Stephen and Mary Lou Feltes (Ña Niní and Don Lalo's surname). But we were married! Ña Niní delighted in the wedding photos we sent her. I had been corresponding with her by letter every couple of months since our departure from Paraguay.

After the intimate, joyful ceremony, we traveled a couple of icy blocks to our reception at Yale's Graduate Club on the New Haven Green. A welcoming fire was blazing in the massive brick fireplace as we entered the wood-paneled dining room and accepted a glass of wine before sitting down to a dinner of Chicken Kiev. Our wedding cake was a simple but delicious Italian cream cake with some extra squiggles of icing to represent roundworms. A cute joke.

Since our wedding, when people ask us how we first met, we reply that it was in the Peace Corps. And we relate the story of the first time we did anything together, which might be considered our first date, certainly a bizarre one, although neither of us thought of it as a first date at that moment in time. We tell that when we were sidetracked on our way to Paraguay in 1974, we visited the Larco Museum in Lima, Perú, to see the amazing collection of pre-Colombian erotic art!

∞∞∞∞

In late November 1979, I eagerly opened a letter from Paraguay written by Peggy (Margarita), a health education and SENASA Volunteer assigned to Ybycuí in 1977. The previous August, Stephen and I had moved to New Haven, Connecticut, after he was accepted at Yale Medical School. For the past year, I had occasionally received letters from Peggy. Ña Niní insisted that she write to me after hearing repeated complaints about how tired she was hearing the local people talk in glowing terms about "Marilú y Esteban." The two of us had become "Ghosts of Peace Corps Past" to Peggy.

The letter I held in my hands told me that upon completing her Peace Corps service, Peggy would return to her family's home in Long Island, New York, accompanied by Tomasa and Ña Niní's daughter Nidia for their first visit to the U.S. They would be only an 80-minute ferry ride across Long Island Sound to Bridgeport, Connecticut, a mere 20 miles from New Haven. The three of them wanted to visit us.

Barely two weeks later and after a flurry of phone calls, Stephen and I drove our chocolate brown Toyota Corolla to the ferry dock in Bridgeport to greet them with a round of hugs, cheek kisses, and exclamations in Guaraní and Spanish. We piled our guests and their suitcases into our small vehicle, which we had purchased with wedding gift money. The sub-compact car, described in *Consumer Reports* as having a back seat for "children and adults you don't like," was adequate for our happy guests for the short trip to our apartment. Tomasa was still the same sweet, observant woman with a zest for life whom we had last seen three years before. Nidia, meticulous about her makeup, took in her new surroundings with the exactness of the math teacher she was by profession. Smiling most of the time, Peggy was a trim young woman with a stylish flair about her. She seemed most curious to meet her two Peace Corps ghosts.

Peggy, Stephen, and I conversed in Spanish, occasionally laughing until we cried, recalling and sharing experiences, until becoming serious again about the sanitation problems that we had addressed. Peggy had worked with a SENASA inspector counterpart, which wasn't always easy, but they did help families build latrines. Lots of them. She didn't know how many, but people were actually interested in latrines because of the intensive education campaign Stephen and I, along with Dave and Martina initially, had conducted. Peggy said that everyone knew about *cevo-í* because of "Marilú y Esteban," and they wanted their children to be healthier. Stephen and I were impressed, and my heart still warms when I think about those few days with Peggy and the realization that we had quite likely made a positive difference in the welfare of Ybycuí's population.

Tomasa and Nidia had a grand time as well, particularly when we took them to see snow for the first time. As it had been a dry winter, the artificially produced snow at a ski resort in nearby Middletown had to suffice. There was enough to have a snowball fight, ending with the five of us covered in cold white flakes and laughing. Before returning to Paraguay, Tomasa and Nidia visited Paraguayan friends in the D.C. area and experienced a heavy snowfall of the real stuff that almost delayed their flight home but fulfilled their wish to see real snow. Our time with Peggy, Tomasa, and Nidia was the first of several examples of how Paraguay persistently popped into our lives in interesting ways after our Peace Corps service.

After the delightful three-day visit, Stephen returned his focus to his medical studies while I worked at the Fair Haven Community Health Clinic as their childbirth educator and prenatal coordinator. I had been hired by Katrina Clark, an RPCV from Colombia and the clinic's director. The clinic occupied an appealing three-story old New England building that had previously been a funeral parlor but was extensively remodeled into an outpatient medical facility. It served a mix of working-class Puerto Ricans, African Americans, Italians, and Anglos. Less than a mile from the clinic was a cluster of outstanding Italian restaurants, including Frank Pepe's Pizzeria Napoletana, founded in 1925 and claimed by some of the locals as the place where pizza was invented. There were a number of other small but outstanding Italian eateries serving delicious pizzas and calzones, too.

When I had entered the clinic the first time for an interview with Katrina, I heard a boisterous string of words identifiable only as Puerto Rican Spanish followed by a crazy cackling. I didn't understand a word of it, and the thought of dealing with the rapid-fire Spanish I struggled with in Ponce during Peace Corps training almost made me turn around and walk out. However, a certain charm and welcoming aura about the place compelled me to keep my appointment. Katrina was willing to take the risk of hiring me, in spite of my not meeting all of the job qualifications. I couldn't refuse the challenge. Although holding a flashlight for a Cesarean section done with only a local anesthetic was not something I'd do in my new position, my fluency in Spanish was helpful.

∞∞∞∞∞

"Marilú, ¿Mba-éi-xa-pa?" Ña Niní's voice on the telephone startled me. It was June 1981, and Stephen was completing his second year of medical school. After a brief exchange of pleasantries, Ña Niní surprised me with the news that she was in northern Virginia near Washington, D.C. Her son Tonio had finished his neurosurgery residency in Arkansas and was preparing to return to Paraguay with his wife Nuchi and two sons. While Tonio was arranging to have their belongings shipped home, they were all staying with Dr. Gonzalez, a Paraguayan psychiatrist employed by the U.S. Army in Northern Virginia. Ña Niní had flown north to join them almost two weeks earlier, fulfilling a dream of hers to visit the U.S. Sadly, nobody had had the time to take her sightseeing in our nation's capital. "We will, Ña Niní," I exclaimed. Stephen set aside his summer research project for a few days and I quickly arranged some time off from the clinic. We drove south in our Corolla to see Ña Niní during the long 4th of July weekend. A phone call to an aunt and uncle of mine in suburban Maryland near the nation's capital assured us of a place to sleep.

Arriving late in the afternoon, we received big bear hugs and cheek kisses from Ña Niní, shed a few joyful tears, and underwent introductions to all of the others. I quickly realized that Tonio was struggling to make his shipping arrangements. He had spent hours on the phone without connecting with someone who could make things happen. Putting practicalities before the pleasure of planning sightseeing for Ña Niní, I telephoned my sister Cynthia, who worked for a major shipping company in Virginia Beach. Could she help? While her company did not ship to Paraguay, Cynthia quickly determined who did. Although it took some phone networking, she figured things out and made the right connections for Tonio. (It would take a couple of months for his Mercedes Benz and household goods to reach Paraguay, but everything made it.)

Ña Niní, an eager tourist, yearned to visit John F. Kennedy's gravesite in Arlington National Cemetery as well as the White House. Nuchi, who had the responsibility of her sons, 11-year-old Carlos and nine-month old Mario, also wanted to see the sights. Fortunately, Dr. Gonzalez offered us his much larger sedan for our touring.

The following morning, we arrived at the Gonzalez home at the crack of dawn in the rain. With our tourists in the back seat of the borrowed car, Stephen drove and I navigated, with the White House as our first destination. Having recently lived in the area, we knew there would be no chance of finding a place to park near the White House. But we had a plan. Today, White House tickets must be requested months in advance from one's senator or congressional representative, but in 1981 it was simpler.

Stephen dropped off the five of us, along with three umbrellas, at the White House tour staging area where bleachers were set up to organize the visitors. Inquiring at the kiosk about ticket availability, I secured four tickets, ushered Ña Niní, Nuchi with infant Mario in arms, and Carlos to a covered area of the bleachers, and waited with them until their tour began. I assured them I would be waiting outside at the end of their quick tour, which only involved two or three rooms of the presidential mansion. Jogging outside the fence around the White House grounds to the mansion's main entrance on Pennsylvania Avenue, I watched for Stephen in the borrowed car. (Cell phones would have helped, but we wouldn't have them for another couple of decades.) I spotted him, waved my arm, and pumped my umbrella. When he saw me, I signaled him to continue his circling. Eventually, when I spotted our Paraguayan friends exiting the Executive Mansion, I signaled Stephen to pull up to the curb on his next loop.

As we piled into the car, Ña Niní was beaming, and Nuchi and Carlos grinned. When I asked how it was, Ña Niní excitedly replied, "¡Yo me senté en la Casa Blanca!" (I sat down in the White House!). She proceeded to relate that the guards had cautioned them not to touch anything. When they weren't looking, she quickly sat down on a chair, jumping up before she could be caught, just so she could make the remark as if she had been an invited guest at the White House. We all laughed, except for infant Mario, who had fallen asleep. The tour had included a mere three rooms, but it was thrilling nonetheless.

When the rain cleared, Stephen drove us across the Potomac River toward Arlington National Cemetery. Upon arrival at the solemn grounds that had been used as the final resting place for thousands of soldiers since 1863 when the Civil War raged, we used the shuttle bus service to ride up the hillside, covered with rows upon rows of white crosses. Our small group quietly stepped off the shuttle and followed the clusters of tourists making their way by foot.

Remembering the reverence she had for President Kennedy, I watched Ña Niní out of the corner of my eye as we approached the simple gravesite with its eternal flame. For her, this was a pilgrimage. Along with her boys, Nuchi stood back a short distance, watching her mother-in-law kneel on the cement at the black chain marking where sacred ground began. I felt Stephen's presence beside me. As Ña Niní prayed, tears flowed down her cheeks, perhaps a combination of homage and peacefulness for being present at this place. When she rose from her knees, we walked as a small group to the area below the gravesite where the panorama of Washington, D.C., spread out before us. Stephen and I pointed out the Washington Monument, the Lincoln Memorial, and the Capitol Building to them, with a promise we would drive past these landmarks for closeup views before returning to the Gonzalez home.

As we gazed at the view, Ña Niní pivoted to look again at Kennedy's grave and to speak to me softly in Spanish. "He was very much loved and revered in Paraguay. Everyone was so delighted when he was elected. We felt he cared about Latin America."

"Did the fact that he was Catholic make a difference for Paraguayans?" I asked.

"Oh, yes," she replied. "Because most of us are Catholics, we felt a special bond to your first president of our faith." She continued, "And when the news came that he had been assassinated, everyone cried. People walking down the roads of Ybycuí had tears streaming down their faces."

I whispered to her, "You know, he's the reason I met you, Ña Niní. If President Kennedy hadn't founded the Peace Corps, I never would have gone to Ybycuí. And I would not have met Stephen."

We lingered awhile longer at this special place, breathing the humid July air and watching as the sun appeared from behind the diminishing clouds, before taking the shuttle bus to the Tomb of the Unknown Soldier. There, we witnessed the precision marching of the Army soldier maintaining the 24-hour vigil at the Tomb and the Changing of the Honor Guard. During this solemn ceremony, the crowd was asked to show respect for those fallen soldiers "known only to God" by remaining silent. I smiled to myself, remembering being in this same place over 20 years earlier when my four-year-old cousin Kenneth edged under the black chain marking the off-limits area. The pacing Honor Guard had abruptly stopped, readied his rifle, and demanded of my cousin, "Halt! Who goes there?" Kenneth froze in place, eyes filled with fear, before slowly backing away.

After a late afternoon driving tour of the major memorials and monuments of the city, our tired tourists were ready to call it a day. Although there were more sites that we could have shown them, Ña Niní and Nuchi were both pleased and satisfied with their touring. We returned them and the large borrowed sedan to the Gonzalez house with a promise that we'd be back the following day to spend the morning with them before heading back to New Haven.

When Stephen and I arrived at my aunt's home that evening, we were surprised to find my mother waiting for us! I had telephoned her after receiving Ña Niní's call, and Mom had decided to fly from Detroit to the Washington, D.C., area to meet her. The following morning, she did just that. Now, four decades later, when I think about that meeting of my two mothers, I choke up with emotion. I translated as they held each other's hands, expressed their joy and appreciation for the Peace Corps and for me, and chatted about President Kennedy and Arlington National Cemetery.

After we took some photographs of the momentous event and before I knew it, Stephen and I had to head back to New Haven. The next day, my mother had a reservation to fly home, and Ña Niní had to return to Paraguay within a few days. I promised to continue corresponding with Ña Niní, and I would definitely send her copies of photos taken during our visit.

On our wedding day, January 14, 1978
(Courtesy of Ken Cowhey)

CHAPTER 8

Did We Make a Positive Difference?

Real change, enduring change, happens one step at a time.
—Ruth Bader Ginsburg

Five months later before dinner, I announced to Stephen, "I have a crazy idea." As I unwrapped take-out food from a neighborhood restaurant, my emotions fluctuated between confidence I could carry out my idea and fear that it bordered on the impossible. In late 1981, I was half-way through the coursework for a master's degree in public health (M.P.H.) at Yale Medical School's Department of Epidemiology and Public Health. I had been accepted as a student after Katrina, a graduate of the program whose work at the Fair Haven Community Health Clinic was often showcased by Yale, wrote one of my letters of recommendation. I still worked full-time and would finish the two-year program in three years, which would coincide with Stephen's completion of his medical degree.

My master's degree required a thesis, referred to as an "essay" by the program, ideally involving some original research. I had been drafting some protocols for possible topics while taking a course in research methodology with Professor Kyle Grazier. She and my advisor, Dr. Jim Jekel, had discouraged me from trying to extract data from Connecticut birth certificates for my thesis due to the many barriers one has to overcome to access such data. It could be done, but it would take months, if not years, to obtain permission. I could not afford long delays and uncertainty.

"Stephen, I have a brilliant topic for my public health thesis. I want us to return to Paraguay for a month next summer." I reminded him of Peggy's words about helping numerous families build latrines. I continued, "I will research the changes in sanitation conditions in Ybycuí from 1974 to 1982. I still have copies of the data from 1974. We could conduct another census of the town." He looked at me in utter disbelief, recalling that he and Dave had taken several months to complete their census. "I have about a month of vacation time from the clinic," I explained. "And you would have to come with me. You have some flexible time this summer. Maybe we could get Peace Corps and SENASA to help us. What do you think?" He eyes reflected incredulity, but he gulped and suggested that I continue developing my idea.

Thinking aloud with Stephen during dinner helped me outline the structure and parameters of a research protocol. After dinner, I began drafting my idea onto paper, along with a lengthy list of things to do. Next, I found our bin of Paraguay mementos and reviewed the 1974 census data on the 662 houses in Ybycuí. Stephen and I guessed that now there could be as many as 1,000 home visits required. I would need about five people who could each conduct an average of 20 successful inspections a day over a two-week period. During the original census, Dave and Stephen had to talk with people about the special project while collecting census data. This time, a home visit would only involve a quick latrine inspection. My mind raced through possible scenarios for making it all happen. Fair Haven Clinic would have to give me time off. I'd need help from Peace Corps and SENASA, as well as money for plane fare and some materials. I hoped we could stay with Feltes family members in Asunción and Ybycuí. My job barely covered our living expenses, we had only meager savings, and I was taking out loans to pay my Yale tuition. Stephen had a National Health Service Corps Scholarship for three of his four years that paid his tuition and some expenses, and he would borrow money for the fourth year.

Stephen had a research idea of his own. Through his father, he had made friends with Fernando, a Chilean neonatologist at Yale, who suggested Stephen study malnutrition in children with a colleague of his in Chile while staying with Fernando's family in the capital of Santiago. The School of Medicine did have scholarships available for medical students' international research projects. As a student in its Department of Epidemiology and Public Health, I was eligible to apply, too.

Our planning began in earnest. Stephen and I each applied for scholarships offered by the School of Medicine. Working through the Paraguay Desk at the Peace Corps Office in Washington, D.C., I began making inquiries and arrangements. What a pleasant surprise it was to learn that Kate from Itacurubí del Rosario was the assistant country director in Peace Corps Paraguay! With her support for my research proposal, Country Co-Director Ann quickly approved it. On my behalf, Kate approached SENASA for the sanitation agency's collaboration. Margarita, still an important figure in that agency, was enthusiastic about my proposed research and offered the participation of SENASA inspectors. Professor Kyle reviewed my proposal and wholeheartedly supported it. She encouraged me to also interview a handful of town leaders to document any significant activities or changes in Ybycuí since the initial census, such as economic factors, health education, sanitation efforts, and community perceptions about sanitation. Katrina promised me adequate time off from my clinic job during the upcoming summer.

However, a setback occurred in the spring of 1982. The international research scholarship committee approved Stephen's idea for funding, but the professor who controlled the funds responded negatively to my proposal. I can still recall the look on his face when I presented my research protocol. It was like he smelled a fetid, overflowing and roofless latrine baking in the Paraguayan sun. I surmised that he thought my topic below the dignity of a Yale graduate student. We were fortunate that Stephen had his plane ticket to Chile paid for through the scholarship fund, and a stopover in Paraguay for several weeks would cost him little additional money. Stephen and I would somehow figure out how to finance my plane ticket and other expenses we might have.

After some phone calls to Paraguay during that spring, my plans began to materialize. Ña Niní was thrilled at the prospect of our visit. She arranged for us to stay with Tonio and Nuchi while we were in Asunción. Of course, in Ybycuí we would stay with her. In addition, she planned to celebrate the grand opening of her new hotel in town during our visit. She and Don Lalo had sold his family's property and cattle in a remote area outside of Ybycuí that they referred to as the *Cordillera* (mountain range). With the proceeds, they were building the *Hotel Py-tu-ú Rendá* (The Place to Rest Hotel). Ña Niní wanted us there for her special event.

The Peace Corps would lend us Daniel, a Volunteer from nearby La Colmena, to work on the census. Margarita promised us three SENASA inspectors for the research. Peace Corps and SENASA both pledged to cover the expenses of their personnel while in Ybycuí. With Stephen, I would have five people under my supervision to conduct the census. I began believing I could pull off the research. Although my plane ticket would wipe out our savings, I felt like I had won the lottery.

∞∞∞

When Stephen left for Chile in early June, we began our longest separation since I had moved to Ybycuí in 1974. We wrote letters and managed a few pre-arranged phone calls. He spent time in some of Santiago's major hospitals seeing children with varying degrees of nutritional deficiencies, including some suffering from kwashiorkor (malnutrition due to lack of protein) and marasmus (wasting away due to lack of protein and carbohydrates). Stephen wrote to me that it was gut-wrenching.

In the privacy of the home of Fernando's parents, he had the opportunity to ask questions about contemporary Chilean politics. General Pinochet was still in power, brutally persecuting those showing any hint of opposition. People attempted to keep a low profile and meet the challenges they faced. However, life for many Chileans remained difficult, and the suffering of malnourished children was one of the consequences of hard economic times and political repression.

In late June, as my plane descended to land in Luque at Paraguay's new international airport, I saw the old terminal through which Stephen and I had left in 1976. It was the first of many changes I would see. For the next month, my eyes searched for the familiar and assessed the new.

My palpable excitement stemmed from a yearning to see Stephen, the anticipated reunion with dear friends, and the urge to plunge into my research project. While I felt confident about getting everything done in a month, I remembered in the back of my mind some advice from an anonymous sage about timelines: "Estimate to the best of your ability the time it will take until completion, and then double it."

Stephen and Tonio met me inside the new airport with strong welcoming hugs. As we left for Tonio's house, I noticed the increase in traffic and the expansion of paved roads. There had been considerable new construction in and around the capital in the past six years. The urban sprawl of Asunción was evident beyond San Lorenzo, now reaching out to encompass Itaguá, Ellen's town where the spiderweb lace was made. The electrical grid had expanded, reaching the homes of very poor communities and into more rural areas. However, in outlying parts of the country, we still saw ox carts, palm trees, termite hills, and fields of *mandioca*, cotton, and tobacco. Also, the welcoming people of Paraguay seemed the same.

A month at a frenzied pace promptly commenced, much like the first months on the Ybycuí project. During the first few days in Paraguay, Stephen and I met with Kate and Ann at the Peace Corps office and Margarita at SENASA to confirm the general work plan and fill in necessary details. Dr. Orihuela, advised of my research, graciously conveyed to the Peace Corps that he would make the sanitation room at the health center available to me. Margarita suggested we might want an updated map of Ybycuí, and she just happened to have one available that I could copy at one of the new Xerox stores in Asunción. Recalling how I had typed stencils and laboriously traced pictures with carbon paper only six years earlier, I jumped at the opportunity to get a couple of accurate copies of a current Ybycuí map. While out on that errand, I purchased blank newsprint and markers for myself and tote bags and ink pens for the inspectors.

A few days later on an overcast day, Stephen and I set out for Ybycuí without worrying about a possible *clausura* because the road was now paved all the way to town. Tonio, the only board-certified neurosurgeon in Paraguay, chauffeured us in his Mercedes Benz, shipped from the U.S.A. with my sister's help. Approaching the outskirts of Ybycuí, we took note of the new cotton factory, mentioned in Ña Niní's letters, that had brought jobs along with workers' lung problems likely caused by cotton dust particles and inadequate ventilation. Proceeding along the main street, we noticed it had been turned into a lovely avenue with an ornamental water fountain at the site where Bernardino Caballero's statue had been. His likeness was moved to the intersection where the homes of Ña Niní and Tomasa stood. Before I knew it, Tonio parked in front of the Feltes' home adjacent to Ña Niní's new hotel. She emerged from her front door to greet us with open arms.

Ña Niní hadn't changed a bit. In my mind, she would never change. There would always be that twinkle in her eyes, the hint of a smile on her face, and her welcoming bear hugs and cheek kisses. Those images are forever imbedded in my memory.

After lunch, Tonio returned to Asunción. Stephen and I settled into Ña Niní and Don Lalo's home, enjoying the conversation, warmth, and love surrounding us. In the late afternoon, Ña Niní handed me the keys to her small Toyota pick-up truck and announced, "You and I are going to pay a social visit to Ña Elisa."

With a pained voice, I asked, "Do we have to?"

She replied, "Sí, Marilú, it's best we get it over with." As I drove us a short distance to the house where I had first lived, bad memories of that woman flooded my brain, including my stolen bras, her red face glowering at me, and her outrageous claim that *I* was gossiping about *her*.

Just before leaving the vehicle, I asked with a twinge of panic in my voice, "What do I say?"

Ña Niní responded, "Don't worry. This visit will make it clear that you are still under my protection. It's a subtle way to minimize her gossiping about you." With that, Ña Niní took charge, clapped her hands at the gate, and dominated our brief conversation with a surprised and cowed Ña Elisa. It was over before I knew it, and I drove us back to the refuge of the Feltes' home with a sense of relief. It would be the last time I'd ever see Ña Elisa.

For the next few weeks, I would face almost nonstop census work, but I was buoyed by being in Ybycuí and staying in Ña Niní's home. One personal thing had changed. Although close friends still called me *"Marilú,"* acquaintances addressed me as *"Ña Marilú,"* as I was now a respectable married woman.

The first morning, Stephen and I were up early. Walking together at a swift pace down the roads of Ybycuí to the health center, we greeted passersby with smiles and the traditional greeting of *"adiós."* Upon arrival, we were welcomed by Dr. Orihuela, Ña Irma, nurse María Luisa, Miriam, and Nimia, along with the background noise of construction workers building a new two-story addition to the health center. After exchanging appropriate salutations, we proceeded to the sanitation room to meet Daniel from La Colmena and the three SENASA inspectors, Alberto, Benicio, and Martín.

As we neared the room, I heard them nervously talking in Spanish about the important North American researcher and her husband who had arrived in a Mercedes Benz the day before. Stifling a smile, I strode into the room with Stephen and saw uncomfortable faces awaiting us. I thought to myself, "This is good, and I will take advantage of it." If they were nervous, they would likely work hard. In my best professional demeanor, I introduced myself and Stephen, thanked them for their willingness to participate in the research, and immediately got down to business.

Spreading out my new map of Ybycuí onto a table along with a large stack of blank SENASA inspection forms, I outlined the purpose of the research. Together we would efficiently and professionally document changes in sanitation conditions from 1974 to 1982. I emphasized that both Peace Corps and SENASA were very interested in this research, as was Yale University in North America. I reviewed with them how they were to rate the sanitation facilities, utilizing the same SENASA standards they had been trained in and that Dave and Stephen had used in 1974.

In the previous weeks, I had thought through the research methodology, refining it with input from Kyle and Stephen. A few days earlier, when I offered Stephen his choice of barrios to inspect, he selected Sanja León, his favorite section of town and the neighborhood where my pink house was. The Ledezma family lived in that area, and Stephen was eager to visit with them. Sanja León was the farthest barrio from the health center but it had fewer houses than the other assignments. He wanted time to make small talk and drink *yerba mate* on occasion. After all, Stephen was on vacation from medical school.

I assigned each of the other four inspectors a neighborhood, indicating on my large map the blocks of homes each would visit, with one inspection form used for each house. If an inspector skipped a house for whatever reason, he should make a note on the form and revisit the property until the latrine had been inspected. Based on the number of homes and walking distances in each barrio in the 1974 census, I had a good idea of how many inspections had to be done by each man during a half-day session in order for the census to be completed on time. I gave them target numbers but encouraged them to exceed my expectations if possible. After completing a half-day of inspections, an inspector was to return to the sanitation room and submit his forms to me.

My team of inspectors listened intently with serious faces. After accepting the totes, ink pens, and blank forms I offered them, we left the health center together, walking to a starting point for the first inspector and reviewing the boundaries of his neighborhood. While he set to work, I led the other four to the next closest barrio, pointing out landmarks and orienting them before continuing to another section of town. When the third and fourth inspectors began their work, I gave Stephen a quick hug and kiss before he proceeded to Sanja León. It was a liberty I had never dared to take in public as a single woman.

Returning to the health center and alone with my thoughts for the first time since landing in Paraguay, I closed the door to the sanitation room and sat down at the big table. Over in the corner were the inspection forms completed by Dave and Stephen in 1974. I had already recorded the results of the first census in my master notebook. My morning task was to organize and prepare the notebook for the tallying of the 1982 census as the first of the inspections were happening.

I completed my work and opened the door moments before Daniel, Martín, Benicio, and Alberto appeared in quick succession. With serious looks on their faces, each one handed over a stack of papers to me. As they left for lunch, I asked that they return by 2:30. Stephen crossed paths with them on their way out. Although his stack was slightly smaller, the grin on his face told me everything. He was having fun.

I looked at my piles of latrine forms and took a deep breath. Stephen pulled up a chair to sit beside me, and we counted the forms in the five stacks. All five inspectors had slightly surpassed their first target numbers! Feeling giddy, I took his arm, and we walked across town to Ña Niní's house for lunch. I paid particular attention to the latrines in the backyards along the way. One lot made me grin—the foundation of a new home had been started, but a solid brick latrine had already been completed. I wholeheartedly approved of that family's priority.

Back at the health center in the afternoon, I dispatched my crew with blank forms, target numbers, and a warm smile before proceeding to tally their morning's work. Upon their return three hours later, the men looked tired and worn. I asked them to sit down and tell me how it was going. They all replied that things were going well. No complaints, no problems. After they submitted their afternoon forms, I gave them positive feedback for their morning accomplishments. From the data in my notebook, I was summarizing the results by neighborhood on the newsprint, and they could see in a glance the fruits of their labors. We still had a lot of work to do, but at the pace they were going, it would be completed on time. Although there was rain in the forecast that might slow us down, it wouldn't stop us. I thanked them for their work and told them I'd give them daily updates of our progress. "Good job! Let's keep it up! See you here tomorrow morning at 7:30." It was obvious that SENASA had sent me three of their best. Daniel, an earnest, pleasant Volunteer, seemed pleased to be working with us. My sweet Stephen rounded out my stellar team.

That evening, I conducted my first of seven interviews of town leaders to ask their opinions about sanitation in town and to document changes that had occurred in Ybycuí in the eight years since the first census. I began with Ña Niní. She had already helped me identify the other six leaders to approach, and she was pleased to be the first interviewee. Based on her feedback, I adjusted some of my wording of the interview questions. Afterwards, she and I talked about the day. Ña Niní was busy planning the hotel's grand opening, which was to take place on Saturday. I told her about how the inspectors had nervously reacted to me. And then we laughed. Stephen joined us, and we laughed some more. The three of us were optimistic that this was going to work out well.

The second and third days of the census-taking were as good as the first. The team worked hard, slightly exceeding their target numbers, and appreciated my positive feedback about their progress. When the rain came, my inspectors were willing to work through it. It slowed them down slightly, but they slogged on. Because people stayed home when it rained, the men saved some time by avoiding multiple visits to a property with nobody at home. The rain also affected Stephen in a funny way. He had lingered at a home in Sanja León to join the family in a circle to drink tea. As they were getting settled and amiably chatting, he asked about the quality of the well water, one of the topics on the sanitation form. "Oh, Esteban, the water is good here. It's good most of the time. Yes, it's good except when it rains, and then we find little bugs in the water."

While Stephen looked out into the rain falling onto the muddy ground, he was offered the container of *yerba mate*. Remembering the "hot-cold" qualities of food and drink that shouldn't be mixed, he politely responded, "Gracias, but I just ate some meat."

By the end of the first week, we had made formidable progress. After Daniel and the three SENASA inspectors left for the weekend, Stephen and I watched the bustle of the preparations for the hotel's grand opening while trying not to get in the way. On Saturday morning, the food began appearing—lots of bite-sized food of all sorts, including meats, cheese, crackers with spread, little sandwiches, *sopa paraguaya*, cakes and other sweets. Vases of colorful flowers graced the tables. Pitchers of beverages were set out, along with small plates, napkins, and glasses. Out-of-town friends and relatives arrived, including Carlitos (the youngest Feltes), Tonio, Nuchi, and their children. Stephen and I were introduced to some people for the first time, and I hoped I wouldn't be quizzed on their names afterwards. The threatening clouds released rain early in the morning, but only some sprinkles fell as the hour of the ribbon-cutting ceremony approached. People gathered on the paved road outside the new hotel.

When the priest and town officials arrived, Ña Niní and Don Lalo appeared at the red, white, and blue ribbon (the colors of the Paraguayan flag) stretched across the double-door entrance to the hotel. With a large pair of sewing scissors in her hand, Ña Niní waited for the priest to complete his blessing in Guaraní. The crowd cheered as she and Don Lalo cut the ribbon together. I was grateful to be present for the special celebration and was especially happy for Ña Niní and Don Lalo. They would no longer be separated by Don Lalo's need to tend the herd of cattle in the *Cordillera*.

The guests then streamed inside to help themselves to the abundance of food before wandering around the new building. The main area was the dining room, lined with chairs along the walls and ample for eating and gathering. Family members were at stations outside some of the guest rooms in the rural two-story hotel to show the furnishings and amenities. Some rooms had private bathrooms, while guests in other rooms would use communal indoor facilities. There was also access to the flat roof with a brick floor and ample drains for rainwater. Parties and dances could be held on the rooftop, with lovely views of Ybycuí from two tall stories high. During our stay, Stephen and I returned to the roof a few times during daylight to enjoy the vista and by starlight to marvel at the immensity of the galaxies.

By Monday, the weather was sunny, and we forged ahead on the census. My team, while continuing at a brisk pace, began to smile. They were now more relaxed as they settled into their work routine. I continued daily briefings on the census progress. They worked their way through the town house-by-house, clapping their hands outside the fence or doorway, inspecting the facilities, and recording the data.

One mid-afternoon when Stephen returned early from Sanja León, I asked him to accompany me on an interview with Don Jorge, one of the town officials. He lived near the center of Ybycuí in an old building with a whitewashed façade and a tall double-door entrance. The dirt road in front of the edifice had eroded from rain, causing a 15-inch drop from the brick walkway at door level to the road. As we stood on the road, I clapped my hands, we waited, and I clapped my hands again. A teenaged girl in a white school uniform opened the heavy wooden door and looked down at us before shyly shifting her glance to avoid eye contact.

"Hello, how are you?" I greeted the girl in Guaraní while peering up at her. "We're looking for Don Jorge. Is he home?" Still averting her eyes, she shook her head in the negative. "Do you know when he might return?" Again, she shook her head to indicate no. "Well, I'd very much like to talk to him." This brought no response from her. Looking up at her and thinking she was old enough to be in elementary school when we were Volunteers, I asked her, "Do you know who we are?" She glanced our way before shaking her head yet again. I persisted, "Do you remember the *'Cevo-i* Song?'" Her body slightly straightened, and she stared directly at me, then at Stephen, and back to me again. I smiled and said, "We're Esteban and Marilú." Her eyes enlarged as she gaped at us.

Finally, her face broke into a huge grin, after which she replied, "Don Jorge will be back soon. Maybe in fifteen minutes. Come back then. I'll tell him you're coming." We returned a short time later, and I got my interview. It felt good that one of our students from seven years earlier had clearly remembered "The Hookworm Song" and the two of us.

In nine days, before the end of the second full week in Ybycuí, my amazing team had completed the sanitation census of 1982. In anticipation, I had notified SENASA and the Peace Corps in Asunción. Kate and three SENASA representatives arrived on Friday morning for a celebration at the health center. Along with Dr. Orihuela, the dignitaries from Asunción listened attentively as I presented my hand-tabulated overall results to them on newsprint. I explained my methodology and reported that the rate of sanitary facilities in town increased from 48% in 1974 to 73% in 1982. Enthusiastically, I sang the praises of my five-man team, SENASA, and the Peace Corps. Also, I acknowledged the work that Peggy and her counterpart had done to improve conditions in town. Back in New Haven, I would do a thorough computer analysis of the census and the leadership interviews before writing my thesis in English and translating it to Spanish. I promised copies to the Peace Corps, SENASA, and the Municipality, where later that day I gave the same presentation to a group of town leaders.

At Ña Niní's insistence, she prepared special refreshments in her hotel restaurant that day for my five inspectors, Kate, the SENASA dignitaries, and me. I felt I was living a dream. Stephen and I now knew that along with Dave, Martina, and Peggy, we had truly contributed something significant as Peace Corps Volunteers. I had the data to prove it.

Next came the difficult part—leaving Ña Niní again. This was my third good-bye, and it didn't get easier. "How can I thank you enough? We'll try to come back again," I whispered in her ear as we embraced. "I just don't know when."

Returning to Asunción for a few days, Stephen and I visited Margarita in the SENASA office to personally thank her for her support. I presented the same brief summary of the research project and preliminary results to other top officials there, emphasizing how helpful it was to have determined the extent of sanitation needs in 1974 and then to re-evaluate conditions eight years later. Our last stop was the Peace Corps office to thank Kate, Ann, and the staff there. Their support had been crucial to the success of the project. Before boarding the plane, I tucked my notebook filled with the data inside my jacket. If the plane were to crash and I somehow survived, I would have my data with me.

∞∞∞

Back in Connecticut, I returned to my full-time clinic job. After work, I punched the computer cards, one for each house in Ybycuí, to feed into the big mainframe at the Yale Computer Center. I wrote my computer program and submitted it to the computer along with my punched cards. Then, I poured over the printouts. (Even if personal computers had been readily available back in 1983, I could not have afforded one.) I then drafted my thesis in English with pencil and paper, preparing my final copy on an electric typewriter at Fair Haven Clinic.

Translating it into Spanish was tedious, but the prospect of typing it in Spanish was odious. While I typed in English almost as fast as I usually talked, typing in Spanish was challenging. My fingers tripped over themselves and automatically typed English combinations. For example, instead of "ción" at the end of a Spanish word, I would invariably type "tion." Because erasing and retyping made a messy document, I opted to learn a word processing software program with the help of Alicia from Argentina, a Yale undergraduate and Fair Haven Clinic volunteer. After a couple of lessons from Alicia at the Computer Center, I was cruising with word processing on the computer. I easily backspaced and corrected my English-oriented keystrokes to clean Spanish words, complete with appropriate accents and tildes, the squiggly symbols over the "n." I translated and typed through the autumn and into the winter, finally being true to my word and sending thesis copies to Paraguay via the Peace Corps office in Washington, D.C., in the early spring of 1983.

My in-depth analyses of sanitation conditions verified the rough tallies I had done while in Ybycuí and also provided more detailed information. My computer analysis confirmed the improvement from 48% sanitary facilities in 1974 to 73% in 1982, a 35% increase. The findings were statistically significant, meaning that the improvement was highly unlikely to have occurred by chance. When I looked at the data by neighborhood, I found that all of the barrios had experienced an increase in sanitary latrines, ranging from a 24% improvement in the center of town to a 100% improvement in the southeastern neighborhood of Santa Teresita. Although there were still 27% of the homes with unsanitary latrines or no facility at all, the improvements during the eight previous years were impressive.

Access to running water had also improved. Since Stephen and I had left in 1976, the town of Ybycuí had installed two elevated water tanks and piping that provided running water to a portion of the town. There were 107 residences (11% of the total) that had tapped into the system and were rated as a #1 facility (modern bathroom on the town's water system.) These were concentrated in and around the center of town.

The interviews that I conducted with the seven town leaders identified health education, sanitation work by Peace Corps Volunteers and SENASA inspectors, economic improvements, and social pressure as helpful factors influencing improved sanitation. Overall, the leaders perceived that sanitation and public health had greatly improved. My study, "A Description and Analysis of the Changes in Sanitation Conditions in a Rural Paraguayan Town, 1974 and 1982," suggested that concerted efforts can foster changes in basic health practices and lead to improved health in the developing world.

It was a glorious feeling to document the impressive progress in improving sanitation conditions in Ybycuí. Peggy and her SENASA counterpart had built on the intensive educational campaign begun by Martina and Dave and continued by Stephen and me according to Chuck's proposal. I had provided evidence of the positive contribution by Peace Corps Volunteers in a developing country. Collectively, we represented some significant steps in the process of improving health in Paraguay. At the time, I wondered if our teacher training had also helped to better conditions in other parts of Paraguay. Stephen and I also hoped that other Volunteers had utilized our materials and curriculum. I had to wait six years for a letter indicating that they had.

In August 1988, an RPCV from Paraguay named David Einhorn wrote to me. He had met our friend and fellow RPCV Burl (A.K.A. Reynaldo) at the Pan American Health Organization in Washington, D.C. Burl suggested he write to us about his Peace Corps experience. David had lived and worked in a town halfway between Villarrica and Caaguazú, in the Ybytyruzú Mountains, which he described as "the world's most unpronounceable mountain chain." He had become involved with the "making of a documentary film commemorating Peace Corps' 20th anniversary in Paraguay." The Peace Corps had selected David's site for the film, which featured a home visit, latrine construction, and David playing the guitar and singing "The Hookworm Song" with school children. He wrote us that our song, "*La Canción de Cevo-í,*" was immortalized in the film. David had added a hookworm dance between the two verses so that the kids could squirm around in imitation of blood-sucking parasites.

During his Peace Corps service, David said that 150 latrines were built and 200 cement floors were sold in his town. He concluded:

"The anti-parasite program has by now become so fine-tuned and well-developed that Volunteers pretty much need only to follow the directions…I write with no other motive other than this.

Burl tells me you are his good friends and that you have continued to maintain an active interest in Paraguay, a country I think all of us have come to love to some degree or another."

David's letter, which I returned to its envelope and tucked into the hard-bound copy of my thesis, left me with a warm glow of happiness.

∞∞∞

On a mild, sunny day in May of 1983, Stephen and I graduated from Yale. My parents, with pride gleaming in their eyes, witnessed our graduation. While we both wore black caps and gowns, Stephen's tassel and hood, the velvety sash covering indicating the graduate's school, were green for medicine; mine were salmon for public health. Stephen and I first attended the massive, all-encompassing graduation speeches on the largest grassy area at Yale. Next, we found my parents, and the four of us went to part of the public health ceremony so that I could be acknowledged and receive my diploma along with graduates receiving joint degrees before proceeding to Stephen's ceremony. As we were leaving the public health event, students who had received international scholarships were being acknowledged by the professor who had selected the recipients. I was sorry I wasn't part of that group, but I had returned to Paraguay anyway.

Dashing over to a tented grassy area near the medical school, we found my in-laws along with the seats they had saved for us. Stephen received his diploma and also an award for the best medical school thesis in his class. The award had nothing to do with child nutrition in Chile, although he had written up a brief summary of his experience for the scholarship committee. Upon his return from Chile and Paraguay in the summer of 1982, he had worked in a genetics laboratory and had discovered the chromosome responsible for producing alpha-1 antitrypsin, an important human protein.

∞∞∞

Stephen opted to pursue pediatrics, not because he wanted to follow in his father's footsteps but rather because he enjoyed dealing with children and felt he could play a positive role in their lives. While his dad had a stellar career in medical academia, Stephen preferred community health with low-income families. He was placed in the program at Children's Hospital National Medical Center in Washington, D.C., for his three-year residency training. In June 1983, we returned to the D.C. area, this time finding a comfortable red brick house to rent in Hyattsville, Maryland, a mere 15 minutes from the hospital. With a loan from my parents, we purchased a new blue Toyota Tercel station wagon. I drove the new car while Stephen commuted in our brown Corolla.

On his first rotation, Stephen was assigned to adolescent medicine and befriended Ozzie, a pediatrician specializing in that field. I soon met Ozzie, who told me about La Clínica del Pueblo/Wilson Community Health Center, a free clinic for undocumented refugees from El Salvador displaced by war, at which he volunteered. He thought I might be interested in helping out.

Located in the Adams-Morgan neighborhood of the District of Columbia, La Clínica was a makeshift medical service open one evening a week. Organized by a handful of volunteers, it had a shoestring budget for supplies, materials, and essential expenses. Funding sources were donations and small grants from private foundations. I began as a volunteer and dove into the work with a passion. In early

1984, I became its part-time, paid director. When Stephen became a licensed physician in his second year of residency, he volunteered when his demanding schedule permitted.

Looking back on the experience, I can see my time at La Clínica as a natural sequel to my work in Paraguay and the Fair Haven Clinic. At La Clínica, I made two major contributions: 1) I improved the physical setup by making dividers of wood and fabric, styled after the ones in Ybycuí's health center, to provide visual privacy in the large room we used for intakes; and 2) I developed and taught a health promoter training course for a dozen community volunteers using two resources written by the Hesperian Foundation, *Where There is No Doctor* and *Helping Health Workers Learn*. I taught the course in Spanish for the predominantly Salvadoran volunteers. Those who hoped to return to El Salvador someday wanted skills that would be needed in a war-torn country, but the immediacy of refugee needs compelled all of the volunteers to learn as much as they could as quickly as possible. They learned to do effective intakes at La Clínica, including writing the chief complaint and taking vital signs. In addition to serving as translators for English-speaking medical volunteers, they helped with follow-up steps to the care provided onsite. I remember them fondly for their dedication and devotion to people in need.

Sonia, a regular volunteer nurse who witnessed the brutal execution of her fiancé by the military in El Salvador before she fled, gave her time and energy as part of her own healing from personal trauma. In turn, I helped her by making her wedding dress when I heard she was to marry. After taking her measurements, we drove to a fabric store where she selected a pattern for a long dress and an elegant ivory satin brocade fabric. Thinking about the special dress Ña Niní had made for me, I gave Sonia's dress to her as a wedding gift.

At La Clínica, we tended to the basic health needs of a population affected by war. Some patients had minor aches, pains, and infections. Many had emotional anxieties. Others had multiple medical needs. For instance, adults had diabetes, hypertension, and sometimes cardiac problems. Also, children needed vaccines. When a small child came in with a live cockroach in his ear, a physician carefully extracted it with long tweezers.

A two-year-old boy sticks out in my mind as a victim of his circumstances. He and an older brother had fled El Salvador for the D.C. area to join their parents, who had barely escaped with their lives six months earlier. The two boys had been held by Mexican immigration for several weeks in threatening, unhealthy conditions before they successfully entered the U.S. The mother brought the toddler to us asking for vaccinations, treatment of a respiratory infection, a dental referral, and help with insomnia. It was the insomnia that got to me—the thought of a little boy unable to sleep due to emotional trauma brought tears to my eyes. Our medical providers did what they could, and our patient population was grateful as well as understanding about our limitations.

As I write about this program thirty-five years later, La Clínica del Pueblo is a Federally Qualified Health Center in its own facility in the Adams-Morgan neighborhood with over 110 employees dedicated to "build a healthy Latino community through culturally appropriate health services, focusing on those most in need."

In August of 1984, I became pregnant. Anticipating increased stress on our family budget, I sought to supplement our income with short-term work in addition to Stephen's salary as a pediatric resident and what I earned at La Clínica. Upon inquiring at the Peace Corps Office about job postings in the area, I was directed to Creative Associates, a for-profit corporation owned by four women. Creative Associates intended to respond to a Request for Proposals (RFP) from the Peace Corps to develop a *Peace Corps In-Service Training Manual*, and they needed a grant writer. I immediately applied and was hired. Good luck stayed with me. Our proposal, the only one submitted, was funded. I was promptly employed as one of two writers for the project. The other writer was a slender, tenacious man named Daniel. Even though he had not served in the Peace Corps, he had extensive community development experience in Africa. Our skills and backgrounds were complementary and our personalities compatible.

Daniel and I began writing in the latter part of 1984, following the format and developing the topics that the Peace Corps had suggested. The manual would be used worldwide by trainers expecting to pick up the materials and conduct sessions with minimal preparation. In-service training took place around the half-way (one-year) mark of the Peace Corps service. This is the time when Volunteers were long past the honeymoon period and wondered what and how they might ever accomplish anything. I remembered it vividly.

The two of us divided up the topics and began developing the sessions. Once a section was drafted, we'd edit it together, assuring our ideas were applicable to a variety of cultures and potentially helpful to Volunteers. Daniel and I proposed group discussions and problem-solving sessions guided by trainers as well as role playing by Volunteers. In addition, we included handouts for Volunteers to use when they returned to their assignments. Daniel wrote an insightful session on identifying natural leaders in a community, which triggered my thoughts about how the Ybycuí project might have been handled differently. Next, we developed the sessions dealing with stress, bribes, loneliness, and frustration, including recognizing when counseling might help and tips on being a peer counselor to fellow Volunteers. I drafted the segment on "How to Write a Funding Proposal" and included a sample proposal embedded with flaws for Volunteers to find and critique. Building on my positive as well as challenging experiences in Paraguay, low-income housing development, and health, I provided helpful parameters for clearly defining the need, budgeting time and resources, and building true ownership of the project.

As I grew in size during my third trimester in early 1985, my energy declined considerably. At noontime, I ate a quick lunch, closed my office door, and spread my coat on the floor for a needed nap. After completing our work in late March of 1985, Daniel and I received praise from Creative Associates and Peace Corps. In April, Stephen and I welcomed our son Matthew into the world.

With Stephen's demanding schedule as a pediatric resident, I opted to become a stay-at-home mom. As much as I loved La Clínica del Pueblo, I loved my infant more. Before resigning as part-time director, I trained Ed and Gretta to assume my responsibilities. Both were dedicated and reliable clinic volunteers who had taken my health promoter training course. The clinic's board hired Ed to replace me. Gretta helped out until she moved to Central America to work as a health promotor.

Once the transition was completed, I became a full-time mom and amateur photographer, with my baby as the subject. After each roll of film was developed, I ordered copies of the best pictures to send to Ña Niní and Tomasa. Both were faithful letter correspondents.

With my census team in front of Ybycuí's health center;
(the man in the upper right is a SENASA supervisor)

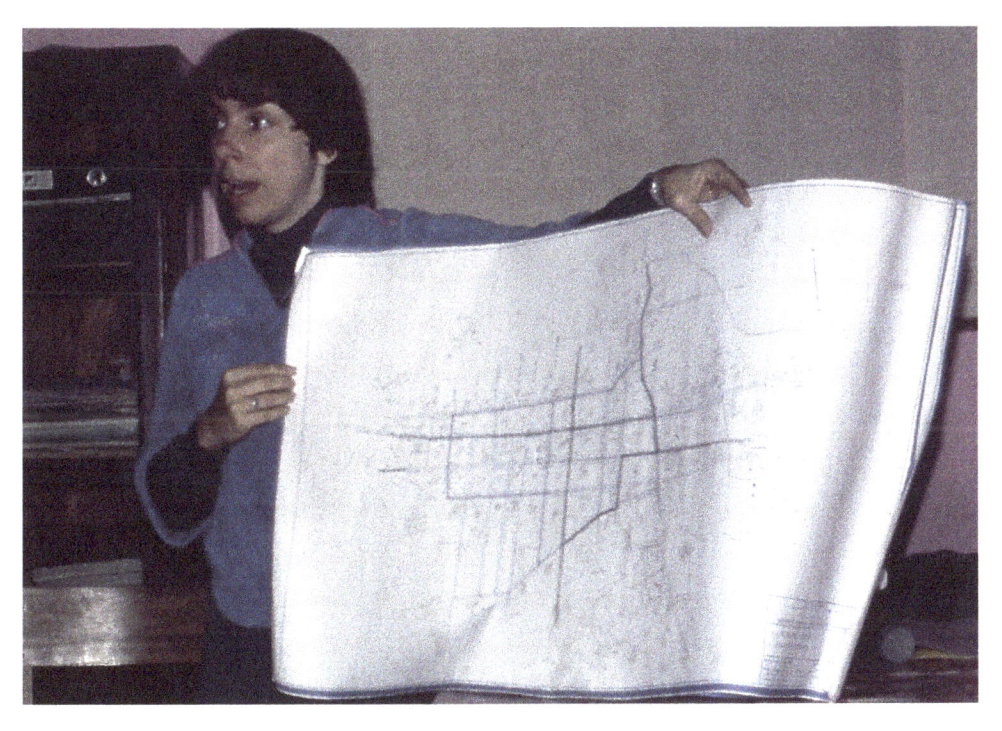

Presenting the results of my research to Ybycuí's town leaders

The priest blessing the new hotel, with Ña Niní on the right holding the ribbon and Don Lalo on the far right

Ña Niní's new hotel

The two of us, wearing Paraguayan *aho po-í*, celebrating our graduation from Yale University

CHAPTER 9

Growing Families

I sustain myself with the love of family.
–Maya Angelou

In early 1986, I heard my sister's voice over the phone. "We're trying to adopt from Paraguay," Cynthia told me. I was aware that she and her husband Henry had been wanting to begin a family for several years. After multiple attempts at medical interventions, Cynthia began dealing with adoption bureaucracies and governmental requirements. Over the age of 40, Henry was considered too old by domestic adoption agencies in their area. Cynthia happened upon an organization dealing with Paraguayan adoptions that was willing to work with them. Matthew turned a year old in April, and I was expecting again. I fervently hoped an adoption would happen for them before our second child arrived in November. However, their agency began fizzling out in mid-1986 and soon closed. Cynthia was devastated.

I was in the middle of packing up our household in Maryland when Cynthia called me about their dashed hope for a Paraguayan adoption. Stephen was about to complete his pediatric residency, and we were moving to rural south-central Florida for his three-year National Health Service Corps commitment in a medically-underserved area. He was placed at a community health center in Frostproof, in the heart of Florida where citrus orchards flourished. We had found a house in nearby Avon Park close to the hospital where Stephen would admit ill children. Also, he was required to cover outpatient pediatric services in a clinic 20 miles away in Wauchula. Fortunately, my parents had retired to a mobile home senior community less than two hours from us in Apollo Beach, just south of Tampa. Their house was on a canal leading to Tampa Bay, and Dad's newly purchased fishing boat was always ready at their dock just outside the back door. I looked forward to living closer to them.

Rural Florida, a far cry from the major beach and urban areas on the peninsula's Atlantic and Gulf coasts, is home to vast orange and grapefruit groves, endless rows of tomatoes and strawberries, and a variety of other produce. Inland and away from the urban areas, one finds the groves mixed into a rural vastness of sandy landscapes, palm trees, pine scrubs, and poverty. The area needed medical providers for Hispanic farm workers, the white rural poor, low-income African Americans, and Haitian immigrants. There were aspects of the scenery that reminded me of rural Paraguay—the palm trees, summer heat, humidity, and a sense of remoteness from urban life. Like Paraguay, Florida had fire ants, causing me to be on the alert for where I placed my feet.

While taking a break from unpacking boxes and gazing out the window of my Avon Park home to the view of subtropical greenery, I called Tomasa in Paraguay to talk about adoptions. "Hello, Tomasa, how are you?" I asked in Guaraní before switching to Spanish. It was always a thrill to hear her voice on the phone. After our usual pleasantries, I brought up Cynthia and Henry's situation. I could hear the heightened interest in Tomasa's voice as she told me she'd make some inquiries. She was living in Asunción with her sister Nena and brother-in-law Arturo. Being in the capital would make it easy to obtain information. We would talk again soon, she assured me.

Less than two weeks later, Tomasa called me back with hope in her voice. She had a cousin who knew the right people and understood the adoption system in Paraguay for foreigners. We began to exchange legal information by certified mail and made a series of phone calls to nudge along the process. Tomasa assured me that something good would happen. And when it did, she told me, Cynthia and Henry would travel to Paraguay and stay with her, Nena, and Arturo.

During one of our phone calls in mid-July, Tomasa asked if she could visit us in Avon Park for the month of August. I was thrilled beyond words! "Fly into Orlando and I will pick you up at the airport! Just let me know when!" I replied. It was surprising that her mother and brothers would let her travel by herself. Although Tomasa was 37 years old, they were overly protective of her because of her lupus diagnosis. Tomasa told me that she had to promise them she'd take good care of herself and not go on any risky rides at Disney World, like Space Mountain or the roller coaster. I excitedly told Stephen, my parents, and Cynthia of Tomasa's impending visit.

I was almost six months pregnant when I put Matthew in his car seat for the drive to the Orlando airport one humid, sweltering August day. Thankfully, my blue car was air conditioned. Only air conditioning made Florida livable…barely. Shortly after we had moved to Florida, Stephen discovered a problem with the brown car. It lacked air conditioning. And now, the heat would not shut off. Too busy and with money too tight to have the car looked at, he rolled down all of the windows and let the wind evaporate his sweat while going from our house to Wauchula to the hospital and so forth. I was ever so grateful for my air-conditioned vehicle and home. I didn't have to suffer through the heat and humidity almost as severe as what I had experienced in Paraguay.

Hugs, cheek kisses, and loving greetings in Guaraní were followed by Tomasa cooing to little Matthew. Although tired after her long journey by air, Tomasa doted on Matthew during the drive to Avon Park. Once back home, I put Matthew down for a nap and found the free lupus resource in Spanish that I had sent for after seeing an advertisement in the *Parade* supplement to the Sunday newspaper a few weeks earlier. "This is for you to look at while I fix dinner," I told her. Settling onto the couch, she began reading. Several minutes later, Stephen arrived home. I called out to Tomasa, but she didn't answer. I peered around to see her on the couch completely absorbed in the lupus resource. I spoke again. When she didn't respond, I thought it best to let her read.

An hour after I had handed the information to her, she looked up with tears of joy in her eyes, as if awakening from a miraculous dream. The first words she uttered were, "You have changed my life with this!" She sprung up to greet Stephen with a hug before leafing through the papers to read us some excerpts, the most important one being that people with lupus can lead a normal life, including marrying and having children. Although pregnancy could carry risks and some complications, her lupus did not prohibit Tomasa from trying. "I'm taking this home with me for my mother to read," she stated with a determined look in her eyes that I hadn't previously seen. She disappeared into the guest room to place the document in her suitcase and reappeared with a special gift for me made by Ña Niní—a frilly orange and white cotton maternity dress that fit me perfectly. Whenever I wore it during the remainder of my pregnancy, I felt enveloped with her love.

With Tomasa as my constant companion, the month of August flew by. My parents drove over from Apollo Beach to take care of Matthew while I took Tomasa to Disney World. The sun was fiercely hot and the humidity oppressively high, but we were protected with large hats and hydrated via water bottles. The two of us frequently rested in the shade to people-watch and enjoy each other's company. Also, we stuck to the gentle attractions like "It's a Small World" and the train ride around the park, fulfilling her life-time dream to visit Disney World.

In the evenings in Avon Park, we dined at home with Stephen before he returned to the hospital to do his rounds. We spent time in Apollo Beach, fishing on Tampa Bay with Dad while Mom tended Matthew. Cynthia flew down for a weekend to meet Tomasa for the first time and talk about the status of the adoption effort. At the end of the month, I was saddened to have my dear Paraguayan friend leave, but we parted with high hopes for a bright future. Tomasa was determined to live a normal life in spite of lupus, and she was upbeat about Cynthia and Henry's adoption prospects.

∞∞∞

On November 5th, Stephen and I welcomed our son Daniel into the world in a hospital near my parents' home in Apollo Beach. We were filled with joy at our family of four! Daniel's birth meant more photos and letters to Ña Niní and Tomasa.

Cynthia, Henry, and I were still waiting to hear from Tomasa about an adoption. Although all of the paperwork had been completed, an available baby had not yet appeared. Then, just before Thanksgiving, Tomasa called me with the news that a healthy newborn girl had been found on a bench of the Itaguá health center five days after I delivered Daniel. The birth mother was nowhere to be found and had likely thought a health center would be a safe place to leave her infant. Tomasa asked, "Did Cynthia and Henry want this baby girl?" After a quick phone call to my sister, consisting mostly of happy, hysterical sobbing, I called back Tomasa to do some tentative planning. Cynthia and Henry would travel to Paraguay in early December for a three-week stay, which was the estimated time in-country for completing the adoption process.

Except for December's heat and humidity, my sister and brother-in-law's trip to Paraguay was a dream come true. With their English-Spanish dictionary and pantomiming, they dealt with the language barrier. When an attorney fluent in German appeared, they had an easier time, as German was Henry's first language. From Spanish to German to English and then the reverse, legalities were understood. The moment they saw their daughter Sara and held her, it was love at first sight. They were allowed to keep her with them from that initial visit, and the household of Tomasa, Nena, and Arturo promptly adapted to the new addition. Henry and Arturo had bonded immediately, helped by hand signals. Arturo would make the brief motions to ask, "Do you want a beer?" Henry would cock his head and grin, prompting Arturo to uncap two ice-cold beers for them to sip in the heat of the Paraguayan summer.

One evening Tomasa, Nena, and Arturo took their visitors to dinner at a restaurant specializing in grilled meats. Cynthia was in the process of cutting a piece of beef when it mysteriously curled up in the manner that a live tongue would. She stopped cutting, caught Tomasa's eye and stuck out her tongue, pointing to her plate with a questioning look on her face. Stifling a giggle, Tomasa affirmed Cynthia's fear that she was eating a cow's tongue. Everyone at the table broke out in laughter, with Tomasa laughing the hardest. My sister couldn't continue with that exotic culinary experience and looked for a cut of beef she would normally eat. Henry ate the tongue.

While waiting for the attorneys to complete the documentation filings, Tomasa drove Cynthia, Henry, and baby Sara to Ybycuí. Of course, Ña Niní wanted to meet them. When she saw Cynthia for the first time, Ña Niní immediately noticed the family resemblance and exclaimed, "She's a younger Marilú!" They stayed as non-paying guests in one of the air-conditioned rooms at Ña Niní's hotel and briefly got a taste of the food, culture, and hospitality of rural Paraguay. It had been a decade since we left the Peace Corps and six years since our return visit, but our ties to this landlocked country in the heart of South America were definitely lifelong.

Cynthia, Henry, and Sara flew to Tampa on December 23rd and drove out to Avon Park with my parents on Christmas Eve. What a chaotic, joyous celebration we had that year, with Matthew toddling around and two infants making their presence known.

∞∞∞∞

"I'm getting married!" Tomasa announced excitedly over the phone. Upon returning to Paraguay from her month's visit with us, Tomasa insisted her mother read the lupus information we had given her. After Cynthia and Henry's visit in December, Tomasa met and began dating Silvio, an agronomist who would initiate innovative agricultural practices in Paraguay. To my knowledge, he was the first Paraguayan to use drip irrigation and screens to shade crops from the intense Paraguayan sun. Tomasa and Silvio married in mid-1987 and moved to Lambaré, formerly a rural town that had been engulfed by Asunción's growth. For a wedding gift, Cynthia and I split the cost of fine Oneida stainless steel flatware, purchased and sent by my sister to Paraguay through a safe shipping industry contact she had.

∞∞∞∞

In 1988, presidential elections were held in Paraguay. General Stroessner and his Colorado Party candidates were elected again by large margins. Those in opposition maintained that elections were rigged, but with a reported 89% of the vote, Stroessner remained in power.

On February 3, 1989, six months into Stroessner's eighth term, I was astonished to hear on National Public Radio (NPR) that the general had been overthrown by his longtime friend and close advisor, General Andrés Rodríguez. My immediate phone calls to Paraguayan friends confirmed that they were all safe and hopeful for a future with a democratic form of government. They confirmed the NPR reporting that there had been brief fighting in downtown Asunción, but Rodríguez quickly consolidated his power. Stroessner was granted political asylum in Brazil a few days later. I expected General Rodriguez to become a dictator. However, elections were held in May 1993. The Colorado Party candidate, Juan Carlos Wasmosy, was inaugurated as the first civilian to hold the office in four decades.

I did not learn of what might have been behind Rodriguez's betrayal of Stroessner until researching the overthrow for this memoir. I found an explanation that rang true in Wikipedia's entry on Stroessner: "One reason for the *coup* was that the generals feared one of Stroessner's offspring would succeed him. Of the two, Alfredo (aka 'Freddie'), was a cocaine addict and Gustavo, a pilot, was loathed for being homosexual."

∞∞∞∞

In August 1989, Tomasa and Silvio adopted a baby daughter they named Silvana. Letters back and forth contained photos of our adorable children. During Silvana's first year of life, Stephen brought home a free colorful set of infant dinnerware—plate, bowl, spoon, and fork—that was too babyish for our boys. I decided to send the set to Paraguay for Silvana. Knowing that the Paraguayan postal service was still unreliable, I sent a certified letter separately to Tomasa and Silvio to let them know the box was on its way. When it didn't arrive within a reasonable period of time, Silvio took the letter to their local post office, read it to the clerk, and demanded his package, insisting that he would not leave the building without it. Luck was with him—the clerk appeared a short time later with the set. Silvio guessed that it soon would have disappeared into someone else's home had he not gone looking for it with a stern, determined face.

I maintained contact with my Paraguayan loved ones. In addition to Tomasa, Ña Niní continued writing. Her hotel was doing well, as were family members. Her son Carlitos had received a doctorate in biochemistry. In addition to working in the humble lab at the health center in Ybycuí, he also opened his own small laboratory in one of the storefront rooms of his mother's hotel. His wife Cesia had biochemistry and pharmacology degrees. By the early 1990s, Cesia and Carlitos had a set of identical twin boys, whom they named Soel and Abel.

Carlitos and Cesia had also begun researching the prevalence of Chagas disease in the rural areas around Ybycuí. Chagas is an ugly illness found mainly in poor rural areas of South and Central America. Insects called triatomine bugs transmit *Trypanosoma cruzi (T. cruzi)*, the parasite that causes Chagas. Via its feces, an infected bug can pass the parasite to a human. The bugs typically live in houses made of mud or adobe with palm thatch roofs. They hide in the roofs and wall crevices during the day. At night, they crawl out and tend to bite people's faces, giving them the nickname "kissing bugs." After they bite for some blood, they defecate on the person. An individual can develop Chagas disease if the parasite passes through a mucous membrane or break in the skin, possibly done through some scratching or rubbing during sleep. Most people have no symptoms for several years or even decades, but later in life, Chagas disease can cause serious cardiac or gastrointestinal complications. It is hypothesized that Charles Darwin suffered from Chagas disease. In March 1835, he noted in his journal that he was bitten by an insect that could have been a "kissing bug" while in the Argentine Andes. Darwin subsequently suffered from symptoms common to Chagas disease, but modern science hasn't confirmed or dispelled it. (See Wikipedia's entry on the health of Charles Darwin.)

I recall hearing about Chagas during Peace Corps training, but in 1974, its presence in Paraguay was not readily recognized. We trainees were told, "Oh, it's in Bolivia and parts of Brazil but not Paraguay." However, within a handful of years after our service, it was often identified in people throughout the rural areas of the country. Doctors were diagnosing and treating it but had no idea of how prevalent it was. With backing from some governmental agencies, Carlitos and Cesia conducted research in the outlying areas of Ybycuí to determine the prevalence of Chagas disease. They found it was quite common and, in many cases, very debilitating. (For more information on this disease, see cdc.gov, who.int, and Wikipedia's entry.)

Tonio and Nuchi, still living in Asunción, had their third son by the early 1990s. Tonio remained busy as the only board-certified neurosurgeon in the country. With strong ties to Ybycuí, Tonio built a lovely country home on his land outside of town where he and his family could escape the pressures of his career and spend time with his parents.

∞∞∞

In June 1989, Stephen and I relocated our family to the Yakima Valley in Washington State, where Stephen began working for a community health center. Once Matthew and Daniel were both in elementary school, I started teaching at Heritage College, a private institution with a nontraditional student body. The college needed an adjunct faculty member to teach introductory Spanish courses during the day. Although my master's degree was in public health, my undergraduate studies were in Spanish and secondary education. With my experience studying and working abroad in Spanish-speaking countries, I felt confident I could handle the teaching.

Most of the students in my Spanish classes were Native American or Hispanic working mothers. I tried my utmost to inspire my students through Hispanic culture, food, and music. I translated recipes into Spanish and prepared the particular food to share with them. After we discussed the recipe in Spanish, the students sampled the food. *Sopa paraguaya*, the tasty cornbread, was on my list, as was the caramelized milk called *dulce de leche*. I presented song lyrics in Spanish, along with a vocabulary list. I brought my guitar and cassette tapes to class so we could sing together, and my students often belted out a few Paraguayan songs (in Spanish, not Guaraní), as well as some from Mexico, Spain, and Chile. I told them simple jokes, most of which they understood. I also shared with them vocabulary variations from country to country, using as an example Pat's mistake of saying "*Hay un bicho en la ensalada*" ("There's a bug in my salad") during our Puerto Rican Peace Corps training.

It was particularly rewarding to help students of Mexican descent who were fluent in spoken Spanish become literate in their first language. I encouraged students whenever and however I could. When one woman told me she suffered from lupus, I set her up as a pen pal to Tomasa. The two-week delay for airmail letters was annoying, but when they did appear, life was sweet for the two pen pals. Teaching was a pleasure, especially when I expanded my courses beyond Spanish to include grant writing (for which I used the sessions from the *Peace Corps In-Service Training Manual*), demography, and health care management classes.

Throughout these years, Paraguay was ever-present in my mind and heart but particularly so when milestones in our lives occurred. In 1995, Ña Niní's husband Don Lalo passed away at the age of 78. By phone, Mary, Peggy, and I compiled a list of Returned Peace Corps Volunteers from Ybycuí and set about trying to contact them about Ña Niní's loss. Through Friends of Paraguay, a group based in Washington, D.C. of RPCVs, we found a number of them. We collected donations totaling over $500 to send to Ña Niní, with the intent that she would use the money to honor Don Lalo in some way. I purchased a cashier's check made out to her legal name, Haydee Cáceres de Feltes, and sent it by certified mail.

When I called her two weeks later, I was dismayed to hear that she had not yet received it. I returned to my bank, and they informed me the check had been endorsed and cashed in Montevideo,

Uruguay. They showed me a photocopy of the endorsement. Corruption in Paraguay had not gone away. It was Ña Niní's legal name, but it wasn't her handwriting. I raced home and returned to the bank with one of her letters to prove that. Furthermore, I had sent the check to Paraguay, not Uruguay. Because I had mailed it certified with insurance and still had the receipt, the bank was able to recoup the value of the cashier's check. I then purchased a second one. That check arrived safely, and Ña Niní, president of the town's committee to improve the health center at the time, donated it to the center in Don Lalo's name.

An interesting side story to that tale came through Mary from one of our Ybycuí RPCV contributors named Beto. On September 17, 1980, Beto left Peace Corps Paraguay and arrived at the Los Angeles airport, where he was detained for about 24 hours without being told why. When he was finally released, he learned that former Nicaraguan dictator Anastasio Somoza, who had been denied refuge in the U.S. by Jimmy Carter but received it from Stroessner in 1979, had been assassinated in Asunción a few hours before Beto's plane had taken off. Because Beto's passport lacked a required exit stamp, he was detained until it was confirmed who he was. It was soon learned that Somoza had been ambushed by a Sandinista commando team of four men and three women. According to the Wikipedia entry on Somoza, six of the seven escaped. The Sandinistas had forced the dictator out of Nicaragua 14 months earlier, but Somoza had apparently absconded with most of the money in the country's treasury.

∞∞∞∞∞

During my years raising our boys, I continued corresponding with Ña Niní and Tomasa, frequently sending them photographs of us. Their letters told me how their families were faring, along with Paraguay in general. As my children were vaccinated, I hoped that little Paraguayans were getting their needed protection against the common childhood diseases. As Paraguay's economy improved, I hoped that the health and welfare of its population were also doing better. Much of a good life depends on the places and circumstances under which children are born. However, there is also a question of happenstance, both good and bad. It might be referred to as serendipity or karma. I have had my share of advantages. Perhaps because of my own fortunate birth in the United States of America to parents who loved and wanted me, I grew up with empathy and wanted to share and give of myself.

Words to articulate this empathy came to my attention in 2012, when I began co-authoring a book with my father-in-law, Dr. Howard Pearson, the founding medical director of actor and philanthropist Paul Newman's The Hole in the Wall Gang Camp in Ashford, Connecticut. Paul established "Camp" for children with cancer and other life-threatening diseases, and it opened for its first sessions in the summer of 1988. My father-in-law was Camp Doc for the first 14 summers.

Something poignant we mentioned in the book, *Fulfilling Paul Newman's Dream—"Raising a Little Hell" and Healing at The Hole in the Wall Gang Camp*, was Paul Newman's reason for establishing Camp: "LUCK...How lucky are we who are blessed to have it, and how brutal it is in the lives of unlucky young kids who are struck by serious diseases who don't have time to turn it around." Children who had been through various medical hells were allowed to just be kids, having a riot of a time at a grand summer camp built just for them.

Paul's words reflect, in part, my own motivation for joining the Peace Corps and afterwards pursuing work in programs that attempt to help low-income people, particularly children, rise out of poverty. Being born into poverty or happening to be a member of a disadvantaged minority is a matter of not-so-good luck. Mitigating poverty-related problems like hookworm and dilapidated, overcrowded low-income housing or helping children through early learning programs like Head Start can make a remarkable difference in the lives of others. I have purposefully sought out these kinds of job opportunities for myself, hoping to make positive differences in the lives of others. In the process, Stephen and I did our best to instill good values in our children by example.

Pregnant and at my parents' home in Florida, with Tomasa, toddler Matthew, and Stephen

CHAPTER 10

Adventurous Vacations

The world is round so that friendship may encircle it.
–Pierre Teilhard de Chardin

Late one evening in the spring of 2003, I murmured to Stephen, "I'd like the four of us to vacation in Paraguay." It had been on my mind for several weeks. Also, it had been 21 years since Stephen and I had last been to Paraguay. Although Matthew and Daniel had heard us talk about the Peace Corps over the years and had met Paraguayans and a number of RPCVs, Paraguay wasn't real to them. They would have to smell it, taste it, and live it themselves in order for it to become real.

Stephen agreed it was time to take our boys, now 18 and 16 years old, for a two-week visit. Matthew was graduating from high school with honors and was preparing to attend Whitman College in Walla Walla, Washington. Daniel was completing his junior year in high school. Although they were willing to make the trip with us out of curiosity, neither was particularly gung-ho. Both had taken Spanish in high school and could speak a little of it, but they had never before experienced a language and cultural immersion. The idea of being language-dependent upon their parents likely lacked appeal, and they were reluctant to leave their girlfriends for two weeks.

While letters, photographs, and occasional phone calls had kept us up-to-date with our friends' lives, the gradual changes Paraguay had undergone hit Stephen and me all at once when we landed after the fatiguing air journey. We arrived on a Sunday in late June.

Our shuffle through customs and baggage claim, with the boys straggling behind us, was interrupted briefly by Ministry of Health staffers in white lab coats with surgical masks on their faces. Pausing as a group, we returned their stares and answered their questions in the negative. They were screening for people displaying any flu-like symptoms who might possibly have severe acute respiratory syndrome (SARS), a newly identified viral disease with a fatality rate of almost 10%. SARS had recently been identified in southern China, and it was classified as a corona virus. (No cases of this particular corona virus have been reported in the world since 2004. In 2017, scientists discovered that the 2002-

2003 outbreak was caused by horseshoe bats in Chinese caves. Given the horrors of the COVID-19 pandemic almost two decades later, the Paraguayans were wisely being cautious of SARS.) With the appropriate stamps on our passports, we were allowed to proceed toward the exit.

Tomasa and Silvio greeted us with bear hugs. In spite of their fatigue and wariness about the next two weeks, the boys returned the hugs and vigorous back slaps. Upon leaving the airport in Luque, Stephen and I immediately noticed the growth the country had experienced since our visit two decades earlier. Briefly closing my eyes to avoid gasping at the dodge-car craziness of the traffic, I heard the myriad noises—honking horns, screeching brakes—and felt Silvio swerving his vehicle with occasional jerks.

After some slow deep breathing to calm myself, I opened my eyes to take in the familiar mixed in with the new. The road system had greatly improved but was barely adequate for the increase in vehicles—buses packed with people and exuding diesel fumes, over-loaded trucks, cars of all makes and sizes, jeeps, motorcycles, and even occasional horse and ox carts. New buildings were under construction everywhere my eyes scanned, and they were evidence of the economic boom brought on by the establishment in 1991 of the southern common market called Mercosur. (While Paraguay, Brazil, Argentina, and Uruguay were the original full members of the trading bloc, today other countries in South America are associate members, and Mexico and New Zealand are observing countries. Venezuela, an early full member, was suspended from the agreement in 2016 for political reasons, as that country was perceived as communistic.)

The free flow of goods and people allowed for tremendous economic growth in Paraguay. My favorite mental image of "modernization," etched in my brain early in our visit, was that of a horse-drawn cart whose driver was holding the reins in one hand and talking on a cell phone with the other. During our stay, we would observe the day-to-day benefits of Mercosur in the small malls and large supermarkets, akin to Walmart supercenters, found throughout the capital's urban sprawl.

The four of us spent the first half of our visit with Tomasa, Silvio, and Silvana in Lambaré, now in the metropolitan area of Asunción. In the weeks prior to our arrival, Tomasa had pumped me for information about the boys' interests. Knowing that Matthew and Daniel lifted weights, she had arranged for them to work out at a small gym two blocks from the house for an hour each day while in Lambaré. Our sons somehow survived the experience and communicated with other young people in the gym, evidenced by one teenaged girl calling me *suegra* (mother-in-law) when I fetched the boys after a session. A few days later, Stephen walked into the gym to get the boys and heard some girls applauding Daniel's weightlifting and smiling flirtatiously at our younger son. A girl then turned to Stephen and addressed him as *suegro* (father-in-law). The attention somewhat embarrassed the boys, but it shocked me—during my previous times in this country, only males would flirt like that.

Stephen, the boys, and I spent our days touring around the immediate area, shopping in malls for souvenirs, eating, and talking with our friends. In addition to the traditional Paraguayan items of *aho po-í*, *ñandutí*, and tooled leather, the boys wanted to buy machetes, causing chuckles among our Paraguayan hosts. Accompanied by Stephen and guided by Roberto, one of Silvio's employees, the boys made a trip to an old-fashioned marketplace where the only machetes to be found were from Brazil and China. Although the boys wanted a Paraguayan machete like their father had in his Peace Corps days, they settled for the Brazilian brand.

One afternoon, we filled two vehicles for a foray to the old downtown area of Asunción. Silvio's nephew Mario, who had been an exchange student in New Zealand, accompanied us to help translate for the boys. We toured the main plaza, gawked at the run-down and vacant Hotel Guaraní, saw the cathedral and Pantheon of the Heroes, and noticed small statues of mythological figures for sale, making us discuss and chuckle about *Pombero* legends. City noises, diesel fumes, and traffic congestion were at their height, but Stephen and I felt more at home as we recognized the old parts of the city.

Later that evening, Silvio, Tomasa, and Mario took us to the same restaurant where my sister Cynthia had been served tongue. Tomasa retold the story with dramatic pantomiming, causing even the boys to laugh. I hadn't eaten beef in years, but I did have a piece of tongue for the humor of it. Live music provided by a Paraguayan band from Ybycuí entertained us with traditional music. I sang along when they performed "*Che Pueblo Porã*," one of my favorite songs about Ybycuí. The boys enjoyed the evening, in part because Silvio's nephew Mario conversed in English with them but also because they enjoyed Paraguayan meat. Though tougher than what they were accustomed to, the beef was grass-fed and had been grilled with lime juice. Matthew and Daniel described it as very tasty.

Another day, when the boys weren't getting along well, as was prone to happen at home, Stephen and Matthew went with Roberto in a big truck to help unload Silvio's fresh produce coming in from his countryside fields. I took Daniel to the supermarket down the street from Tomasa's house. Tomasa had given us a shopping list for dinner, providing me an opportunity to walk the aisles with my younger son.

While Daniel helped me find the items, I encouraged him to select additional things that interested him. Our purchases included *surubí* (the mild white fish common in Paraguay), *dulce de leche*, cookies, and *yerba mate*. As we pushed our grocery cart along, Daniel noticed a man doing the same while slurping *yerba mate* through a silver straw, refilling the *guampa* container frequently. "How much of that stuff will he drink?" Daniel asked with curiosity.

I replied, "I suspect he'll drink it until the water in the thermos is gone." What amazed me was that a man was shopping for food, something I never had seen before in Paraguay because it had been considered women's work.

One morning, we were up before 3 a.m. for a trip to the Itaipú Dam on the border with Brazil. Traveling in two cars, we intended to tour the dam during the day, stay that night with Tomasa's brother, also named Silvio, before returning to Lambaré. I traveled in the back seat of a small pickup truck sandwiched between my sons, who dozed with their heads shifting from my shoulders to their windows while I tried not to squirm and awaken them. Nidia traveled shotgun and served *mate* to her boyfriend Gustavo while he drove.

Following Silvio, Tomasa, Stephen, and Silvana, we zoomed along on the paved highway that had little traffic early on that Saturday morning. About halfway to the border, Silvio pulled over, as did Gustavo. The drivers jumped out, each with a large thermos in hand, and disappeared into the dark. They reappeared a short time later with filled thermoses, ready to continue the journey. Most likely, they paused to empty their bladders in the darkness while on their mission for more water.

It was past dawn as we drove through Mallorquín, and I couldn't help but recall my mistake in calculating travel time to that town years before. We arrived at Ciudad del Este (City of the East, formerly called Puerto Presidente Stroessner and changed when the dictator was deposed) at 8 a.m. After a hearty breakfast at the brother Silvio's house, we proceeded to a tour of the dam.

Itaipú Dam and the vast area it flooded was on a scale that I hadn't quite imagined, even though I had seen it under construction in 1976. After glimpsing the enormity of the dam and reservoir, we entered the visitors' center with our friends. Upon learning that the Itaipú movie was offered in English upstairs and Spanish downstairs, I muttered to Stephen, "That's a relief." We took the boys upstairs for the brief but informative introduction that didn't need translation. The movie had our rapt attention. It showed various views of the vast reservoir created by the dam that extended into the horizon as if it were an endless ocean. When the dam construction was completed, 520 square miles of land were flooded, with the water rising 330 feet in elevation and inundating the magnificent Guairá Falls about 130 miles up the Paraná River. The dam electrified almost all of southern Brazil, northern Argentina, and 90% of Paraguay.

Reuniting with our Paraguayans, we lined up for a tour by bus. Silvio the husband connected with his brother Ediberto, an engineer, who became our familial guide. At the time of our visit, there were 18 functioning turbines with two more in the process of being installed. Paraguay was using electricity generated from only one of the turbines. Ediberto explained details of the dam's operation, far too complicated for me to remember. As the bus drove along the top of the dam, it presented us with a view of its face below to the south and the vast flooded area to the north. Matthew and Daniel stared at the scenery, taking in the enormity of Itaipú and showing more interest in the visual panoramas than a translation.

On the return trip, I was again sandwiched between my boys. While Nidia was absorbed in Guaraní conversation with Gustavo, our backseat conversation in English focused on questions the boys had about our Peace Corps days. I responded to their curiosity, so long in coming, by reminiscing about the Ybycuí project, working well with their father, having the winning ticket in the raffle for a steer, teaching children and training teachers about hookworms and roundworms, and appearing on national television. Although they had heard many of the anecdotes before, they seemed to comprehend them for the first time. They now knew how Paraguay looked, smelled, and tasted. They had seen the urban and some of the rural. But they had not yet seen Ybycuí.

By midafternoon, we were only twenty miles from Lambaré when both vehicles stopped in Itaguá, where we could buy *ñandutí*. Tomasa and Nidia had made an earlier trip to the town to select the best place based on quality. Behind the counter, Eduardo, a mustachioed and goateed man in his forties, patiently waited on us by bringing out stacks of spiderweb lace in all colors of the rainbow. As I began setting aside pieces for gifts as well as keepers for me, I asked if he knew Elena (Ellen), a Volunteer who had lived in his town in the mid-1970s. "Oh, yes!" Eduardo replied in Spanish with surprised delight. He remembered that she had purchased many lovely pieces of *ñandutí* from his grandmother, who had made much of it herself and had owned the store back then. We began chatting about Ellen and his own family, some of whom lived in the U.S., while the boys added some lace pieces for their girlfriends to our pile. By the end of our shopping spree, I walked out with a large pile of the lace carefully wrapped in tissue paper, the phone number of his brother Nene (an industrial electrician in the D.C. area), whom I was to call just to say "hello," and more money left in my purse than I had anticipated due to the reasonable prices he charged. I later sent Ellen a photograph of Eduardo showing us *ñandutí*. She clearly remembered the teenaged Eduardo and his grandmother.

A week after arriving in Paraguay, we boarded a bus to Ybycuí and a reunion with Ña Niní. It would be the first time she would see her North American grandsons, other than in photographs, and I telepathically sensed her anxious anticipation.

While Matthew seemed relaxed with his natural curiosity, Daniel was edgy. I took a window seat near the front of the bus, and Daniel sat beside me in the aisle seat. More passengers boarded. I felt my son tense up and then heard him seethe at me through clenched teeth, "That woman is touching me. I don't like it here. People make me feel uncomfortable! Why did you make me come with you?" A woman walking down the bus aisle had brushed up against him, a violation of his own personal space but not of a Paraguayan. After I glanced at Stephen and Matthew, who had found seats together a couple of rows back, I realized I was on my own to resolve this problem.

"Switch seats with me so you can look out the window," I told him.

The bus pulled out onto the main highway, but Daniel continued in a low, angry voice, "It stinks like diesel fuel here, and the traffic is noisy and irritating!"

I replied, "You're right. I know what you mean, but we're going to Ybycuí now. It'll be different."

As we passed through Ellen's town of Itaguá, I pointed out Eduardo's *ñandutí* shop and reminded Daniel of our spiderweb lace purchases and other beautiful, pleasant aspects of our visit so far in Paraguay. "We'll leave the urban noise and diesel smells behind us soon." I continued, "Perhaps you don't know that when I lived here, I often had feelings of anger and discomfort. There were times when I was riding on this bus line back to Ybycuí, and I really didn't want to be here."

Daniel asked, "Well, then why did you stay?"

I replied, "I had made a two-year commitment to the Peace Corps, and I felt our work was important. But the main reason was because of your father. I knew that he wanted to complete his service. I hated this place when I realized that the woman in whose house I was living had been meanly gossiping about me. However, I had Ña Niní, Mary, and your father to support me. I knew they cared about me." Daniel remembered who Mary was. She, her husband, and their two daughters had visited us in Toppenish a decade earlier.

Daniel was quiet for a time, seemingly absorbed in the scenery that was changing from urban to rural, with more palm trees, termite hills, small houses with thatched roofs, and an occasional ox cart. I felt him beginning to relax somewhat, but then he blurted, "I don't understand the language. Dad doesn't translate for me." I knew that wasn't true. I had heard Stephen translate extensively for both boys.

I simply replied, "We'll both try harder to translate for you, Daniel."

We turned left off the main highway at Carapeguá, proceeding to Ybycuí. I pointed out the hills that formed the "Lady of Acahay," and commented that except for the paved road replacing the dusty red one, the scenery looked much the same as when we lived here. As we approached the outskirts of Ybycuí, I leaned into the aisle, got the attention of the *guarda* (bus driver's assistant), and asked in Spanish if we could be dropped off at Ña Niní's house. When the man nodded his head to acknowledge my request, Daniel asked me in a surprised voice, "He knows her?" Hmm, so he understood *some* Spanish.

I explained, "Everybody in town knows her, Daniel. She is a remarkable woman. I think you'll like her."

Tomasa had telephoned Ña Niní to let her know what time we were due to arrive. The bus turned at the corner in front of her property, and I saw Ña Niní rise from her chair in front of the hotel, eager to greet us. "There she is, Daniel," I said softly as my eyes started to glisten.

As soon as the bus rolled to a stop, I jumped up and dashed out the front door, with Daniel, Stephen, and Matthew close behind. Ña Niní ran across the road with open arms and tears streaming down her face. Falling into her arms for her big bear hug and loving streams of Guaraní, I was soon surrounded by my three males, awaiting their turns. While our luggage was unloaded from the cargo area beneath the bus, Stephen got his hug. Then Ña Niní paused and sized up her North American grandsons, who were shyly waiting. With a grin growing on her face and twinkles in her eyes, she called each one by name, Mateo and then Daniel, knowing them from the photographs I had sent her over the years. They fell into her warm embrace as she pounded them on their backs to make sure they were really with her in the flesh. The boys took this greeting quite well, particularly considering Daniel's mood at the beginning of the bus ride. Ña Niní beamed with the pleasure and delight of grateful grandmother.

The three Pearson males gathered up our baggage and followed Ña Niní and me across the street and into the hotel. She instructed them to leave the boys' suitcases in the hotel dining area and bring mine and Stephen's through the doorway leading into the house. As we walked through the Feltes home, we passed the china cabinet displaying some fragile items as well as family photographs, including some of us. I glanced at the boys, Yes, there were noticing the photos. We proceeded through Ña Niní's bedroom, where Matthew and Daniel could see additional family photos, some of themselves, on the shelf at the head of her bed frame. It was obvious they had been there awhile, some for years. I saw the boys make eye contact with a glint of understanding of what we four meant to her. After Stephen's and my belongings were dropped in the bedroom where we would sleep, we retraced our steps to the hotel dining area.

"Let me show you where you will sleep," Ña Niní said to the boys in Spanish. Gathering up their baggage and with Stephen and me bringing up the rear, the boys followed her to the second floor of the hotel and down the tiled hallway to a room with two single beds, a private bathroom, a television, and a window air conditioner. Although it was winter in Paraguay and air conditioning wouldn't be needed, she had obviously selected her very best room for Matthew and Daniel. Ña Niní told them in Spanish, "Your television has cable networks, so you'll have choices in Spanish and Guaraní." She clicked the TV on with the remote. "Let me know if there's anything you need. We'll let you rest here for a bit."

They nodded their heads while replying, "Gracias, Ña Niní," without looking to their parents for a translation.

Cesia and the twins were in Asunción, but Carlitos came to Ybycuí in time for lunch and remained for the duration of our visit. Carlitos, having known several Peace Corps Volunteers over the years, spoke slowly and patiently in Spanish with our sons, successfully engaging them in simple conversation. It was in sharp contrast to Silvio's fast barrages and teasing in Spanish and Guaraní with Stephen, often impossible for me to understand.

Our first lunch was a feast. Ña Niní served us *locro* (corn soup), *milanesa* (breaded beef), a salad, boiled *mandioca*, sodas with ice, and a double dessert offering of *arroz con leche* (a pudding of rice and milk) and *flan* (vanilla custard with a caramel sauce). She won the hearts and stomachs of Matthew and Daniel with the desserts. When needed, I earnestly translated between my Paraguayan mother and brother and my sons, with Stephen helping out as well. Ña Niní couldn't take her eyes off the boys as they spoke, smiled at her, sipped their sodas, and savored the food.

Stephen and I left Matthew and Daniel to themselves in their room after lunch, and we brought out gifts for Ña Niní. I had made her a lap quilt, and we had letters and gifts from Mary and Peggy. She tucked the letters in her pocket for a private reading later and then opened the gifts, including a wind chime from Peggy. Appreciation and grateful tears filled her eyes as she opened each thoughtful gift that she would cherish always. The tender expression on her face reinforced how much she loved us all.

After a brief siesta, Carlitos drove Stephen and the boys to nearby towns looking for a gym where they might lift weights. No gym could be found, but the countryside tour around Ybycuí was worthwhile for them.

While the males were away, Ña Niní and I had time for quiet conversation. She was pleased to the core to see us again and finally meet Matthew and Daniel. Ña Niní was grateful Carlitos lived in Ybycuí much of the time, and the hotel was doing okay. She talked about Don Lalo's death and adjusting to life without him. I had felt the void he left when I initially walked into the Feltes home. Ña Niní couldn't sew much anymore, but she still sold veterinarian medications and vaccines. She asked for details about the September 11, 2001, terrorist attacks on the United States, and we commiserated about the lack of peace on earth. "We need more Peace Corps Volunteers around the world helping people to understand each other," she wistfully commented.

Dinner was a feast of chicken, boiled *mandioca*, mashed potatoes, and flan. While eating, Ña Niní proposed her plan for the following day. She wanted to take us to Posito, her dairy farm where Mary and I had celebrated our 24th birthday, to watch her dairy herd get vaccinated. The boys mused this might be interesting, but when finished eating, they promptly disappeared to their hotel room until morning. Ña Niní also retired to her bedroom. Carlitos observed that the excitement had worn her out, but she'd be back to her old self in the morning.

Stephen and I stayed up with my "little brother" Carlitos, listening to him talk about missing his father, how he and his own immediate family were doing, and getting updates about his brother, Tonio. Cesia, Soel, and Abel were living in Asunción so that the boys could attend a good school there. Cesia continued working for the Ministry of Health in the capital. Carlitos still did laboratory work at Ybycuí's health center and in his own private lab. Since Don Lalo's passing, he felt responsible for his mother. Most weekends he was able to spend time with Cesia and the twins. Although this situation wasn't ideal, it was working out for everyone.

Tonio was keeping busy with his neurosurgery practice. Auto accidents were prevalent, and his skills were needed. He, Nuchi, and their sons visited Ybycuí when they could, staying in their lovely country home on land adjacent to where his cattle grazed. Tonio's property abutted Posito and a tract of land that Carlitos owned. As it grew late, Stephen and I reluctantly retired to our bedroom, knowing we needed a good night's rest to prepare for the following day.

Letting the boys sleep in the following morning, Stephen and I arose early and walked around town before breakfast. We stopped in some of the small businesses on the main avenue to greet friends. I pointed out an Anglo-looking young man to Stephen, instantly guessing he was North American. We approached him, and I asked in English, "Hello! Are you a Peace Corps Volunteer by any chance?"

He jerked his head and stared at us a moment before replying, "Yes, I'm Benji, a recently arrived Volunteer. My wife and I are supposed to be working in youth development. Who are you?" Stephen and I walked with Benji back to his small rented house off of the avenue to meet Alyssa. The two of them were struggling to integrate themselves into the town and figure out how to "develop the youth."

With knowing smiles, Stephen and I briefly related our challenge of eradicating hookworm in the town. Volunteers often muddle through job descriptions on their own. I asked an obvious question from my perspective, "You've met Ña Niní Feltes, haven't you?" They responded in the negative. "Well, you must be introduced," I insisted. "She has been the protector of most of the early Volunteers in this town. Would you like to go with us to her small dairy farm later this morning?" They were both interested.

When Stephen and I returned to the house and told Ña Niní about the Volunteers, she was delighted we had invited them to Posito. I woke up the boys and we readied for our little excursion. It took two trips to transport Ña Niní with her vaccination supply, the new couple, Matthew, Daniel, Stephen and me to the dairy farm. Dani, a man in his early twenties living in the Feltes home, also went along. Stephen drove, which was fine because there was no chance of a *clausura*—it wasn't raining and the road to the entrance of Posito was now paved.

Upon our arrival, the dairy ranch hands had the milk herd of about 35 cows ready and waiting in the holding pens. After Ña Niní passed the vaccinations to her workers, we sat down on chairs to watch the action. The boys were invited to climb up on the wooden fencing for a closer look as the mild-mannered cows walked in single file through the chute, pausing for vaccinations applied by the workers.

As the last of the cows exited the chute to join the herd in an enclosed pasture, Ña Niní settled into a chair to relax and enjoy some *yerba mate*. She was about to invite everyone to join her, but Dani distracted us by asking Stephen if he could show Matthew and Daniel how to "fish for tarantulas, something all Paraguayan boys do for fun." Of course, the idea appealed to our sons, and Dani explained the process slowly in Spanish as he demonstrated the steps. "First, chew some gum into a small ball. Next, tie the ball of gum onto a string. Then, look around for a hole." He led the boys off the bricked patio area and onto bare earth, with Benji, Alyssa, Stephen, and me following. All of us scanned the ground for holes. For the first time in Paraguay, I noticed with a shiver that there was an abundance of holes all around us, many of them about the size of a nickel. Matthew and Daniel huddled around one such opening and watched as Dani dropped his chewing gum on the string down a couple of inches into the hole, with the slight weight of the gum keeping the string taut. It didn't take long for the string to jerk, much like a fishing rod does when a fish bites the bait. Our sons backed away as Dani quickly yanked the string upward and away from the hole, causing the tarantula clasping the chewing gum to land on the dirt. Dani promptly captured it in a tin can and placed a cover on it.

"Now what?" we North American spectators asked almost in unison.

Dani replied, "We fish for another tarantula and then make them fight." A few moments later, Dani had landed a second one, scooped it into another can, and then jostled the two spiders out of their respective cans to face each other on the brick patio. He pulled a stick out of his back pocket, ready to prod them if necessary. Dani commented that tarantulas don't like to come out in the daylight, and they fight viciously against whatever is in front of them. We watched in fascinated horror as the two hairy tarantulas angrily went after each other as if they were boxers vying for prize money. It didn't take long for the larger of the two to dominate and kill its opponent.

"What's next?" asked Benji.

Dani scooped up the surviving spider with a can and replied, "Oh, I'll just kill the winner." Alyssa was appalled and appealed to him to let the tarantula go free. His eyes showed disbelief but he said, "Okay." As our small spectator crowd dispersed, I was the only one watching Dani walk a short distance away, shake the spider out of the can, and squash it with his shoe.

Speaking of shoes, the Paraguayans I saw during our 2003 visit wore shoes, with the exception of an older woman working at Posito. Perhaps in more remote areas, people still went barefoot. However, I wish I had asked Dani how Paraguayan boys had taken care of the winning tarantula in days of yore, when shoes in rural areas were a rarity. Did they squash it with a bare foot?

Later that evening, Benji and Alyssa joined us for dinner at Ña Niní's and lingered for an evening of our favorite Paraguayan songs, with Carlitos on the guitar. After our guests left and our sons retired to their room, Stephen and I climbed the stairs to the hotel roof to gaze at the night sky. "Look, Esteban, there's the Southern Cross and Scorpius," I whispered. Searching the sky, Stephen pointed out a bright glow moving across the heavens. I asked, "Might that be the International Space Station?" He nodded. Launched five years earlier, it was circling the earth about 250 miles above us, traveling fast enough to make a complete orbit every 90-some minutes.

"Boys, how about a visit to the health center?" I suggested the following morning after breakfast. Although less than enthusiastic, they piled into the vehicle Stephen and I borrowed from Ña Niní, and we drove across town.

As we entered, a stunned face stared at us from behind a desk, stopping us in our tracks. The woman's jaw was dropped and her mouth hung open as if she were seeing ghosts. Stephen's voice calling her name woke her from her shocked state. Nurse María Luisa's gaze went from Stephen's face to mine and then back again. Her mouth grew into a huge smile as she rose from her chair to greet us in the Paraguayan customary way. "Is it really you? I'm retiring in a couple of weeks, and I'm so glad I am still here to see you!" she exclaimed. We introduced her to the boys, who clammed up somewhat.

A few years prior to our visit, we had heard that Dr. Orihuela was no longer living in Ybycuí. His wife Ña Irma had passed away, as had Nimia, the lab technician. The health center was now staffed by some younger physicians. When Stephen asked María Luisa if we could talk with one of the doctors, she disappeared to inquire. I asked the boys if they wanted to wait together on a bench or tag along with us. They preferred their own company on a bench.

María Luisa promptly reappeared and motioned for us to follow her. On the way, Stephen and I were introduced to the young midwife who immediately recognized us. She had been one of the contest winners in Ybycuí and still had the photo prize we had taken of her and her family. We walked through the enlarged, modernized facility and noticed that it was sparkling clean. María Luisa led us to the doorway of the doctor's office, introduced us, and returned to her duties.

Dr. Melgarejo, a neat and serious young man in a white lab coat, shook our hands, offered us chairs, and sat down behind his desk with a professional flair. "What might I help you with today?" he asked politely in Spanish.

I responded, "Well, we were Peace Corps Volunteers working in health education and sanitation here in 1974, and we are interested in learning what medical problems you are seeing today. We are back for a visit with our teenaged sons."

Stephen added, "I'm a pediatrician now, and Marilú is a public health specialist. When we lived here, we knew there were problems with *cevo-i*, both hookworms and roundworms. What kinds of diseases do you see now?"

The doctor proceeded to talk about prenatal care for about 300 women a year, problem deliveries, performing Cesarean sections at a rate of 14%, and dealing with both viral and bacterial infections. He spoke slowly and thoughtfully with a serious look on his face, only occasionally making eye contact with us. Just as I noticed his mouth starting to twitch, he abruptly stopped and looked directly at us. Attempting to hide a smile, he confessed, "I was six years old and in second grade when you lived here. I used to walk several kilometers into town to attend school back then. I remember the *Cevo-i* Song. I remember you both!" His face, completely dropping its serious professional demeanor, warmed into a shy smile. The three of us broke into delighted laughter. The rest of our conversation and the health center tour he personally gave us is a blur in my memory, but the warmth and delight in his eyes will stay with me forever.

We collected our boys from their temporary boredom on the bench and returned to Ña Niní's house, where she greeted us with an offer to help her roll out the *chipá*, bread made with *mandioca* flour and corn meal. Following a handwashing, the boys and I joined her. We subsequently enjoyed what we had helped with for lunch, along with rice soup, salad, chicken, and a fresh fruit salad.

After a siesta, Carlitos announced he wanted to drive us out into the countryside. "Ja-jhá" (jah-HAH, Let's go in Guaraní), I exclaimed. Stephen rode in the front, while I was sandwiched in the back between the boys. To his credit, Stephen did much of the translating as we stopped at the iron foundry of Minas Cué, which we had seen inaugurated by Stroessner in 1975. Carlitos, proud and knowledgeable of Paraguayan history and the role of the iron foundry during the War of the Triple Alliance, explained what we were seeing as we walked through the site. The next stop was Salto Cristal, the lovely waterfall where Stephen and I once camped with Mary, Lee, and Tom over a quarter of a century before. Daniel energetically hopped across the creek and down the slopes to the pool below the falling water like a free soul, taking in the greenery and enjoying the moment. Matthew walked around the peaceful setting with a thoughtful, calm air about him. I felt at peace.

Too soon came the time for preparing our belongings for the bus ride back to Asunción. I became emotionally distraught with the thought of leaving Ña Niní. She quietly accepted our departure, thanking us for our visit and hugging each of us. I waited to be the last, feeling that we would never return to Paraguay again. I thought this was the last time I'd ever see her. As she embraced me with her bear hug, she begged at my ear, "Please come back before I die."

I couldn't speak. I didn't know. But I nodded my head slightly, fighting back tears. I softly told her, "Thank you so very much. I love you."

Back in Asunción, the four of us spent time with Cesia and twins Soel and Abel. Cesia spoke enthusiastically about her work against Chagas disease, while her pre-adolescent sons, identical to the point that their parents had difficulty telling one from another, listened as attentively as we did. Cesia and her staff were winning the fight to eradicate new cases of the disease in eastern Paraguay and had recently begun a similar effort in the Chaco.

Before returning us to Tomasa's home in Lambaré, Cesia helped us with some last-minute shopping so that Stephen and our boys could buy some souvenir mythical creature figurines, including the *Pombero*. These were carved of light-weight balsa wood and measured up to ten inches tall. (Today, Stephen's purchases occupy a bookcase shelf in his home office.) By early afternoon, we were packing suitcases for our departure for home the next day. We accommodated the machetes, spiderweb lace, *aho po-í*, and some thoughtful gifts from our friends into our luggage. Unfortunately, the jar of homemade *dulce de leche* Ña Niní had given Daniel had to be ditched. Ants had gotten into it.

Late in the afternoon, Nidia's boyfriend Gustavo, a police officer by occupation, appeared at the house and invited Stephen and the boys to visit his jailhouse. Thinking it would be a different cultural experience for Matthew and Daniel, Stephen accepted the offer. As he later related to me, the visit was awkward but interesting.

Upon entering the dank, dark building, they were introduced to three uniformed police officers on duty and one inmate, all seated at a table in a large common area. They were eating dinner and congenially talking. Gustavo declined the invitation for the four of them to partake in the meal, explaining they had dinner plans for the evening. The boys stood agape at the barred, unoccupied jail cells at the far end of the darkly painted room while Stephen attempted to politely converse in a mixture of Spanish and Guaraní.

The police officers were discussing the array of stolen cars and untaxed illegal vehicles in the country. They had been pulling in a lot of them lately—Mercedes Benz, Toyota pickup trucks, various SUVs. Yes, there was still a considerable flow of contraband in Paraguay. One officer explained that the sole inmate at the time was routinely invited to eat meals with the officers, but he was always returned to his locked cell to sleep. Although curious but not wanting to adversely affect the casual, relaxed atmosphere, Stephen refrained from asking what crime the inmate had committed. The brief visit ended none too soon for Stephen but with words of thanks to Gustavo for the experience. The boys looked relieved when the visit concluded.

After their return from the jailhouse, we readied ourselves for our last evening in Paraguay. Tomasa and Silvio hosted a lovely dinner party for us with 16 other guests at their home. We feasted on more Paraguayan grilled meat, *sopa paraguaya*, *mandioca*, salad, and an array of sweet desserts. Silvio hired the Paraguayan band we had enjoyed at the restaurant, and the musicians filled the air and our hearts with our favorite *guaranias* and polkas. For Stephen and me, the evening doubled as our going-away party and our 25th wedding anniversary celebration about six months after the fact. The eating, singing, dancing, and conversations along with the company and hospitality of our friends nurtured our souls.

Saying good-bye to Tomasa was bittersweet—so sad we had to leave but thrilled we had been able to visit. On our return flight, the boys were happy. "They survived Paraguay, Esteban," I whispered in his ear. Although they had not experienced the unsanitary conditions of our Peace Corps service, Matthew and Daniel had definitely acquired a deeper insight into the earlier lives of their parents. As we had hoped, the feel and smell of Paraguay, the taste of its food, the culture of its people, and the love between us and our Paraguayan families had become a reality for our children. Now that we were on the way home, our sons conveyed to us that it had been a meaningful visit. Both said they understood us better for having seen firsthand the place where our relationship had developed. For Stephen and me, it was a satisfying dream-come-true for our children to visit Paraguay and learn what it meant to us.

∞∞∞∞

"¡Hola, María-í. ¿Mba-éi-xa-pa?" I said to Mary by phone upon our return. After filling her in on our memorable vacation, I said, "I will mail you some lovely gifts from our Paraguayan families." Moved by our experience, Mary declared that she would take her husband Thomas and their girls next year. I repeated a similar conversation with Peggy. Both listened intently and asked myriad questions.

Late in our summer of 2004, Mary was true to her word and took Thomas and daughters Gabrielle and Alexis to visit Paraguay. While in Lambaré, they attended Silvana's *quinceañera*, the special fifteenth birthday celebration in Hispanic culture to recognize a girl had become a woman. Mary and I had pitched in together to buy her a pearl earrings and necklace set for the occasion.

Mary also collected some medical supplies for victims of the tragic August 1st Ycuá Bolaños supermarket fire in Asunción that killed almost 400 people and injured over 500. Not only had the supermarket lacked adequate fire protection systems, but also the exit doors were locked after the fire started to prevent possible looting. The president of the company and some of his employees received prison terms for their behavior. One of Silvio's employees had been in the supermarket when the fire broke out but had escaped with relatively minor injuries.

Except for the aftermath of the supermarket tragedy, Mary and her family had a memorable vacation following in our footsteps by spending time in Lambaré with Tomasa and in Ybycuí with Ña Niní. In spite of the cool winter weather in Paraguay, Ña Niní filled her hotel's newly built swimming pool so the girls could swim. One afternoon they rode horses around town, arranged by some of Mary's friends, to give the girls a rustic, rural Paraguayan experience. Thomas loved it so much that he told Mary he wanted to retire there some day.

∞∞∞

After our trip to Paraguay, our family life was in transition. We drove Matthew to Whitman College to begin his undergraduate studies, causing me to suffer "empty nest syndrome." Although he was only two hours away, I missed him terribly. I was consoled by knowing that Daniel would still be at home for another year.

Stephen resumed working as a pediatrician but switched jobs to Central Washington Family Medicine, a family-practice residency training program. I began a position with the local Head Start program as the Assistant Director of Community Development. Head Start had been launched by the federal government in 1965 to help break the cycle of poverty by providing disadvantaged preschool children from low-income families with a comprehensive program to meet their emotional, social, health, nutritional, and psychological needs.

My new position involved technical and grant writing, as well as developing special projects, one of which was writing small bilingual books for preschoolers. Although educators talk repeatedly about the importance of reading to young children, oftentimes low-income families don't have anything appropriate to read to them. I recalled how well received *Barefoot Pepe and the Hookworm* had been in Ybycuí. It was a story with a positive health message that children could take home and read with their parents. I wanted to develop similar stories for Head Start preschoolers.

My most successful book turned out to be *My Healthy Heart*, a teaching tool for staying healthy. The impetus for the book and its accompanying curriculum was Stephen's offer to have a family practice resident at Head Start for a half-day per month. When the residents were assigned to outpatient pediatrics under his supervision, they were to learn about important pediatric services in the community, including early learning programs.

"May I take the residents into the Head Start classrooms?" I asked Stephen.

"To do what?" he inquired. I responded a short time later with a one-page curriculum and the draft of a 16-page bilingual book, *My Healthy Heart*. He enthusiastically supported my idea.

At the time, general obesity rates had been increasing in the United States, and preschool children were not exempt. Washington State's early learning program had begun promoting two messages for young children to avoid obesity—eat at least five fruits and vegetables and have fun exercise every day. The curriculum and the little book, with drawings and photos, conveyed those messages along with simple anatomical concepts. The one-page curriculum for a 20-minute lesson paralleled the book but also included the opportunity for the children to listen to their hearts with inexpensive stethoscopes. The program was a hit.

I developed an array of other books, including *Hands* to teach hand washing and *Our Healthy Smiles* to promote oral hygiene, but *My Healthy Heart* has had the most enduring success. Seventeen years after I wrote it, the curriculum and book are still being used in our local Head Start program. Perhaps some of the children will remember the book in years to come, much like Dr. Melgarejo and others remembered *Barefoot Pepe and the Hookworm* and the *Cevo-i* Song years afterwards.

∞∞∞∞

"Let me take your picture," pleaded Tomasa in our summer of 2008, when she saw the colorful outdoor Toppenish mural with a latrine in it. "A Halloween Prank," depicting an old-time outhouse, is one of my personal favorites. Painted on the side of the public restrooms labeled as "West Rooms," the mural shows pranksters pushing over an occupied outhouse. "*Cevo-í, cevo-í...*You have to have a clean latrine to poop in!" Peggy, Stephen, and I sang in Guaraní. Tomasa snapped a staged photo of we three sanitation RPCVs, along with Peggy's fiancé Rich, pretending to participate in the prank. Peggy and Rich had flown to the Pacific Northwest to see Tomasa and her sister-in-law Marta during their 2008 visit to the West Coast. Although his Spanish was limited, Rich was an old pro at interacting with people of other cultures because of his career in international development with the World Bank.

When Tomasa had called me two months earlier about a potential visit, I was missing both sons. Matthew had graduated from Whitman College in May 2007 with a studio art major. He was a whiz with computers and had worked part-time in tech support at the college. After receiving his degree, he was hired by Whitman as a full-time technology employee.

In the spring of 2008, Daniel had graduated from Willamette (pronounced "will-AM-it, rhymes with "damn it," as we were informed during parent orientation at the beginning of his freshman year) University in Salem, Oregon. Shortly after receiving his diploma, he left us for the National Institutes of Health (NIH) in Bethesda, Maryland. Daniel had landed an internship in the genetics laboratory of Dr. Francis Collins, the pediatrician/geneticist who had successfully led the government's program to map the human genome and who would letter become the NIH director. The internship program was designed for young people considering medical school, a doctoral program in science, or both. Dan, as we now called him, was thinking about both. Although Stephen and I rejoiced that Matthew and Dan were now independent, living on their own, and pursuing their dreams, I felt a sense of loss. My days as a hands-on mother were over.

One midnight in August of 2008, Tomasa and Marta arrived at the airport in Portland, Oregon, where Stephen and I greeted them. The morning after their arrival, our guests were giddy, likely from excitement combined with fatigue from their journey and a lack of sleep. The four of us headed by car east along the Columbia River. We stopped about 30 minutes out of Portland at Multnomah Falls for a photo opportunity with the scenic backdrop of a tall waterfall. Although the Iguazú Falls drastically dwarfed it, it was the first glimpse of the Cascade Mountains for both visitors. Their small digital cameras were clicking to capture scenic photos through the windshield.

Before arriving at Multnomah Falls, Tomasa and Marta attempted to describe one of the souvenirs they both wanted to buy during their visit. Their descriptions were puzzling, but Stephen and I finally figured it out—souvenir orange traffic cones. "Seriously?" I asked. Giggling, they both answered in the affirmative. Oddly, the gift shop at the Multnomah Falls Lodge provided an opportunity for them to purchase not only beautiful postcards, but also miniature souvenir orange traffic cones. I never did figure out their fascination with the cones (or "witches' hats," as my mother used to call them). I was relieved that we had found versions only three inches tall on our first tourist stop.

Our visitors enjoyed the diverse landscape of the Columbia Gorge, the majestic Cascade Mountains, and the irrigated agricultural acreage of the Yakima Valley on the way to our home on top of Cherry Hill in Granger. As we reached the top of the hill, Stephen stopped the car to point out the flagpole of a neighbor's home. We had offered to buy a Paraguayan flag for Bill, a flag aficionado, but he refused our money and took it upon himself to welcome our friends with their country's flag. Tomasa and Marta were delighted, snapping photos before we proceeded to our home on the far edge of the hill. Our western view of Mt. Adams and Mt. Rainier on the horizon with the backdrop of a clear blue sky was another marvelous greeting for them. Peggy and Rich arrived the following day.

Stephen, Peggy, and I recalled our own interests in the culture and arts of Paraguay, as well as its geographical beauty. We intended to provide Tomasa and Marta with parallel experiences in Washington State. The City of Toppenish, known as the Town of Murals, was at the top of the list. Stephen, the boys, and I had lived in Toppenish for nine years before moving to Granger. Before ending up with our visitors at "The Halloween Prank" mural, the six of us had taken a city tour in a horse-drawn covered wagon to see a number of the 76 murals, illustrating the colorful history of the area, scattered around town on the sides of buildings. Stephen, Peggy, and I translated the wagon driver's entertaining narration of the murals.

Since its founding in 1989, the Toppenish Mural Society has required the well-known western artists painting the murals to correctly depict them, according to Northwest history. In one instance, an artist, after painting the image of John Wayne as a cowboy in a cattle round-up, was forced to disguise the famous actor's face with a beard. However, the resemblance on the face is easy to see once it is pointed out.

One mural commemorates The Treaty of 1855, negotiated between the U.S. government and the Native Americans living in the area. The treaty created peace between the United States and the confederated 14 tribes of the Yakama Nation while taking away most of the land the tribes and their ancestors had occupied for millennia. Tomasa and Marta spoke of the way the Paraguayan government and powerful politicians were mistreating small, indigenous tribes—exploiting and stealing their land. It was generally recognized that almost 60,000 people in Paraguay and Brazil had been displaced by the Itaipú Dam alone.

Ironically, on the building which used to house Pacific Power and Light in Toppenish, there is a mural of Native Americans fishing at Celilo Falls on the Columbia River. Sadly, those falls were destroyed in 1954 when The Dalles Dam, an important source of hydroelectrical power in the Pacific Northwest, flooded them. Traditional fishing villages were lost, indigenous families were displaced, and the migration and spawning of salmon were disrupted. Oldtimers claim that the salmon used to be so plentiful that you could "walk across the river on their backs." It is common knowledge that wild salmon runs on the Columbia are a small fraction of what they used to be and are likely on the verge of extinction, due to a variety of reasons but most prominently the installation of dams, including the Grand Coulee, Chief Joseph, Bonneville, and The Dalles. While hydroelectric dams have provided electricity to modernize the world, they have also caused losses, the worst of which are often suffered by indigenous people.

Some Toppenish murals honor Indian culture, battles, and leaders. But in the end, White culture has dominated. Indigenous tribes in Paraguay have similarly suffered. Tomasa commented, "At least we have preserved our Guaraní culture and language in Paraguay." She added that the isolation of Paraguay by 18th century dictators had enabled the preservation of the Guaraní language among the Native women who had married Spaniards. But other indigenous tribes in Paraguay, such as the Aché and Macá, suffered much the same as Native Americans in North America. (For more information, see iwgia.org/en/paraguay.)

To conclude our Toppenish tour, Stephen and I took our friends to the local McDonald's to gawk at a rogue mural painted on an inside wall, described by a friend as weird and somewhat creepy. It was not a Toppenish Mural Society work of art as it did not reflect true history. It was what might be considered a politically incorrect mural of Ronald McDonald interacting with Indian children among tepees, with snow-capped Mt. Adams as a backdrop. (After a renovation a few years ago, the controversial mural no longer graces the McDonald's interior.)

"The Spanish and the English were cruel to Native Americans," we all agreed. The six of us had driven to the Yakama Nation Cultural Center on the outskirts of Toppenish. It is a sobering place, with displays of the Yakama Indian lifestyle and plaques explaining the loss of their land to White men. When Stephen and I lived in Toppenish on the Yakama Reservation, we learned of the pain and losses that the local Native Americans have suffered over the years. In the United States, Native American languages and cultures are at risk of disappearing. Beginning in the late 19th century, it was common practice to forbid Native children from speaking their languages in school and to outlaw their cultural practices. The Yakama Nation Cultural Center is a small island of hope to preserve the local language, Sahaptin, and the Yakama culture.

Checking out the dinosaurs in Granger involved another tour. In the early 1990s, people in Granger bandied around ideas for a community theme that would put the town of 2,000 inhabitants on the map, much like the murals had done for Toppenish. As one citizen confided to us in 2000 when Matthew developed explanatory plaques for each dinosaur statue in town for his Eagle Scout project, dinosaurs seemed to be the only theme that most people could agree upon. Although no dinosaur fossils have been discovered in the Yakima Valley, there is a general fascination with the extinct animals.

In 1994, Granger's Public Works Department built and displayed the town's first dinosaur, a baby Brontosaurus true to scale according to fossils, as are the subsequent thirty-some statues scattered around town as of 2020. Some statues are placed in parks for children to play on, while others are less accessible. For example, the *Spinosaurus* is on a pedestal close to the freeway to greet visitors as they exit Interstate-82 at Granger. When freezing fog descends upon the valley in winter, the wires of *Spinosaurus* become coated with frost, giving the ancient animal an aspect as cold and biting as the weather. Our guests were enthralled with the statues of the extinct creatures around town, but their favorite was the *Tyrannosaurus rex* bursting out of one of the public works buildings, where they proudly and laughingly posed for photos.

Although Tomasa had seen snow on her first U.S. visit, Marta, like most Paraguayans, had not yet had that pleasure. To give her the experience, we drove in two cars to Mt. Rainier National Park, stopping at Tipsoo Lake at the top of Chinook Pass, an elevation of almost 5,300 feet. Laughing and shouting with joy, we had a friendly mid-July snowball fight. We proceeded to the Sunrise Visitor Center, on the northeast side of Mt. Rainier at an altitude of 6,400 feet, for spectacular views. An active volcano at 14,411 feet above sea level, Mt. Rainier is the highest mountain in Washington State. Impressed and awed, we lingered to enjoy the view and the company of friends. Peggy and Rich left us there and headed to Seattle in their rental car for their flight home. All of us were grateful for our time together.

Back in Granger, I asked Tomasa and Marta, "Are you interested in assembling a jigsaw puzzle?" I set down the *yerba mate* we were sharing and pulled out a scenic puzzle I had purchased of Mt. Rainier. The women's faces lit up, but Stephen retreated, mumbling he had an aversion to those things. With three of us working on the puzzle, it didn't take long. I then promptly disassembled it in order to present the box and its 500 pieces to them as a gift to take back to Paraguay.

All too soon, it was time to return them to the Portland airport for their flight to San Diego, where Mary anxiously awaited their arrival. During the second half of their vacation, Tomasa and Marta visited the San Diego Zoo, walked sandy beaches while watching surfers, and enjoyed the company of Mary, Thomas, and their daughters. Our connection to Paraguay remained strong. One thing we all agreed upon—their visit wasn't long enough. However, it had helped ease my pain of missing Matthew and Dan.

∞∞∞

Two months later, in October 2008, my father passed away. Mom and Dad had moved from Florida to Virginia Beach a few years earlier to be in close proximity to Cynthia and Henry. When Mom and Dad were no longer able to live alone, they moved in with my sister and brother-in-law. Dad had cancer. Although chemotherapy effectively killed the tumor, Dad never recovered his strength from the chemical treatment. Knowing my father's end on this earth was near, Stephen and I traveled to Virginia to help. Mom, Cynthia, Henry, Stephen, and I were all there to tell him we loved him and then let go. He was 86 years old.

In February 2010, I returned to Virginia Beach for the last days of my mother's life. She slipped away peacefully one afternoon lying on her bed, embraced by Cynthia on one side and me on the other. She had turned 87 three months earlier.

My parents had given me the greatest gift in life—they loved me unconditionally. Also, they encouraged me to follow my dreams and conveyed that they had true confidence in me. My parents had nurtured and supported me, allowing me to develop the courage to take risks, like joining the Peace Corps. Even in far-away Paraguay, I felt their love and sensed that part of them was with me during my times of trouble, as well as at moments of joy. I shared the grief of my losses with Ña Niní and Tomasa by long-distance telephone, and I felt their loving support across the miles.

A Peace Corp Memoir

Buying spiderweb lace from Eduardo, who remembered Volunteer Ellen

At the dinner where I ate tongue; from left to right,
Daniel, Matthew, Mary Lou, Stephen, Silvio, and Tomasa

At Posito with Ña Niní and Volunteers Alyssa and Benji

Matthew, watching the vaccination of the cows at Posito

Making *chipá* with Ña Niní

Daniel, Carlitos, and Matthew near Salto Cristal

At the Toppenish mural, "A Halloween Prank,"
from left to right, Rich, Peggy, Mary Lou, and Stephen

Tomasa, Marta, and Peggy on the Granger dinosaur tour

In our Granger home, Peggy, Tomasa, Marta, Stephen, and Mary Lou

CHAPTER 11

Celebrating the Peace Corps and Reflecting

How lucky am I to have something that makes saying goodbye so hard.
—Winnie the Pooh

In March of 2011, Mary visited us from her home near San Diego to celebrate the 50th anniversary of the Peace Corps. After the end of World War II in 1945, there were discussions in the United States Congress about establishing a program to send volunteers to developing countries. In late 1951, Representative John F. Kennedy suggested, "…young college graduates would find a full life in bringing technical advice and assistance to the underprivileged and backward Middle East…" Senator Hubert Humphrey later introduced a bill to create the Peace Corps Program. His bill never came up for a vote in the Senate, but he was responsible for the name. In his memoir, *The Education of a Public Man,* Humphrey wrote:

> "I introduced the first Peace Corps bill in 1957. It did not meet with much enthusiasm. Some traditional diplomats quaked at the thought of thousands of young Americans scattered across their world. Many senators, including liberal ones, thought it silly and an unworkable idea…It is fashionable now to suggest that Peace Corps Volunteers gained as much or more from their experience as the countries [where] they worked. That may be true, but it ought not demean their work. They touched many lives and made them better."

After a long day of campaigning for the presidency, then-Senator John F. Kennedy presented the idea of an international volunteer program at 2 a.m. on October 14, 1960 in Ann Arbor, Michigan. The press had left, but 10,000 University of Michigan students awaited the candidate. He didn't let them down. His short speech included the following:

> "How many of you who are going to be doctors, are willing to spend your days in Ghana?

Technicians or engineers, how many of you are willing to work in the Foreign Service and spend your lives traveling around the world? On your willingness to do that, not merely to serve one year or two years in the service, but on your willingness to contribute part of your life to this country, I think will depend the answer whether a free society can compete. I think it can! And I think Americans are willing to contribute. But the effort must be far greater than we have ever made in the past."

During that hard-fought presidential campaign, Alan and Judy Guskin, Ann Arbor supporters of the Peace Corps idea, took the concept to Kennedy's opponent, Richard Nixon, in case Kennedy lost the election. (peacecorps.umich.edu/Tobin.html) Nixon nixed the idea, referring to it as a "cult of escapism and a haven for draft dodgers." (peacecorps.gov/about/history/founding-moment)

On March 1, 1961, less than six weeks after taking the oath of office, President Kennedy established the Peace Corps by an executive order. Three days later, he named his brother-in-law, R. Sargent Shriver, its first director. Volunteers began serving in nine countries in 1961. Within six years, more than 14,500 Volunteers had served in 55 countries. A peak was reached in 1966, with 15,000 Volunteers in service, coinciding with the time Volunteers first entered Paraguay. (See the milestone fact sheet on Peace Corps' website.) In 1974, only eight years later, Mary, Stephen, and I were serving in Ybycuí. Peggy would follow us with her two years of service from 1977 to 1979. Before the COVID-19 pandemic struck in early 2020, there were over 200 Volunteers in Paraguay, and they had pushed the total number having served there to over 4,000.

Prior to the Peace Corps, the U.S. State Department had been described as "Pale, Male, and Yale." According to John Coyne (Peace Corps Ethiopia 1962-64) in his 2018 article, "How the Peace Corps Transformed the Foreign Service," published in *American Diplomacy*, more than 60 RPCVs have served as U.S. Ambassadors. Surely, many others have served in additional State Department capacities around the world. I recall at least four Paraguay Volunteers I served with who joined the Foreign Service. RPCVs speak the languages and understand the cultures of the countries in which they served. Also, they can readily adapt to additional foreign countries because of their Peace Corps experience. As President Kennedy predicted, the Peace Corps has transformed the State Department to include men and women "from every race and walk of life."

In 2011, our local Yakima Valley group of about 18 returned Peace Corps Volunteers, representing countries around the world, met for a potluck celebration wearing traditional clothing of our host countries. Mary, Stephen, and I wore *aho po-í*. With each of us bringing a traditional dish from our country of service, the food was diverse and delicious. We took two pans of *sopa paraguaya*. All present shared a memory and the passion for our service and our host countries. It was clear that we all had left a part of our hearts in our countries of service and had maintained a strong bond to our adopted cultures and dear friends in faraway places.

∞∞∞∞

Darkness had already fallen in mid-2012 when Stephen and I set out for Ybycuí with Carlitos and Cesia. It was our first full day back in Paraguay, and we were anxious to see Ña Niní. My "little brother" Carlitos drove his diesel Toyota 4-Runner southeast out of Asunción on the two-lane paved highway, with Stephen in the front passenger seat and Cesia and me in the back. As we neared the Carapeguá turnoff but still surrounded by the dark, the 4-Runner's headlights started dimming. Alarmed, Carlitos pulled to the side of the highway. When the headlights completely went out, he shut off the engine, said some bad words in Guaraní, and stated he had just had his vehicle serviced to avoid such a problem.

Cesia pulled out her cell phone to frantically call friends and colleagues who lived in Carapeguá, only a few kilometers ahead. After several minutes, Carlitos started the car, relieved to find he had headlights again. He pulled back onto the highway and proceeded another kilometer. Unfortunately, the same dimming reoccurred. Seeing the lights of Carapeguá in the distance, he continued driving while Cesia talked in Guaraní on her cell phone. City streetlights finally welcomed us, and Carlitos pulled into the gas station indicated by Cesia. In very short order, a couple of cars pulled up beside us. A small group of men jumped out to greet Carlitos and tackle the problem of the vehicle's headlights. Cesia took Stephen and me into the small store adjacent to the gas station, where we purchased snacks and used the facilities. And then we waited.

Earlier in 2012, two years after my mother's passing, Tomasa and Carlitos had both advised me by phone that Ña Niní's health was deteriorating. Carlitos bluntly said, "If you want to see her again, you had better plan a visit." My heart ached to go. Ña Niní's last-minute plea in 2003 to return before she died kept replaying in my mind. Matthew was happily living and working in Seattle. Dan was in the MD/PhD program at Harvard, fully funded and with a stipend. Stephen and I could afford the vacation time and the expense. "*Ja-jhá*" (Let's go), Stephen said to me.

I called Mary and Peggy, updating them about Ña Niní and our plans, and both decided to join us. Tomasa, Carlitos, and especially Ña Niní were thrilled at the prospect. Peggy's plans were first to travel to Argentina, where she had lived for a few years, after which she would join us in Asunción. Mary booked a flight from San Diego to Houston, with only 45 minutes to connect with a flight to São Paulo, Brazil. Stephen and I secured reservations from Seattle to Chicago, connecting with a flight to São Paulo and then onto a plane to Asunción with Mary. Carlitos, Tomasa, and their families would meet us at the airport.

In the weeks prior to the trip, I made two wall-hanging photo quilts for gifts. Tomasa's had photos from her Connecticut, Florida, and Washington visits with us, and I embroidered at the top in Spanish, "When will the next trip be?" For Ña Niní's quilt, I collected a photograph each from Mary and Peggy taken during their Peace Corps days, as well as a current photo. For the recent ones, Mary sent a family photo with Thomas and their daughters, and Peggy emailed me one of Rich and her on their wedding day. I selected our photos. I displayed the old pictures at the top of the quilt and the contemporary photos underneath. Ña Niní's four "Volunteer children" and our families would be with her at a glance.

While our 2003 trip had been funded by frequent flier miles except for the taxes, this time Stephen and I opted to use our miles for an upgrade to business class on our Chicago to Sao Paolo flight. With two large suitcases crammed with clothing and gifts, we flew out of Seattle in mid-July. After boarding our connecting flight in Chicago on time, we settled into comfortable business-class seats that would completely recline into beds for the overnight flight to Brazil. As Stephen and I awaited our departure, a flight attendant took our orders for drinks and dinner and gave us each a packet containing a small pillow, blanket, and eye mask. We stowed our belongings for take-off and began taxiing toward the runway. Suddenly, the jet came to an abrupt halt, seeming to dig its wheels into the pavement to brace us for the onslaught of an impressive storm, with thunder and lightning crashing at the same time indicating we were in the middle of a bad one. While torrential rain and winds pounded the exterior of the plane, the pilot's voice informed us that we would have to sit it out where we were, due to the ferocity of the winds. In business class, we were promptly served dinner with drinks, an indication that it wasn't a quickly passing summer shower. We could also select from an array of movies to watch on our own private screens.

By the time my first movie concluded, I realized we had been waiting on the ground for the storm to pass for over two hours. I glanced toward the coach section of the plane with compassion for the passengers crowded together with few amenities, as well as with relief that we had upgraded our seats. Complimentary after-dinner drinks were served to those of us in business class. Just before I started my second movie, the pilot announced that we would remain stationary for an undetermined amount of time. The storm had passed beyond us only to turn around and aim straight at us from the other direction. Whatever the second movie was, it could not keep my attention, as I frequently looked at my watch to calculate whether or not we would make our connecting flight in São Paulo. Finally, almost six hours after our scheduled departure, we were cleared to proceed. Once airborne, I fully reclined for a restless night's sleep. Stephen did the same.

The sun was up as the wing flaps slowed the plane and we turned to taxi toward the terminal in Brazil's largest city. I looked out the window at a Paraguayan TAM airplane taxiing for departure. "Look, Stephen, I'll bet Mary's on that flight," I murmured. Whether I was right or not in identifying the plane, we had missed our connection.

After booking a flight leaving later that evening and scheduled to arrive in Asunción around midnight, Stephen and I were directed to the business class lounge with plenty of free food and drinks, an internet connection, and restrooms with soft toilet paper. Settling into a comfortable lounge chair and booting up my laptop, I emailed Tomasa and Carlitos to let them know of our delay with the hope that at least one of the messages would get through to them. We knew that Tomasa and Silvio had planned a dinner party in their home that evening, complete with live Paraguayan music, to celebrate the homecoming of the four of us. I hoped we'd arrive at the party before everyone left.

Thankfully, the TAM flight to Asunción was uneventful and on time. Stephen and I cleared immigration and proceeded to the baggage claim area. There, we patiently waited, watching the circling conveyor belt with the sinking feeling that our luggage would not arrive. When all of the other passengers had left with their bags, I suggested to Stephen that I would deal with the lost luggage if he would proceed through the airport to meet our awaiting friends. After giving the TAM attendants our luggage tag numbers, I was advised to return to the airport the following day as our baggage would likely be on the next flight scheduled to arrive in the late morning. I dragged myself past an empty customs desk to the exit door and was enthusiastically greeted by Carlitos, waiting with Stephen. Carlitos assured us that the dinner party was still going strong, with plenty of food remaining for us.

Zooming through the streets of the city with little traffic due to the late hour, we arrived at Tomasa and Silvio's house in Lambaré to the loud sound of beautiful Paraguayan harp and guitar music and the chattering of friends waiting to greet us. Mary and Peggy, both happily partying, hugged and welcomed us along with the others. Mary related that when she was greeted at the airport, our friends were clapping her on the back, hugging her, first saying in Spanish, "Hello, hello, Mary!" followed by a puzzled, "But where are Marilú and Esteban?" as they looked for us over her shoulder. They collectively surmised that we must have missed the flight.

When Tomasa had checked at the TAM desk, the agent informed her that we would arrive on the late flight. Stephen laughed and added, "When I finally arrived and was greeted by Carlitos, it was much the same. He gave me a bear hug, then looked over my shoulder and asked in an alarmed voice, "But where is Marilú?"

We ate, sang, drank, and danced into the wee hours until finally collapsing onto our beds, exhausted but deliriously happy. The following morning, Silvio took Stephen to the airport in search of our lost luggage. They returned with only one large suitcase. We'd have to check later in the day for the other one.

Our friends had made plans to transport us to Ybycuí to see Ña Niní that first full day. Mary, Peggy, Tomasa, and Silvio set off in the late afternoon, assuring us they would wait in Tomasa's family home kitty-corner from Ña Niní's until we arrived. The four of us wanted to greet Ña Niní together.

First, Carlitos and Cesia took us back to the airport, where we retrieved our remaining lost suitcase. We proceeded to their home in San Lorenzo on the outskirts of Asunción, where Stephen and I enjoyed a short visit with Soel and Abel. Cesia and Carlitos were rightfully proud of their shy and humble sons. Stephen and I had a high-quality Littman stethoscope for each of the boys. They were both third-year medical students in need of one. (In Paraguay, students start their six-year medical education directly after high school.) I told them, "These are gifts from your North American aunt and uncle! It's the same type of stethoscope that we gave Dan when he entered medical school and similar to the one Stephen's father had given to him in his first year at Yale." Visibly moved by our gifts, Soel and Abel gave us warm hugs. We knew they would treasure and guard them. It was difficult to pull ourselves away, but Stephen and I knew that the others would be waiting for us in Ybycuí, along with Ña Niní.

Whatever the men in Carapeguá did to the vehicle worked temporarily. As long as we could get to Ybycuí, Carlitos could safely drive his car during the day until he returned to his mechanic in Asunción for a permanent repair. Along a dark stretch of road toward our town with the headlights as the only illumination, Carlitos made the mistake of relating to us that a Volunteer had been killed in an auto accident in the general vicinity. I was quiet but hopeful that we would arrive safely. After passing through Acahay, I soon saw the lights of Ybycuí. Carlitos drove through to the other side of town, pulled up in front of Ña Niní's house, and we collectively breathed a sigh of relief.

Stephen and I dashed across the intersection to Tomasa's family home and into the arms of our friends. "What took you so long?" they inquired. Carlitos, close behind us, told them the bad news about the vehicle's lights, but the good news was that we had arrived safely and were ready to see Ña Niní. She was still awake and waiting for us. Hugging her was the homecoming we had been anticipating. Although Ña Niní had aged and her health was poor, her soul was as vibrant and loving as ever.

The following morning, we eagerly jumped out of our beds to enjoy breakfast. While food was abundant and delicious, what fed our spirits was being together. Ña Niní tired easily but was determined to enjoy our visit to the fullest. When she rested mid-morning, Peggy, Mary, Stephen, and I strolled around town reminiscing and occasionally stopping to talk with Paraguayans who remembered us.

The four of us visited the health center, now a regional hospital with modern equipment. I waved in the distance to Dr. Melgarejo, who had remembered "The Hookworm Song" and us during our 2003 visit, still busily working there. Stephen posed in front of the house where he once lived. Looking definitely better than it did in 1975, it housed a private dentist's office. Mary had us take her picture in front of the new agricultural extension building that had replaced the old one housing her office as a Volunteer.

Some of the side roads had been cobblestoned since our last visit, helping to minimize road damage from heavy rains. My pink house, now painted a pale aqua, had an improved road in front of it. However, chickens and cows still roamed through town in their role as sanitation workers, eating garbage as they had in the 1970s and causing us to watch where we placed our feet.

One somewhat negative change that struck all of us that first morning was the large increase in small motorcycles. They seemed to buzz around town constantly, some carrying two or three passengers clinging to each other. Rarely did we see a rider wearing a helmet. Although these little machines were convenient, Carlitos informed us that there were frequent tragic accidents. The only ox cart we saw near town was one with tires rather than the oversized wooden wheels so common forty years earlier.

Ybycuí's main avenue was well maintained as a pedestrian promenade in the middle and pavement for vehicles on each side. The five of us posed for photos along the avenue and at the new welcome sign into town, "*Bienvenidos a Ybycuí, Che Pueblo Porâ*" ("Welcome to Ybycuí, My Beautiful Town," the title of a song in Guaraní).

During the first afternoon, we four North Americans brought out our gifts for Ña Niní. She showed pure delight with each one, appreciating the item and the loving thought behind it. Mary had brought her an 8' by 6' woven tapestry lap blanket with a photograph of Stephen, her, and me taken during Mary's visit to Washington State for the Peace Corps' 50th Anniversary. In the photo, we posed in front of a fine piece of spiderweb lace displayed on the wall. The three of us proudly posed in real life with Ña Niní and the woven blanket as Peggy snapped a number of photos for mementos of the occasion. (After returning to the U.S., Mary had a woven tapestry lap blanket made with *that* photo on it and sent it to me as a birthday present.) Peggy brought some funny little toys for Ña Niní to fiddle with, and fiddle she did, with her fingers kneading and caressing the items. She shed tears of joy upon unwrapping my photo quilt with her Volunteer children and embroidered lettering at the top in Spanish, "Some North American branches of the Feltes family." As we passed the time together in the patio area of Ña Niní's backyard, Cesia set up a table and pulled out the 1,000-piece jigsaw puzzle of the San Diego Zoo that Mary had brought her as a gift. Mary, Peggy, and I took turns drifting to the table to help piece it together.

We drank *yerba mate* every day and talked, reminiscing about our Peace Corps days. One afternoon, I recalled to Ña Niní the first time I walked into her veterinarian pharmacy and saw President Kennedy's framed photograph hanging on her wall. "Oh! I still have that!" she exclaimed, immediately directing one of the household help to bring it out. She cradled it in her arms and waited for me to photograph her with it. When I mentioned how touching it was for me to have her meet my own mother, she had someone bring out her album where she kept the photographs that I had sent her over the years. She promptly found the pictures of that particular encounter, and they brought tears of joy to my eyes. (Unfortunately, today I am unable to locate the best original slides of Ña Niní at JFK's gravesite and the meeting with my mother. After I had photos made to send to Paraguay, I misplaced the original slides.)

During one of Ña Niní's afternoon siestas, Carlitos and Cesia drove us out to Posito, now called *Cabaña Don Lalo* (Don Lalo's Cabin), pointing out the two adjacent properties that were his and Tonio's cattle ranches. I found peace in that lovely place with fond memories of the 1974 birthday party for Mary and me, the cattle vaccination and tarantula fishing with our boys and Dani in 2003, and the beauty and quiet of the Paraguayan countryside. We roamed the property, admiring the palm trees, bamboo, wildflowers, and domestic animals, occasionally sharing in soft voices our random thoughts and feelings. The six of us lingered to watch the crimson sunset.

When Tonio came to Ybycuí for a visit, we all enjoyed a feast of a dinner at his country home. Because he had arranged everything ahead of time, the food began flowing upon our arrival. Ña Niní sat in a chair, soaking up the atmosphere created by her loved ones—the four North Americans she considered her children, her sons Carlitos and Tonio, and daughter-in-law Cesia. Sadly, Tonio's wife Nuchi had passed away a few years prior to our visit. Tonio himself had recently suffered a heart attack, causing him to retire in Asunción where he maintained a lovely home. His three sons, all physicians, lived in or near the capital with their families. That night at Tonio's Ybycuí home on the outskirts of town, he spoke to us in English, telling us of the respect he had for the North American work ethic and his gratitude for having trained as a neurosurgeon in Little Rock, Arkansas. He talked about not allowing Paraguayan acquaintances of his speak negatively about the people of the United States in his presence. Instead, he told them about the good in the people he had known in the States and how hard they worked.

Late one morning, Dani, the young man who had introduced the tarantula fishing to our sons, came to the house proudly driving a red firetruck that had been donated to Ybycuí by the Japanese government. Dani was a volunteer firefighter in town. He was thrilled to see the four of us. Peggy had been a Volunteer when he was a toddler, brought to Ña Niní's home from the countryside to be raised. Now he usually lived and slept at the small firehouse in town, ready to respond in case of an emergency.

Another afternoon, we awoke Ña Niní from a nap with a special surprise. I had changed some of the words to the song, "Pueblo Ybycuí" to make it personal for her. The words to the original song were written by Sosa Cordero, and the music was composed by Mauricio Cardozo Ocampo. Stephen, Peggy, Mary, and I rehearsed the revised, personal rendition on the sly with Carlitos accompanying us on the guitar. Ña Niní beamed with delight at our serenade:

Pueblo Ybycuí, Our Serenade to Ña Niní
O, pueblo Ybycuí, tierra paraguaya que nos vió crecer
O, rincón de Ña Niní, cofre que atesora todo nuestro querer.
En tu amoroso hogar corrieron los años en el Cuerpo de Paz
Hoy parias en nuestro vagar, el anhelo tan solo fue verte otra vez.

Queríamos volverte a encontrar tan resueña cuando te dejamos
Con tu casa exhalando cariño que siempre buscábamos
Y ahora estamos acá, cantando con Carlitos mbaraká.
Rovy-á estar juntos a ti, ore rogustajhá.
O, pueblo de Ña Niní.

English Translation of Ybycuí Town, Our Serenade to Ña Niní
Oh, town of Ybycuí, Paraguayan land that saw us grow
Oh, Ña Niní's corner, a treasure chest containing all our wants.
In your loving home ran our years in the Peace Corps.
Today as we wander around, our longing is only to see you again.

We wanted to return to see you, laughing as when we left you
In your home exuding affection that we always sought.
And now that we are here, singing with Carlitos' guitar,
We're so happy to be with you, we're so very pleased.
Oh, town of Ña Niní.

Music filled an evening after dinner when Carlitos brought home a talented group of three teenagers who performed Paraguayan songs for us in the Feltes' backyard patio. The lead guitarist, Oscar Javier Lezcano, had performed on a tour in the United States. His fingers were a blur on the strings of the guitar as if he had been born playing the instrument. Oscar's younger brother and a friend rounded out the trio. At one point, Carlitos dragged me by the arm to join the group and sing a few traditional Paraguayan songs with them, followed by a rendition of "The Hookworm Song" sung by Stephen and me, with Peggy and Mary joining in. I was able to do it only because of the bit of *Aristócrata* I drank after dinner.

It was heart-wrenching to leave Ña Niní, knowing that we would not see her again in this life. It was tough for me to accept this reality. Peggy, Mary, Stephen, and I were deeply grateful for our time together with this wise, kind woman who had taken us into her home and lovingly treated us as her children. We parted after exchanging hugs and murmurs of love and gratefulness. I remember this 2012 visit every morning when I look at a framed photograph of Ña Niní, drinking *mate,* on my bedroom wall next to a photo of my parents.

Carlitos drove us back to Asunción during daylight but not before stopping in the adjacent town of Acahay to ask about Ña Lali, Mary's agricultural extension counterpart while a Volunteer. Ña Lali and Mary had been the judges in our hookworm and sanitary latrine contest back in 1974. Carlitos, who had recently talked to Ña Lali at Ybycuí's hospital, knew she lived in Acahay. It took several inquiries before we tracked her down west of the town as she was returning from a relative's home. As Mary jumped from Carlitos' vehicle, she called out to her old friend. Ña Lali was stunned upon hearing Mary's voice. Ña Lali was even more shocked when Stephen and I appeared from the 4-Runner for a brief but happy reunion on a remote, rural Paraguayan road.

We dined at Tonio's Asunción home the night before Peggy had to leave. Tonio ordered in an enormous Spanish seafood *paella*, more than plenty to serve all of the guests, including most of Tonio's extended family. Carlitos and Tonio profusely thanked the four of us for coming to visit. They had seen how animated and happy their mother had become after months of physical decline, and they credited us for her improvement. The four of us insisted that we were the ones to thank Ña Niní for all the mothering she had done for us during our Peace Corps years. She watched out for us, protected us from gossip, educated us about Paraguayan culture and its nuances, and she loved us.

The following day, after Peggy left for home, Tomasa and Silvio drove Mary, Stephen, and me two hours from Lambaré to their property near the rural town of Piribebuey (pee-ree-bay-BWEE) to see Silvio's vast productive vegetable fields. They had purchased the land decades before and over the years developed it into a prosperous farm supplying fresh produce to supermarkets in the capital. Silvio, self-educated in drip irrigation and the use of shading material to reduce the light intensity of the hot Paraguayan sun, produced high quality crops and achieved much higher than average yields.

The Authentic Radical Liberal Party under Fernando Lugo had taken power from Stroessner's Colorado Party in 2008 for the first time in 55 years. Because of this change in power, Silvio applied to receive a large grant from the Ministry of Agriculture for a demonstration project to teach small farmers the techniques he was utilizing. As a Liberal, he would never be awarded grant money from a Colorado president or regime. He took advantage of the window of opportunity with the Liberals in office. Tomasa promised to let us know when they heard from the Ministry about his request.

During our brief time on the Piribebuey acreage, we strolled around to admire the lush plants and Silvio's pigs, chickens, and cattle. It was impressive, to say the least. Their two-story country home with a tiled roof had the luxury of running water and lights unless the electricity went out, which it did during a severe storm during that night. In the morning when the sun rose, the creek passing through the property was swollen and fields were a brilliant emerald green, creating an Eden-like vista from the front porch.

On our last full day in Paraguay, Mary, Stephen, and I spent time relaxing with dear friends. Carlitos and Cesia took time to drive us to Ypacaraí Lake in the morning. Located an hour east of Asunción, Ypacaraí is somewhat of a tourist spot for Paraguayans as a place to escape the heat of the city during severe summer temperatures. It was a sunny, mild winter day in July when we visited and strolled the shore of the lake and the roads of the nearby town of Areguá.

In one of the small Areguá shops was a colorful painting displaying Paraguay's natural environment, including flowers, plants, tropical birds, a black panther, a jaguar, and an iridescent blue butterfly. At the top of the painting were the words, "*Sí, mi amor*" (Yes, my love). With his eyes twinkling, Stephen commented to the five of us that the phrase was important for a husband to say with frequency. He had recently read someplace that when the woman in a relationship gets her way most of the time, particularly regarding relatively minor matters, the odds are better for having a happy, harmonious household. Stephen looked me in the eyes. I returned his smile, replying, "*Sí, mi amor.*" Turning to Carlitos, I asked if he said it with frequency. With his arm around Cesia's shoulders, he cooed to her, "*Sí, mi amor.*" Mary laughed in delight and promised she would share this wisdom with Thomas as soon as she returned to California. To this day, Stephen often says, "*Sí, mi amor.*" On my part, I have tried harder to say it with frequency as well.

We spent our last afternoon in Lambaré with Tomasa, Silvio, Silvana, Arturo, Nena, and other friends, celebrating Tomasa and Silvio's 25th wedding anniversary a couple of months after the fact. Mary had brought them a silver cake cutter. Stephen and I gave them a pair of pewter wine goblets. We laughed, ate, talked, and laughed some more. Our Paraguayan friends honored us with a number of thoughtful gifts—*aho po-í* blouses, a *yerba mate* thermos with our names tooled into the leather casing, and spiderweb lace. Sad that it was all coming to an end but elated that the trip had actually happened, Mary, Stephen, and I rejoiced and reflected on our years of friendship.

∞∞∞∞

After our return home, I periodically called Ña Niní. But by late 2012, due to a decline in her health, she no longer could talk on the phone. I reverted to writing her letters and periodically checking with Carlitos and Tomasa by phone.

In December 2012 during a phone call, Carlitos told me Cesia had been invited to attend a conference in New York City as the director of Paraguay's campaign to eliminate Chagas disease. The event, supported by the Bill and Melinda Gates Foundation, was part of a working group on Sustainable Development Goals. Chagas disease was included in the planned discussions. Cesia's expenses were covered, and Carlitos would accompany her at their own expense. Although his mother's health was tenuous, his brother Tonio was on top of the situation, and Carlitos didn't want to pass up the opportunity to visit the United States. "Could you possibly fly to the east coast to see us? Would you call Peggy and let her know?" he asked.

"Of course," I replied.

Peggy opened her home to us in Alexandria, Virginia. Unfortunately, Stephen was unable to accompany me. However, Peggy, Cesia, Carlitos, and I enjoyed Christmas lights and displays in the nation's capital and went to Arlington Cemetery to visit John Kennedy's grave and the Tomb of the Unknown Soldier, as Carlitos' mother had done decades earlier. We had tasty indigenous dishes at the National Museum of the American Indian before enjoying the displays that focused on South America. Carlitos spoke to us at length about his mother's decline in health and how much our 2012 visit had meant to her and all of the Feltes family. The conference Cesia had attended was worthwhile, and she talked about the progress being made against Chagas disease in Paraguay with the help of Doctors Without Borders. The twins were doing well in medical school, and the Littman stethoscopes were the envy of their classmates.

Before returning to Paraguay, Carlitos and Cesia flew to Florida to visit Paraguayan friends. They returned home in time to celebrate Christmas and the New Year with Ña Niní and the rest of the family.

∞∞∞∞

Ña Niní passed away at a hospital in Asunción on February 3, 2013, four days prior to her 88th birthday. As with my own parents, I knew in my heart that it was her time to leave us. While mourning her, I was thankful Ña Niní was relieved of the suffering she had endured in her last days. I will always miss her and my parents, but I am daily grateful for them as I gaze at their photos next to each other on the wall by my bedroom dresser.

∞∞∞∞

On October 8, 2014, Mary and I celebrated our 64th birthday together in her home near San Diego. Stephen was there by my side, along with Mary's husband Thomas, and other family members. I wore the same black Paraguayan *ty-poi* blouse with orange embroidery I had worn at our birthday party at Posito forty years earlier.

As always when we were together, our conversations were a mix of Paraguayan memories and our current lives. Mary, who had earned a master's in public health after returning from the Peace Corps, was a senior planner at Kaiser Permanente in Southern California, still giving of herself for the good of the community by working for one of the largest non-profit managed-care organizations in the country.

During our visit, Mary took us on a tour of an almost-completed hospital she had helped make happen. It was a state-of-the art facility that would soon provide the physical plant necessary for top-quality medical care. Mary belonged to a book club, volunteered to help a senior citizen on a weekly basis, and participated in local Returned Peace Corps Volunteer activities. Like Stephen and me, she had been profoundly affected by her Peace Corps experience, and her work and life reflected it.

Talk of retirement arose. My intermittent contract work involving technical writing and public health consulting for the local Head Start Program could stop at any time, and I would adjust to a retirement schedule. Thomas, a few years older than Mary, was heading toward retirement. Mary and Stephen, however, intended to continue working for the foreseeable future. Mary had projects she wanted to see to the finish, and Stephen simply enjoyed his work.

∞∞∞

In 2019, before the COVID-19 pandemic erupted, 7,367 Peace Corps Volunteers were serving in 62 countries at a cost of $410 million dollars per year, according to the agency's 2020 financial report. That amount of money would purchase less than two F22 Raptor aircrafts, which are estimated at $339 million each to build and cost $60,000 per flight hour. The cost to support a Volunteer is less than $56,000 per year, and that includes the entire Peace Corps bureaucracy. There are many ways to serve one's country and promote the best interests of humankind, and Peace Corps is one excellent possibility.

I often reflect on the commitment to Peace Corps that Stephen and I individually made in the early 1970s, and Paraguay comes up frequently in our household. Words and phrases in Guaraní appear in our daily conversations. The subsequent journeys we have traveled in this life grew out of our Paraguay experience, with each of us selecting slightly different pathways while staying true to ourselves. Our marriage has lovingly endured over the decades, as has our commitment to help make the world a better place.

The pattern in our lives during and after Peace Corps is similar to what other RPCVs have experienced, according to a report published in September 2011 to coincide with the 50th Anniversary of the Peace Corps. "A Call to Peace—Perspectives of Volunteers on the Peace Corps at 50" was written by Civic Enterprises and the National Peace Corps Association in partnership with Peter D. Hart Research Associates. In addition to providing brief histories and anecdotes about Peace Corps, the report provides survey results of over 11,000 RPCVs who were asked, among other things, about what inspired them to join, what their experiences were like, how well they believed they advanced the three Peace Corps goals, and the influence their experiences had on their career choices.

The report presents the survey results of questions about Peace Corps' three goals. The first goal is "To help the people of interested countries in meeting their need for trained men and women," and 59% of RPCVs responded that their service was very or fairly effective. "To help promote a better understanding of Americans on the part of the people served," is the second goal, and 82% of RPCVs rated their service as very or fairly effective in achieving it. The third goal states, "To help promote a better understanding of other people on the part of Americans." (Personally, I prefer describing us as "North Americans from the U.S." because people from Canada to the tip of South America's Cape Horn are all Americans.) This goal was deemed as very or fairly effective by 79% of the RPCVs surveyed. Together, the three goals have the intent of working toward **world peace**, the underlying reason for the establishment of the Peace Corps.

The survey results also show that for RPCVs, their experience was transformative—92% said the Peace Corps changed their lives, with many of those saying it made them more open to people of different races, ethnicities, and religions; and 60% said their service influenced their choice of careers. When asked in an open-ended form to describe their experiences, one third responded by referring to the best aspects of being a Volunteer, including "the people they met, life-long friendships they formed, and being accepted and welcomed by the local community." The top three reasons RPCVs gave for joining were "wanting to live in another culture," "wanting a better understanding of the world," and "wanting to help people build a better life." In other words, their main motivating factors for volunteering were altruism, adventure, and curiosity.

Stephen and I were not surveyed, but we definitely are among those who count the Peace Corps experience as effective. Although our original assignment to conduct the project designed by Chuck did not succeed, we learned a considerable amount during its short life. Based on the project, we turned the positive education campaign into our Traveling Hookworm Show, training teachers in five sites in all corners of eastern Paraguay. When we returned to Paraguay to conduct my public health research project, I determined that the work of Volunteers had made a significant difference in Ybycuí's sanitation conditions from 1974 to 1982. Subsequently, our census method and educational materials were utilized by Peace Corps and SENASA in other parts of the country.

Over the years, Stephen and I have promoted a better understanding between cultures, including opening our home to Paraguayan friends. We also received much in return through gestures in kindnesses, big and small, from Paraguayans we wanted to help. Stephen and I experienced warm hospitality during our times in Paraguay. While some of our enduring friendships are with middle class Paraguayans who have had the means to maintain contact with us over time and distance, during our service and subsequent visits, we connected deeply with people from different political, social, and economic walks of life. I know in my heart that these strong bonds and love that began when we were teaching about hookworms and sanitary latrines in the land of spiderweb lace will last as long as we live. Hopefully, generations to come will continue building bridges across cultures to promote international tolerance and peace. People generally don't wage war against others they understand and care about.

In March 2020, the COVID-19 pandemic caused the United States to evacuate all Peace Corps Volunteers. By early 2021, Peace Corps country directors returned to their posts and are developing plans for the return of Volunteers once the pandemic resolves. I am hopeful for a continued presence of Peace Corps around the world.

∞∞∞

I began this memoir writing about latrines and sanitation, favorite topics of mine but not ones conjuring up pleasant smells and images. Now, I conclude it with my own design for a piece of Paraguay's beautiful spiderweb lace symbolizing the essence of the Peace Corps. (A sketch of my design is found on the book cover.) The eight outer circles neatly enfold an inner one, with all of the circles connected by silken threads to make it a united image.

Four of the circles pertain to common Peace Corps programs—health, agriculture, education, and cooperatives. Woven into the health circle are tiny red worms to represent blood-filled hookworms whose eradication occupied my efforts in Paraguay. (It is at one o-clock in the design, and the others follow clockwise.) The red also symbolizes healthy blood once parasites no longer occupy the body. Depicting hookworm in spiderweb lace is not farfetched; there is a *ñandutí* pattern, shown on page 186 of Annick Sanjurjo's Spanish version of the book, called *letrero* (sign or placard) with an interior design called a *cevo-í* (worm) by one of the author's consultants. I imitated the zig-zag pattern in that design. The growing cornstalks symbolize agricultural extension efforts, as well as my personal memories of *sopa paraguaya* and *chipá* made with local corn. Peace Corps' education program is symbolized with books in various colors, and they carry hope for a better future due to improved education. The cooperative circle shows small hands in different hues of skin colors that work together toward common goals to benefit all.

The remaining exterior circles represent qualities and emotions common to the Peace Corps experience. Silver *bombillas* alternating with gourds containing *yerba mate* tea represent the circle of sharing and friendship so aptly displayed in the custom of drinking *mate* in Paraguay. Next comes the circle filled with waxy, heart-shaped red anthuriums graced with a yellow spike growing from the stem. An anthurium represents the hospitality openly offered by people in our host countries. Happy sunflowers dotting the seventh circle, with their brilliant yellow petals encompassing the brown center seeds, represent good luck. Sunflowers are also associated with truth, loyalty, and honesty. The eighth and last outer circle is emblematic of remembrance with a continuous ring of dark pink and purple gladioli. These large, elegant flowers symbolize memories of Volunteers and host country friends alike.

A ring of green aromatic rosemary sprigs, an herb thought in ancient times to strengthen memory, graces the exterior portion of the center circle. Inside the rosemary is the focal point of my spiderweb lace in red, white, and blue, the colors of the U.S. and Paraguayan flags. The dove in the middle represents the Peace Corps, the program that provides the opportunity to serve, to bridge cultures, and to promote peace and understanding.

While contributing to sanitation improvements in rural areas during my two years of Peace Corps service in Paraguay, I received much in return. To begin with, I learned to think about the world in languages other than English. Also, I observed lives very different from those in my working-class neighborhood in Detroit in the 1950s and 1960s. In addition, I adapted to daily life without running water, electricity, and other amenities. From there, I grew to understand and share Paraguayan pride in their history, culture, music, *yerba mate, aho po-i,* and spiderweb lace. Likewise, I benefitted from Paraguayan hospitality and returned it when possible, with empathy and humility. I treasure my life-long friendships with Stephen, other Volunteers, and Paraguayans who have immensely enriched my life. Often, I was challenged, but those challenges helped me grow. I found joy and love. I will remember. I am grateful.

Ybycuí's main avenue in 2012, with a pedestrian promenade in the median

At the entrance to Ybycuí ("Welcome to Ybycuí, My Beautiful Town");
Mary, Mary Lou, Stephen, and Peggy

Mary holding up her larger-than-life gift to Ña Niní, who hangs onto Mary Lou and Stephen

Ña Niní, with her photo of JFK that had been on her wall
when I first entered her house in 1974

Near Acahay, a surprised Ña Lali, with Mary pointing at Stephen and me

A Peace Corp Memoir

Stephen and Mary in Silvio's massive shaded fields near Piribebuey

Love and Latrines in the Land of Spiderweb Lace

The thermos, *guampa*, and *bombilla* set, a gift to us from Tomasa and Silvio

Cesia and Carlitos at President Kennedy's grave

CHAPTER 12

Where We are Now

Grow old with me! The best is yet to be.
–Robert Browning

After the 1989 *coup d'état*, Stroessner sought exile in Brazil, where he lived until his death in 2006 at the age of 93. Paraguay adopted a new constitution in 1992, establishing a democracy, and elections were subsequently held. Despite the *coup* that deposed Stroessner, the Colorado Party has maintained power continuously, with the exception of 2008-2012, when Fernando Lugo of the Liberal Party served as president. Lugo was impeached by the still powerful Colorado Party, and he was removed from office in June 2012. In August 2013, Horacio Cartes became president, resuming full Colorado control of Paraguay. In August of 2018, Mario Abdo Benitez was elected president. He had been the personal secretary of Alfredo Stroessner.

As I write this in 2021, Carlitos still works at the Ybycuí health center and takes care of the family's property in town. Cesia continues the campaign to eliminate Chagas disease in Paraguay, and twins Soel and Abel are both surgeons. Tonio remains retired from neurosurgery. His three sons are still all practicing physicians. Carlos, the eldest, who clearly remembers when we took him on a tour of the White House and Arlington Cemetery, did a five-year surgical residency in Macon, Georgia, and practices in Asunción.

Carlitos told me that Paraguay fared better than most countries during the first six months of the COVID-19 pandemic because people were taking this virus seriously. They respected and obeyed stay-at-home and facial masks orders. Initially, cases and deaths were mostly confined to the area in and around Asunción. From the beginning, Paraguayans suffered economic consequences from the pandemic. However, in the latter part of 2020, COVID-19 cases began to rise and spread beyond Asunción. When I mentioned in a phone call early in the outbreak that toilet paper was nowhere to be found here, Carlitos laughed and said that Paraguayans were also hoarding toilet paper. As of March 2021, the Russian COVID-19 vaccine, Sputnik V, was beginning to arrive, and the Paraguayan government was hoping to purchase more vaccines through the World Health Organization.

Since the onset of the COVID-19 pandemic, Tomasa spends most of her time in Ybycuí these days, along with her daughter Silvana but without her husband Silvio. In late 2012, Silvio, the successful agronomist and grower, received a large government grant to conduct agricultural demonstration projects with the intent of improving the production of small farmers. A few years after the Colorados regained power, they aggressively prosecuted several politicians from the opposition Liberal party, along with the Minister of Agriculture who had given Silvio the grant, and Silvio himself. In 2017, Silvio was imprisoned with an 11-year sentence. His sentence was recently reduced by two years. In June 2021, he remains incarcerated but hopes his case will be favorably reviewed soon by new top-echelon politicians who have replaced some of the more corrupt ones. Faith sustains Silvio and Tomasa.

Silvio's optimism is reinforced by a *New York Times* article on April 22, 2019, "In Paraguay, Fighting Graft With Eggs and Toilet Paper." A movement, modeled after protests in Argentina three decades earlier by relatives of "disappeared" and killed people, has arisen in Paraguay to denounce corruption. Attorney María Esther Roa and a group of mostly women turned their outrage to action against Senator José María Ibañez. The senator had survived impeachment after admitting he used public funds to pay three people working at his estate in the countryside. Roa and others gathered at his home, banged on pots and pans, threw raw eggs at the structure, and covered it in toilet paper to symbolize that Mr. Ibañez needed to clean himself up. Amazingly, the senator resigned. Emboldened by the result, protestors kept up the pressure, resulting in two more resignations by prominent senators. Subsequently, prosecutors charged five additional government officials with crimes and began investigating others. Videos of the protests spread on social media, encouraging more attacks on governmental corruption. Although some protests have become violent, Ms. Roa and her supporters continue to persist.

Pat McArdle, the experienced Volunteer who helped trained us in Ponce, left the Peace Corps in 1974. She served as an officer in the U.S. Navy and was assigned to a remote base in Morocco for three years. After her military service, she worked for the U.S. State Department as a foreign service officer for 27 years.

Kate Raftery, the Volunteer with whom I lived in Itacurubí del Rosario and who was Peace Corps assistant country director when Stephen and I returned to Paraguay in 1982, has continued in international work. In 2001, she helped in the re-establishment of Peace Corps in Perú after a 26-year absence. The program had left Perú in 1976 due to political and economic instability. Kate also served as the program's country director in Honduras. In the fall of 2018, while country director in Peace Corps Paraguay, Kate emailed me that Jeff and Ricardo, the Volunteers who conducted our teacher training program in hookworm prevention and sanitary latrines after we left in 1976, were in her office singing "The Hookworm Song" to her! In 2019, Kate became a special assistant to the Peace Corps director in Washington, D.C.

Ellen Eiseman, the Volunteer in Itaguá who hosted me for my first experience in the Paraguayan countryside during my Peace Corps training, obtained a master's in public health after her return to the States. She later received a master of science in organization development and has dedicated her life to international health improvement, working in Africa, Asia, and South America. Ellen became Peace Corps country director in Mozambique in late 2018. When the COVID-19 pandemic broke out, she led the evacuation of her Volunteers to the United States through Ethiopia. In December 2020, Ellen traveled back to Mozambique to prepare for the return of Volunteers once the pandemic subsides.

Dave Stanton and Martina Nicholson, who helped launch the effort to eradicate intestinal parasites in Ybycuí, returned to separate areas in California after the Peace Corps. Dave became an immigration attorney in the southern part of the state. Martina fulfilled her dream of being a physician. She served as an obstetrician/gynecologist in Santa Cruz, California, for over thirty years.

Abel Salazar, the agricultural extension Volunteer coordinator who served in Ybycuí, married a Paraguayan woman before returning to the United States in 1976. Abel asked Mary, Stephen, and me to be witnesses at his wedding. We attended and signed papers at the civil marriage the day preceding the religious ceremony in the Catholic Church. Once he left Paraguay, he did not keep in touch with anyone. Years later, Mary and I attempted to find him to inform him of Don Lalo's passing, but we were unsuccessful.

I have been more successful keeping in touch with some of the Volunteers who trained with Stephen and me. Larry Hodgson, who served in Mallorquín, did fulfill his personal dream by opening a restaurant in San Pedro, California. Retired now, he creates artistic photographs and still loves cooking gourmet meals. I'm hoping he will someday write his Peace Corps memoir that includes a rustic rafting trip he took down the Paraguay River with a small group of fellow adventurers.

Burl Wagenheim, the Villa Hayes Volunteer from my hometown of Detroit, earned his PhD in psychology and worked with military veterans and patients suffering from Alzheimer's disease until his recent retirement.

Wyn Lewis, who served in Caraguata-y, became a nutritionist in Santa Fe, New Mexico. As long as the holiday cards I send her aren't returned, I'll continue sending them. She periodically updates us on her life.

For years, I was out of touch with Marty Todd Elwell, the Villa de San Pedro Volunteer. When Mary found a phone number for her in 2014, I jotted down the information and misplaced it until it appeared among some notes in my office in June 2020. Marty responded promptly to my voice mail as I was editing the section of our 1976 trip to her town. She lives in Prescott, Arizona, and is the mother of five children and six grandchildren.

Mary Wirges and I remain close, talking by phone every month or so. She still works full time and is dedicated to her family and active in her community.

Bron and Eric Anders, our Peace Corps physicians, live in Southern California. In addition to exchanging Christmas letters with them over the years, Stephen and I occasionally saw Bron at the national meetings of the American Academy of Pediatrics. At one meeting, I spotted her going down a long escalator while we were ascending on another one, which resulted in the three of us dining together.

Peggy Seufert, who served in Ybycuí in the late 1970s and returned to Paraguay with us in 2012, taught English as a Second Language (ESL) for decades. She served as Peace Corps staff in Romania and Poland as an ESL specialist. She is retired and lives in Alexandria, Virginia.

My sister Cynthia and her husband Henry still live in Virginia Beach. Sadly, their adopted daughter Sara has suffered from mental illness since her teen years. I know my sister and brother-in-law have tried their best. They cherish their happy memories of traveling to Paraguay and the initial years with their adopted daughter.

My father-in-law, Howard Pearson, passed away in October of 2016, five months after he and I finished his memoir, *Fulfilling Paul Newman's Dream—"Raising a Little Hell" and Healing at The Hole in the Wall Gang Camp*. Writing with him gave me confidence to write this Peace Corps memoir.

Our son Matthew, who has a master's degree in information systems, is a technology security specialist for a health care company, and his wife Tasha is employed at a large nonprofit. They reside with their cats in Seattle.

Our son Dan received his PhD in 2018 and earned his M.D. degree in 2020. He is now a resident in pathology and resides in Boston with his wife Laurie, an internal medicine physician specializing in hematology/oncology. In February 2020, their son Oliver was born.

Since the beginning of our Peace Corps service in 1974, the population of Ybycuí has grown by over 50% to just under 5,000 inhabitants. Ybycuí's health center has become a district hospital. I can see on Google Maps that there are many more businesses today, including groceries, clothing stores, appliance vendors, two ice cream parlors, a laundromat, and at least ten small hotels (one is owned and operated by Epí, who used to work for the Feltes family). When Ña Niní could no longer operate her hotel because of declining health, she rented it to a university program. A few years ago, an accounting business occupied it. As I write this, the property is vacant, and the Feltes family is looking for a renter.

According to the Peace Corps' website, the program is recruiting Volunteers for Paraguay for departure in early 2022 in agriculture, community economic development, environment, and health. About 80% of assignments are in rural communities of less than 5,000 inhabitants, and some Volunteers are assigned to communities of less than 200 people. These locations very likely won't have running water or paved roads, but they will have electricity. Volunteers are issued cell phones with a basic plan by the Peace Corps, and they are required to live with a family for the first three months of service. Because of safety concerns, Volunteers are not allowed to drive or ride on two- or three-wheeled motorized vehicles, including motorcycles, for any reason, but they can request that Peace Corps issue them a mountain bike and helmet. Also, Volunteers are prohibited from driving private vehicles.

After the 2011 potluck to celebrate the program's 50th anniversary, the RPCVs in the Yakima Valley have continued to meet at least once a year, except during the COVID-19 pandemic. We have marched as a group in Yakima's Sun Parade, and we have sponsored some community events related to the Peace Corps and its goals. The group has plans for a potluck gathering in the summer of 2021, and we currently number about 50 RPCVs.

Stephen and I are again members of the National Peace Corps Association and its affiliate organization, Friends of Paraguay, after being out of touch for several years. Through online meetings and newsletters, we maintain our lifelong commitment to the Peace Corps, stay connected to old friends, and meet new ones. In early 2021, I participated in a Friends of Paraguay Zoom meeting featuring the work done by RPCVs Jeff Wong and Henry Maillet. Still in Paraguay after their service, they spent about six months rowing a boat 1,300 kilometers down the length of the Paraguay River, finishing just as the pandemic began closing the country. With sponsorship of the World Wildlife Fund and other support, they interviewed people living along the river about the changes in their climate. Along with the interviews, they filmed and photographed their way down this spectacular river, with the intent of developing a documentary entitled, *Rostros del Río/The Faces of the River*. (For more information, see their website: rostrosdelrio.com, and click on the language of your choice.)

Stephen and I attended another Friends of Paraguay Zoom meeting in May 2021 that focused on Peace Corps' health program. We learned that when health Volunteers return to Paraguay after the worst of the pandemic is over, they will work with youth in rural areas to address concerns about obesity, alcohol and tobacco use, and teenage pregnancies. Although hookworm infestation still occurs in rural areas, it is not the problem it used to be.

Nearing seventy, Stephen now works part-time as a salaried pediatrician in a family practice residency training program that is part of a federally qualified health center. He loves what he does, he's good at it, and he uses his Spanish on a daily basis. Some of his current patients are the grandchildren of patients he had thirty years ago. Stephen's curly dark brown hair from his younger years is now a distinguished, relaxed silvery gray. He still has his beard and frequently strokes it while in deep thought, but it has grayed as well. When I look into his eyes, I see the same kind, loving man I fell in love with in Paraguay.

In 2017, Stephen and I moved from Granger to a new home in Yakima. While we miss our spectacular western view, our new location is more convenient for us. I officially retired in January 2020. Before the COVID-19 pandemic, I swam 1.5 miles four or five times a week to fight off old age. I recently returned to the local YMCA pool, open again with pandemic limitations. I'm editing the letters my father wrote to my mother during World War II and developing an historical timeline to accompany them. My current hobby, my contribution to the public's health these days, is making quality cotton masks and giving them as gifts to family and friends. I have sent some to the Feltes and Centurión/Riveros families in Paraguay as well as to Ellen in Mozambique. She has had as much fun giving them away as I have had in making them. Most of all, I enjoy living with Stephen in our Yakima home with family photographs and several intricate pieces of *ñandutí* displayed on our walls, quilts I have sewn draped over the backs of the chairs and couch, and our Paraguayan guitars in their tooled leather cases at hand.

White ñanduti on black velvet, displayed in our home in Yakima

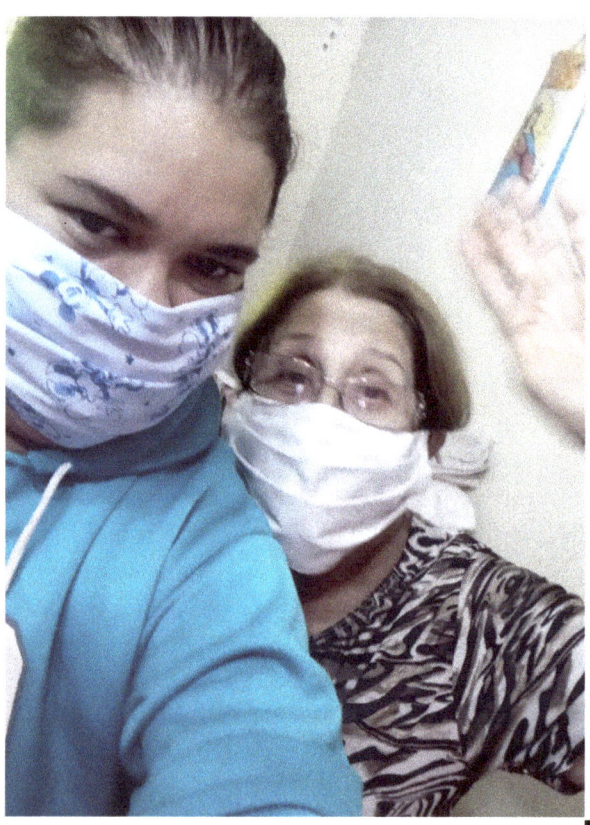

Silvana and Tomasa, wearing masks I made for them (Courtesy of Tomasa Centurión de Riveros).

Carlitos and Cesia wearing my masks (Courtesy of Carlos Feltes Cáceres)

Stephen and Mary Lou, circa 2012
(Courtesy of Matthew Pearson)

Suggested Reading

There have been over a thousand Peace Corps memoirs written since 1961. One of the earliest ones and a favorite of mine is *Living Poor: A Peace Corps Chronicle* by Moritz Thomsen. He served in a small coastal community in Ecuador and wrote about his experience with humility and insight. Thomsen became somewhat of a legend among Volunteers in that country and around the world.

Another favorite is *Monique and the Mango Rains* by Kris Holloway, a Volunteer in Mali in 1989–91. It is a heart-felt tribute to her counterpart, a midwife named Monique. Kris writes with sensitivity and humor, reflecting the passion and soul of the Peace Corps. When Julie, one of our local RPCVs in the Yakima Valley, told me she had served in Mali, I mentioned the book. Tears came to her eyes as she told me she had been assigned to work with Monique after Kris completed her service. It was obvious that Julie also had deeply loved and respected Monique.

Journey to the Heart of the Condor: Love, Loss, and Survival in a South American Dictatorship by Emily Creigh and Martín Almada is a memoir with a unique approach. Emily's service as a Volunteer in Paraguay overlapped with ours. Co-author Martín is a Paraguayan who suffered severely under the Stroessner Regime. The juxtaposition of their writing is riveting, giving insight into what it was like for some Paraguayans during the years of dictatorship.

Mark Salvatore, who arrived in Paraguay to serve in the Peace Corps just before Stroessner was deposed in 1989, starts his memoir as an eyewitness to that historic event. His story, *Shade of the Paraíso: Two Years in Paraguay, South America*, brings to life his experiences in a small, remote community. As I read his memoir, I easily saw the images in my mind's eye. Although I wish he had continued his story beyond his service, I recommend his book as a good reflection of the Peace Corps experience.

Don Haffner, an Albion College classmate (Class of 1972), published his memoir, *Mukho Memories: A Peace Corps/Korea Memoir*, in 2017. His Volunteer journey turned into a decade of living and working in his host country. He does exceptionally well writing about the history and culture of Korea as he tells his personal story.

For deeper insight into Paraguayan history, culture, and contemporary life, *The Paraguayan Reader: History, Culture, Politics* is enlightening. Editors Peter Lambert and Andrew Nickson cover a broad variety of topics by authors with different viewpoints from Paraguay's earliest recorded history to the first part of the 21st century.